Previous *Washington Post* Books
Published by Scribner

Trump Revealed

The Mueller Report

The Mueller Report Illustrated:
The Obstruction Investigation

DONALD TRUMP
AND HIS
ASSAULT ON TRUTH

The President's
Falsehoods, Misleading Claims
and Flat-Out Lies

The Washington Post

GLENN KESSLER
Editor and chief writer of The *Washington Post* Fact Checker

SALVADOR RIZZO
MEG KELLY
Reporters for The Fact Checker

WITHDRAWN

SCRIBNER

New York   London   Toronto   Sydney   New Delhi

Scribner
An Imprint of Simon & Schuster, Inc.
1230 Avenue of the Americas
New York, NY 10020

Copyright © 2020 by WP Company LLC

All rights reserved, including the right to reproduce this book or portions thereof
in any form whatsoever. For information, address Scribner Subsidiary Rights Department,
1230 Avenue of the Americas, New York, NY 10020.

First Scribner trade paperback edition June 2020

SCRIBNER and design are registered trademarks of The Gale Group, Inc.,
used under license by Simon & Schuster, Inc., the publisher of this work.

For information about special discounts for bulk purchases,
please contact Simon & Schuster Special Sales at 1-866-506-1949
or business@simonandschuster.com.

The Simon & Schuster Speakers Bureau can bring authors to your live event.
For more information or to book an event, contact the Simon & Schuster Speakers Bureau
at 1-866-248-3049 or visit our website at www.simonspeakers.com.

Manufactured in the United States of America

3   5   7   9   10   8   6   4   2

Library of Congress Cataloging-in-Publication Data is available.

ISBN 978-1-9821-5107-2
ISBN 978-1-9821-5108-9 (ebook)

Photo Credits
page 52: Senate TV/AP; page 54: Mandel Ngan/AFP/Getty Images; page 57: Melina Mara/
The Washington Post; page 58: Matt McClain/*The Washington Post*; page 60: Matt McClain/
The Washington Post; page 62: Melina Mara/*The Washington Post*; page 64: Melina Mara/
The Washington Post; page 67: Tom Brenner/*The New York Times*/Redux; page 68: Bill O'Leary/
The Washington Post; page 70: Steve Helber/AP; page 71: Andrew Caballero-Reynolds/AFP/
Getty Images (Lisa Page), Manuel Balce Ceneta/AP (Peter Strzok); page 76: Daisuke Tomita/
Yomiuri Shimbun/AP; page 98: Chip Somodevilla/Getty Images

CONTENTS

CONTENTS

CONTENTS

16,000 Falsehoods

"As the vilest writer hath his readers, so the greatest liar hath his believers: and it often happens, that if a lie be believed only for an hour, it hath done its work."
—Jonathan Swift, "The Art of Political Lying," 1710

Every president lies—at some point.

It's the nature of politics and diplomacy. Sometimes, a president might convince himself that a lie is in the national interest. A president might lie to shield the public from damaging information that could undermine sensitive missions. A lie could be a way to protect intelligence vital to national security. Or a presidential falsehood could be inadvertent, the result of sloppy staff work or wishful thinking.

Not every lie is equal. There is the daily fluff of campaigning—marketing embellishments meant to secure political support, such as Barack Obama's "If you like your health-care plan, you'll be able to keep your health-care plan." There are lies to prevent embarrassment, such as John F. Kennedy's denial that he had Addison's disease or Bill Clinton's denial that he had an affair with Monica Lewinsky. There are lies to protect national security, such as Kennedy faking a cold to cancel a campaign tour so he could meet with top aides about the still-secret Cuban Missile Crisis. And at the top of the scale, there are lies to cover up important crimes—such as the Watergate scandal—and lies of policy deception: Lyndon B. Johnson minimizing the war in Vietnam, Richard Nixon hiding the secret bombing of Cambodia, and Ronald Reagan denying the Iran-Contra scandal.

Just about every recent president is associated with one big lie. Sometimes, a falsehood becomes notorious because it seemed out of character for that president.

Dwight Eisenhower, now ranked by many historians as one of the greatest presidents, approved a series of statements designed to cover up secret overflights of the Soviet Union by American U-2 spy planes. The president's misleading comments were based on the mistaken belief that the pilot of a missing U.S. "weather plane" was dead and his aircraft had been destroyed. But the pilot, Gary Powers, had miraculously survived after being shot down by Russian surface-to-air missiles. Eisenhower's error proved to be a propaganda bonanza for Soviet leader Nikita Khrushchev, as the Soviets could disprove U.S. claims with both a live pilot and the plane's wreckage. Years later, Eisenhower was asked what his "greatest regret" as president was. "The lie we told," he said. "I didn't realize how high a price we were going to pay for that lie."

And then there's Donald Trump, the most mendacious president in U.S. history. He almost never expresses regret. He's not known for one big lie—just a constant stream of exaggerated, invented, boastful, purposely outrageous, spiteful, inconsistent, dubious and false claims.

From the start of Trump's presidency, The *Washington Post* Fact Checker team has catalogued every false or misleading statement he has made. As of Jan. 20, 2020, three years after Trump took the oath of office, the count stood at 16,241.

That works out to about 15 claims per day. But the pace of deception has quickened exponentially. He averaged about six claims a day in 2017, nearly 16 a day in 2018 and more than 22 a day in 2019. Indeed, the president made more false or misleading claims in 2019 than he did in 2017 and 2018 combined.

Some days are simply astonishing: On Sept. 7, 2018, he made 125 claims. On Dec. 18, 2019, 126 claims. And on Nov. 5, 2018, 139 claims. October is an especially dangerous month for the truth: In October 2018, the president tallied 1,205 claims, and in October 2019, the count was 1,159.

The pace and frequency of Trump's falsehoods can feel mind-numbing—and many Americans appear to have tuned out the torrent of presidential misstatements. In 2003, George W. Bush's administration was thrown off course for months, with a top official offering his resignation and a presidential aide eventually convicted of perjury, after the president's State of the Union address included 16 words—"The British government has learned that Saddam Hussein recently sought significant quantities of uranium from Africa"— that turned out to be based on inconclusive evidence.

By contrast, Trump routinely says dozens of things in each State of the Union address, campaign rally and major speech that are flat wrong—with barely any consequence.

At a January 2020 rally, Trump casually announced that he had "made a deal. I saved a country." He contended that he should have been awarded the Nobel Peace Prize for achieving peace between Ethiopia and neighboring Eritrea. Ethiopia's prime minister had been given the Nobel for negotiating a peace deal after 20 years of bloody conflict. Trump had had nothing to do with those peace talks.

Trump had confused these negotiations with another set of talks, between Ethiopia and Egypt, and he had maligned the head of another country. In any other presidency, such remarks likely would have resulted in a scandal or at least days of negative news reports. In the Trump presidency, the statement passed by with virtually no notice.

This book is not simply a catalogue of false claims; rather, it is a guide to Trump's attack on the truth. The construction of false but boastful narratives about his achievements is at the core of his political strategy and it is a key to his personality. Trump took office as trust in government institutions was rapidly declining—a drop he has exacerbated with attacks on the FBI, intelligence agencies and what he calls the "deep state." He has constructed a vision of America that connects with the frustrations of his supporters—but leaves little room for opposing viewpoints or even respectful dialogue with people who are not in his base. That laser focus on his base, and his tradition-shattering embrace of lurid rhetoric and coarse insults, helps explain why many of his supporters believe in him with such fervor—and also why a majority of Americans continue to disapprove of his performance, despite economic numbers during his first three years in office, before the coronavirus crisis hit, that would have earned the envy of many past presidents.

Trump's falsehoods can be overwhelming, so we've organized this book to be digested in whatever way readers find useful. Read it straight through to get the full impact and meaning of the president's mendacity. Or dip into the chapters that most intrigue you; each chapter stands on its own. We have strived to avoid repetition, but repetition is one of Trump's favorite tools, and we do want to reflect how and why he uses it to persuade people of his message. The first chapter assembles Trump's most noteworthy falsehoods, across all subjects. The next three chapters document Trump's lies about himself, his attacks on his perceived enemies, and his deception of his political base. Chapter Five examines how Trump uses his favorite transmitter of falsehoods: his Twitter account. The final five chapters detail Trump's major falsehoods about important policy areas: immigration, economics and trade, foreign policy, the Ukraine controversy that led to his impeachment, and the coronavirus crisis that dominated 2020. In between the chapters are quick glimpses at some of the oddest and most oft-repeated themes that emerge from the Trumpian landscape of falsehoods and exaggerations. The conclusion considers Trump's impact on truth in American politics. Finally, at the end of the book, an appendix demonstrates how Trump combines dozens of falsehoods in a single campaign rally, delivering to his followers a rousing but confounding stew of misstatements, lies and the occasional actual fact.

Facts and figures are a critical part of most politicians' arsenals. But whether people actually care if those facts are correct is open to question. Supporting a "blue" or "red" candidate increasingly is an important part of Americans' identity. In the age of Trump, there is evidence that Republicans have grown less concerned about presidents being honest than they were a decade ago. A 2007 Associated Press–Yahoo poll found that 71 percent of Republicans said it was "extremely important" for presidential candidates to be honest, similar to 70 percent of Democrats and 66 percent of independents. Fast-forward to 2018, when a *Washington Post* poll asked the same question and found that identical shares of Democrats and independents still prioritized honesty in presidential candidates, but the share of Republicans who said honesty was extremely important had fallen to 49 percent, 22 points lower than in the poll a decade earlier. That statistically significant shift suggests that many Republicans realize that Trump often lies, yet they have decided that truth-telling is less important than the message he sends about the country's sorry state and the forces he blames for its troubles.

Social science research shows that people are receptive to information that confirms their preconceived notions, especially when it comes to politics. One study quizzed participants on data measuring the effectiveness of a skin-cream product; people with good math skills could interpret the data correctly. But when the same survey participants were shown similar numbers on whether gun control increased or decreased crime, liberals and conservatives who were good at math misinterpreted the results to conform to their political leanings. In other words, once politics was introduced, people could not accept a finding that conflicted with their beliefs.

The Washington Post launched The Fact Checker in 2007, coincidentally at the same time that PolitiFact, another early fact-checking organization, was founded. Both projects were born out of journalistic frustration. Editors and reporters concluded that they had not consistently vetted the claims of politicians and advocacy groups, and they had failed to expose the shaky intelligence on weapons of mass destruction that was used to justify George W. Bush's invasion of Iraq in 2003. Campaign controversies such as the "swift boat" attacks on 2004 Democratic presidential candidate John Kerry and the release of fabricated documents concerning Bush's National Guard service also demonstrated the need for a dedicated fact-checking team.

In politics, you only succeed if you win. After more than three decades of covering government, politics and diplomacy—in the halls of Congress and at the White House and the State, Treasury and Transportation departments—I have found little difference between the two parties on this basic fact: They will both stretch the truth if they believe it will give them a political advantage. The rationale behind The Fact Checker was this: Just like most people would not buy a used car without checking under the hood, neither should people accept what a politician says to advance his or her policy preferences without checking out the facts.

At least five days a week, we take detailed looks at a politicians' statements and examine the facts behind those claims. We dig through government reports, find relevant data, speak to analysts and experts and of course challenge the politician's staff to explain the source of their information. Then, in what at the time was considered a groundbreaking innovation, we make a ruling on how truthful each statement is, using a Pinocchio scale. It is like a reverse restaurant review, ranging from One Pinocchio (selective telling of the truth) to Four Pinocchios (a whopper). Those Pinocchios got politicians' attention. No longer could they expect the newspaper to settle for dueling quotes from both sides, leaving readers puzzling over who was right. Instead, we are the readers' advocate, showing them how we do our research and why a politician's claim is misleading.

We aim to write deeply about policy issues. In many cases, a politician's statement is simply a jumping-off point to educate readers about complicated policy issues—health care, taxes, foreign policy and so forth. Politicians often speak in code or shorthand. We have found that the more complex a subject is, the more likely a politician will try to hoodwink voters about it. Our goal is to make people better informed, not to change votes. (Indeed, one study found that fact checks of Trump improve the accuracy of readers' beliefs about what's true, even among his supporters, but they do not change attitudes toward Trump.)

For political fact-checkers, there's nothing more satisfying than finally figuring out how a politician has manipulated statistics to promote a policy. After all, if a politician has to fiddle with the facts to sell a proposal, maybe something's wrong with the policy.

But we had never encountered a politician like Trump—so cavalier about the facts, so unconcerned with accuracy, so willing to attack people for made-up reasons and so determined to falsely depict his achievements. Presidents previously sought to speak with authority; Trump wants to brag or berate, usually armed with false information.

One hallmark of Trump's dishonesty is that if he thinks a false or incorrect claim is a winner, he will repeat it constantly, no matter how often it has been proven wrong. Many politicians are embarrassed to receive a Four-Pinocchio rating; often, they will drop or refine the offending talking point. Some even apologize for their departure from the truth. Trump digs in and doubles down. He keeps going long after the facts are clear, in what appears to be a deliberate effort to replace the truth with his own, far more favorable, version.

When Trump was elected president, The Fact Checker team faced a conundrum. In fact-checking Trump, we did not want to have our core function—writing about policy—sidelined by chasing down the president's latest tweet or ignorant assertion. We also wanted to note when he simply repeated a false claim without having to constantly write new fact checks to respond to old deceptions. So we decided to create a database, starting with the first 100 days of the new administration, to record every false or misleading claim. Our standard was that it had to be a statement that merited at least Two Pinocchios (essentially "half-true") on our rating scale. The president sometimes repeats the same claim several times in a speech, but to keep it simple we decided we would record only one entry per news event (a speech, rally or remarks to reporters), no matter how often he repeated the same falsehood in that setting.

In those first 100 days, we counted 492 claims, or almost five a day. Readers urged us to keep going. Though maintaining the database was time-consuming, it seemed manageable. We decided to continue at least through Trump's first year. He maintained a pace of about six claims a day. This behavior clearly was not going to go away. We announced we would keep the database going through the rest of his term.

It quickly went downhill from there. In his second year, Trump effectively became his own press secretary. The daily White House media briefings got shorter and shorter and were eventually eliminated. Instead, Trump began talking more to reporters, on the White House lawn or in interviews with friendly TV hosts. His speeches got longer. He tweeted more frequently. The number of false and misleading claims exploded; midway through 2018, the number of monthly claims doubled from the pace earlier in the year. Our weekends and evenings were soon lost to the depressing task of wading through the president's forest of falsehoods.

We eventually realized we needed a better method for tracking Trump's insistent repetition of clearly false claims. We were hesitant to use the label "lie" when we couldn't discern Trump's intent, but we wanted to reflect the fact that he was peddling propaganda. In 2018, we introduced the "Bottomless Pinocchio," a Web page that lists each distinct Trump claim that has earned a rating of Three Pinocchios ("mostly false") or Four Pinocchios—and been repeated at least 20 times. The list was announced on Dec. 10, 2018, with 14 claims. It grew to 32 claims by Jan. 20, 2020.

Maybe because The Fact Checker Pinocchio is such a visually-arresting image—and because our ratings are published in the Sunday edition of *The Washington Post*—Trump can't stop talking about our Pinocchios. He's brought them up nearly 20 times, usually to complain that we are nitpicky. "I have to be always very truthful because if I'm a little bit off, they call me a liar," he said at a December 2019 rally. "They'll say, 'He gets a Pinocchio,' the stupid *Washington Post. They're* Pinocchio." Of course, when we award Pinocchios to Democrats, such as Four Pinocchios to Rep. Adam Schiff (D-Calif.), his nemesis in the House impeachment inquiry, Trump is quick to cite the fact check.

Whether all of Trump's false statements could be considered lies is certainly subject to dispute. Many are exaggerated or factually wrong, but "lie" suggests that a person knows his statements are false. In some cases, the word "lie" is clearly justifiable: Trump lied when he said he didn't know about secret payments to alleged paramours; he had been recorded on tape discussing the payments. He also repeatedly lied about Obama's Hawaiian birth certificate, spreading the fiction that it was fake and that Obama likely was born in Kenya. He knew better.

Trump is also quick to falsely accuse his opponents of lying, a typically Trumpian form of projection: His main GOP primary rival in 2016 was "Lyin' Ted" Cruz; Democratic presidential nominee Hillary Clinton was "a pathological liar"; former FBI director James Comey is a "a liar and a leaker"; and Schiff is a "congenital liar."

But in many cases, Trump appears to have persuaded himself that his falsehoods are true. That's because Trump lives only for the moment—what he said yesterday may be completely different from what he says today, and he sees no problem in the inconsistency. For Trump, his statements are relevant only for today's news cycle and are subject to change, even to total contradiction. In a word one could (once upon a time) never use in a family newspaper, Trump is a bullshitter—a characterization that he has occasionally embraced, though he prefers to call himself a "showman" or "master salesman."

Philippe Reines, an aide to Hillary Clinton who played Trump in mock debates during the 2016 campaign, noticed that an easy way to get under Trump's skin is to quote him back to himself. Clinton sent Trump into a rage during one of the presidential debates when she reminded him that he had once tweeted that climate change was a hoax made in China. Trump's ghostwriters and biographers have often noticed that he has little recollection of what he's previously said—and doesn't care if his new comments are the opposite of what he'd said in the past.

The longer Trump has been president, the more he has confined himself to friendly interview settings, such as Fox News shows, where hosts generally do not challenge—and even encourage—his stream-of-consciousness falsehoods. A contentious interview with Leslie Stahl on "60 Minutes" in 2018 was a rare exception. Trump bobbed and weaved as Stahl challenged his claims. Her first question: Did Trump still think climate change is a hoax? He dodged by saying "something's happening." Then Trump completely reversed course and declared that climate change is no hoax: "I'm not denying climate change."

Whatever the venue, Trump routinely exaggerates his accomplishments. He has claimed that he passed the biggest tax cut ever, presided over the best economy in history, scored massive job-creating deals with Saudi Arabia and all but solved the North Korea nuclear crisis. He then repeats those claims over and over, sometimes hundreds of times. The Fact Checker team has identified more than 400 false or misleading claims that the president has repeated at least three times each.

The president often makes statements that are disconnected from his policies. He said his administration did not have a family-separation policy on the border, when it did. Then he said the policy was required because of existing laws, when it was not.

The president also invents faux facts. He repeatedly said U.S. Steel was building six to eight new steel plants, but that wasn't true. He said that as president, Obama gave citizenship to 2,500 Iranians during the nuclear-deal negotiations. It didn't happen. Over and over, Trump claimed that the Uzbekistan-born man who in 2017 was accused of killing eight people with a pickup truck in New York had brought two dozen relatives to the United States through so-called chain migration. The actual number is zero.

The issue of immigration especially animates the president, making it one of the biggest sources of false claims. He loves to suggest the Mara Salvatrucha gang (commonly known as MS-13), which originated in Los Angeles in the 1980s, is akin to a foreign army that has invaded the country.

"It's like liberating, like a war, like there's a foreign invasion. And they occupy your country. And then you get them out through whatever. And they call it liberation," Trump declared at a Wisconsin rally in 2018, prompting some audience members to begin yelling, "Get the hell out!"

This dystopian vision of a violent gang overrunning cities and towns across the United States is divorced from reality. MS-13 operates in a few areas, including Los Angeles, Long Island and the Washington, D.C., region. The 10,000 members in the United States don't make up even 1 percent of all gang members in the country.

In one of his strangest claims, Trump on four separate occasions has falsely asserted that Obama had such a bad relationship with the Philippines that the country's leaders would not let him land his presidential jet during an official visit, leaving him circling above the airport. Trump often seeks to undo and minimize Obama's accomplishments, but why would he conjure such an implausible scenario? The answer, never certain, could be as simple as "because he can."

Sometimes, Trump attempts to create his own reality. Leaders gathered at the U.N. General Assembly in 2018 burst into laughter when Trump uttered a favorite false claim—that he had accomplished more in less than two years than "almost any administration in the history of our country." The president, visibly startled, remarked that he "didn't expect that reaction." Later, he falsely insisted to reporters that his boast "was meant to get some laughter."

Similarly, Trump's response to the 2020 coronavirus outbreak was hobbled by his consistently upbeat pronouncements that the United States was safe, even as the virus rapidly spread around the globe. "We pretty much shut it down coming in from China," he said on

Feb. 2. Three weeks later, he said the coronavirus "is very well under control in our country." The next day, he confidently predicted that the 15 reported cases in the United States at that point "within a couple of days is going to be down to close to zero." Reality struck when thousands of cases spread across the country, deaths spiked and the scope of the public-health crisis was too large to ignore. Only then did Trump shift his tone. "I felt it was a pandemic long before it was called a pandemic," he said on March 17.

The president is also quick to embrace conspiracy theories, even from the most dubious sources, if he believes he can weaponize the claim to his benefit. Trump refused to accept the U.S. intelligence finding that Russia had interfered in the 2016 U.S. election; instead, he seized on the notion that it was actually Ukraine that was responsible for the interference—a false claim spread by Russian intelligence. Trump raised this theory in his July 25, 2019, phone call with Ukraine's apparently nonplussed president, Volodymyr Zelensky. That was the same call in which he urged Zelensky to investigate his potential 2020 campaign rival, former vice president Joe Biden.

That phone call, of course, led to Trump's impeachment. His statement shocked White House aides who were monitoring the call, prompting a whistleblower to file an official complaint. Trump responded in typical fashion: He had done nothing wrong, and the phone call had been "perfect."

Trump even exaggerates when the facts are on his side.

The economy continued to churn out new jobs through his first three years in office, so Trump could reasonably claim to have overseen the creation of 6.7 million jobs in that period. That's a good record. But instead of stopping there, he routinely touted a number that measures job growth starting back at the November 2016 election, rather than beginning when he took office three months later, thus inflating the cumulative figure by 600,000 jobs.

During his campaign and his presidency, Trump has spun the same government data to make diametrically opposing points, seemingly unconcerned about consistency. Data is merely a weapon to be used to make a rhetorical point, rather than information that might inform policymaking.

For most of his first year in office, for instance, Trump bragged about how sharply apprehensions of undocumented immigrants had fallen on the southern border. Using cherry-picked numbers, he claimed a drop of 40 percent, then 61 percent, and then 78 percent.

The president stuck to the 78 percent statistic for months, even when his own fuzzy accounting was out-of-date. Then, after several months of silence on the matter, as the number of apprehensions climbed, he rolled out a new and opposite claim: "We have set records on arrests at the borders."

Both claims are from the same data maintained by U.S. Customs and Border Protection. It's just that Trump flipped the script, twisting the numbers to present the rosiest picture possible. Whereas a *drop* in arrests previously was cause for celebration, now a *surge* in arrests was declared to be even better.

Of course, when arrest numbers started to go down again in 2019, Trump flipped the script back to his original take. "Thanks to our tireless efforts to secure the border, illegal crossings are down 75 percent since May," he crowed at a January 2020 rally.

Trump has played similar games with economic statistics. In Trump's version of history, he "inherited a mess," with "millions of people out there" seeking jobs, whereupon he "accomplished an economic turnaround of historical proportions."

Actually, it was Obama who inherited an economic crisis, with the country shedding 800,000 jobs a month when he took office in 2009. Eight years later, Trump took over when the economy was adding about 200,000 jobs a month, as it continued to do through his first three years. But Trump sought to persuade Americans that the good economy was entirely his own doing—and that it was the best economy ever.

Trump comes from a real estate background, where what he once called "truthful hyperbole" is regarded as the norm. Real estate developers often hype their properties, describing them in gloriously elaborate language, to lure buyers. But Trump went far beyond the usual sales tactics to hone his (mostly invented) image as a wildly successful Manhattan playboy tycoon, misleading reporters, investors, bankers and customers on a regular basis.

As a business reporter for *Newsday* in 1990, I co-wrote one of the first articles about how Trump's portfolio of real estate, airline and casino holdings was under stress—he later filed for Chapter 11 bankruptcy protection six times. Our article recounted numerous examples of the disconnect between his public statements and reality. So I was familiar with Trump's dysfunctional relationship with the truth. He made it appear as if he had paid $10 million in cash for his Palm Beach estate, Mar-a-Largo, when court records later revealed he had put up only $2,000. (Chase Manhattan Bank helped in this subterfuge by not recording its loan to buy the property in public records, court records showed.) And Trump claimed he paid only $30 million for Manhattan's St. Moritz hotel, but legal filings showed he had paid nearly $74 million—and had an $80 million loan from Bankers Trust.

While running his businesses, Trump rarely faced public consequences for his lack of truthfulness. Apartment buyers who realized they had been misled about condo sales or banks that concluded he had lied about his net worth did not put out news releases; they simply would not do business with him again. A rare instance in which Trump's deceit became public came when he sued a reporter, Timothy O'Brien, for writing a biography that questioned Trump's claims about his net worth. As part of the lawsuit, Trump was forced to endure a two-day deposition in which lawyers for the other side caught him 30 times making false statements—about condo sales, golf-club membership prices, the number of his employees, his debts and his earnings. At one point, he asserted he had been paid $1 million for making a speech, but under oath conceded he'd received only $400,000 in cash. The other $600,000 was his fuzzy estimate of the value of the publicity he had received.

When Trump in 2015 suddenly announced he was running for president, our fact check of his error-filled announcement speech began with these words: "Businessman Donald Trump is a fact checker's dream . . . and nightmare."

That may sound prophetic, but we were unprepared for the tsunami of untruths we would encounter over the course of the campaign. Most politicians earn Four Pinocchios about 15 to 20 percent of the time. Before Trump, only one politician—Rep. Michele Bachmann of Minnesota—had received Four Pinocchios for more than 30 percent of the claims we examined. But 65 percent of Trump's statements received Four-Pinocchio ratings over the course of the campaign.

The list of false claims was endless. Trump said he had watched thousands of Muslims in New Jersey cheer the fall of the World Trade Center; there is no TV footage, no newspaper coverage, just scattered, unconfirmed reports of five or six people celebrating—and they were not necessarily Muslim and probably only teenagers. He said the wives of the 9/11 attackers were sent home from the United States before the attacks; all but one of the attackers was unmarried—and the wife of the married terrorist never visited the United States. He said millions of undocumented immigrants ("illegal aliens") were flooding U.S. borders, even though the estimated number of undocumented immigrants has been static for years.

Trump had been making false statements about his business prowess from the moment he appeared in a *New York Times* profile in 1976. In the presidential campaign 40 years later, he continued to mislead about his career.

During the campaign, Trump said he got his start in business with only a $1 million loan from his father, which he then turned into a $10 billion empire. But most experts who have looked at the available numbers say Trump is not worth anywhere close to $10 billion. And Trump's father gave him more than that single $1 million loan. Trump actually inherited tens of millions. Most famously, when one of Trump's casinos was teetering on the edge, unable to make a mortgage payment, his father bought $3.5 million in gambling chips—and then did not use them, effectively giving his son a cash infusion. The hotel then used the cash to make the mortgage payment. Gambling regulators later called that an illegal loan.

Such falsehoods were part of Trump's secret sauce for getting elected. Most politicians would have been wary of making such claims because they knew they were false. But Trump said many things that his supporters already believed to be true, so he sounded like the first politician who actually told the truth. And having watched his act for 14 seasons as a decisive boss on "The Apprentice," the popular NBC reality-TV show, supporters readily accepted the story that he was a self-made success. His claims often got an extra boost of credibility when right-leaning media outlets such as Fox News and Breitbart amplified them for Americans who get their information in a right-leaning media silo.

Trump had long found many of his pseudo-facts by listening to talk radio, such as Rush Limbaugh's nationwide broadcast or New York's "Bob Grant Show." Sam Nunberg, a Trump campaign aide, recently revealed that a major source for Trump's campaign rhetoric was Mark Levin's syndicated radio show. Nunberg would email Trump about issues that animated Levin's conservative listeners, and then Trump began listening to the show himself. When Trump appeared on the show, as Politico's Michael Kruse put it, he gave "Levin's listeners what they wanted—which essentially was . . . Levin's ideas, studiously collected by Nunberg, consumed by Trump and regurgitated back to the host."

Trump has earned fierce loyalty from his base through such techniques, but he also has trapped himself. His narrow 2016 victory was such a surprise, especially to the Republican establishment, that Trump could have governed as he campaigned—somewhat aloof from party orthodoxy and affiliation. He might have cut bipartisan deals to restructure the Affordable Care Act, fund infrastructure projects and assist the so-called dreamers, undocumented immigrants who had arrived in the United States as children. But while such outreach might have earned Trump support from people who did not vote for him, it also could have angered voters who tuned into Mark Levin's show. While Trump occasionally dabbles in such deal-making—he even briefly considered gun-control legislation—he invariably runs back to positions supported by his base. Trump's inability to reach across the aisle—indeed, his constant effort to deride his opponents as evil, duplicitous people—has exacerbated an already deep partisan divide. The result is that Trump has not been able to expand his support, becoming the first president since World War II who never once has achieved an average approval rating above 50 percent.

To be fair, Trump for decades has held dear to certain lodestones, including a belief that the United States is getting ripped off by international trade deals, that tariffs are good and that foreign alliances are suspect. Those instincts run counter to Republican orthodoxy, but through the force of his personality and the loyalty of his base, he has managed to persuade most Republican lawmakers to adopt his program and support nearly everything he says (or at least to acquiesce publicly, even if they privately hold different beliefs).

Trump's dysfunctional relationship with the truth has made it easier for him to control his own party. And conversely, his party's near-absolute support for him has assured that Trump faces little risk when he makes false statements. During the Obama years, we fact-checked nearly 200 statements by the president. These often were complex checks, because Obama generally spoke carefully and used the full resources of the government to vet his speeches. Obama was not happy to receive Pinocchios, so his White House staff often worked hard to defend his remarks and provide factual backup for his statements. When Obama got in trouble with his facts, it was generally when he spoke off-the-cuff or was in campaign mode, such as making unwarranted attacks on Mitt Romney's business record.

Trump's misstatements are more casual and routine than Obama's, posing a difficult challenge for The Fact Checker team. (The Trump White House also almost never responds to our queries.) Many of Trump's claims are such nonsense that they can be checked in minutes. During the 2016 campaign, for instance, Trump claimed he would save $300 billion a year in Medicare by negotiating for prescription drug prices—but Medicare spent only $78 billion a year on prescription drugs. That was a five-minute fact check. (When Chris Wallace of Fox News called out Trump on his fantastical Medicare math during one of the primary debates, Trump appeared confused about why it was even an issue.)

And the opportunities for the news media to expose or push back against such claims have been sharply curtailed since Trump took office. The president's constant banter with reporters is a poor substitute for a White House briefing. (The administration also largely eliminated State Department and Pentagon briefings.) Past administrations have discovered that the rigor of preparing to brief the press forced officials to confront contradictions in policies and required better coordination among Cabinet agencies. Just as muscles get flabby when you don't work out regularly, an administration's policy process withers without the daily requirement to agree on how to explain its positions to reporters. But there does not appear to be much of a policy process in the Trump White House. Much depends on the whims of the president, who contradicts himself from day to day. Since few officials want to take the risk of advocating a policy position, only to be reversed by the president, the rest of the administration has become largely silent—leaving only one voice of authority.

That voice is distinctive. Trump is needy and boastful; he's often a bully, yet he is easily offended. He makes jokes, often with a nasty tone, but rarely about himself.

Bella DePaulo, a social scientist at the University of California at Santa Barbara, studied Trump's falsehoods using The Fact Checker's database, drawing on claims the president made in his first year in office. Research indicates that most people tell an average of nearly two lies a day, mostly in service of their own self-interest. About half of the lies told by participants in DePaulo's previous surveys were self-serving, compared with about a quarter that were told to advantage, flatter or protect someone else. Only a tiny percentage of falsehoods were labeled as mean-spirited. By contrast, DePaulo found that two-thirds of Trump's falsehoods were self-serving and slightly less than 10 percent were meant to be kind. That meant he told nearly seven times as many self-serving lies as kind ones. Then, when DePaulo catalogued claims by Trump that could be deemed hurtful or disparaging, she found that "instead of adding up to 1 or 2 percent, as in my previous research, they accounted for 50 percent. When I first saw that number appear on my screen, I gasped."

In another surprise, Trump's falsehoods often fell into more than one category: He managed to both belittle others and enhance himself with the same statement. DePaulo offered this tweet as an example: "Senator Bob Corker 'begged' me to endorse him for reelection in Tennessee. I said 'NO' and he dropped out (said he could not win without my endorsement)." Corker said he didn't do any begging; rather, Trump had called him to reconsider his decision not to seek reelection and offered his endorsement.

Trump speaks at the reading level of a 4th or 5th grader (as measured by the Flesch–Kincaid Grade Level Formula), according to an analysis by FactBa.se, a website that tracks Trump's statements. That is the lowest grade level of any president since Herbert Hoover. Obama, Ronald Reagan, George W. Bush and Bill Clinton spoke at an 8th or 9th grade reading level, according to the analysis, which studied at least 100,000 words spoken in unscripted settings such as news conferences and interviews. Yet Trump also has a unique ability to command attention, according to a study that monitored brain activity as participants watched 2016 debate clips.

The full Trump effect is clear at his campaign rallies. He has a collection of favorite falsehoods, which he sprinkles into riffs on perceived insults or malfeasance by his enemies. He alternates between bragging about his supposed successes and pitching himself as a victim of intrigues by Democrats. A little less than one-third of his factual statements are correct, according to a detailed examination The Fact Checker team has made of three rallies. For two rallies in 2018 and one in 2019, we catalogued every assertion by the president, and the results were stunning: Two-thirds to three-quarters of the claims were false, mostly false or unsupported by evidence. His pitter-patter of data points and outraged stories are intended to suggest a degree of verisimilitude to his supporters. At a two-hour rally in Michigan in December 2019, Trump presented 179 statements as facts, more than one a minute, of which 67 percent were false or misleading.

At his rallies, Trump depicts himself as a political superhero, able to bend the will of government, the economy or other nations with a force previous presidents have lacked. More than 100 times, for instance, Trump has falsely claimed he passed into law the Veterans Choice Act. At one rally in 2018, Trump suggested the law was the result of a brilliant brainstorm. "I said, 'I have the greatest idea. We're going to do this. If a veteran has to wait, we're going to send them to a private doctor. We'll pay the bill.' What a genius—I said, I said, 'How good is that?' They said, 'Sir, we've been trying to get it passed for 44 years.'"

Actually, Barack Obama signed into law the Veterans Choice Act in 2014, two years before Trump became president. Trump merely signed an expansion of that law.

When Trump inserts the word "sir" in a story, it's often a sign that he's telling a fairy tale. (Almost 100 claims in The Fact Checker database involve a story in which some hapless soul calls Trump "sir," only to learn of his brilliance.) He regales his audiences with tales of tough, beefy men who collapse into tears because of something he has accomplished. Usually, the alleged tears happened backstage, making it difficult to verify. But on three occasions, Trump has claimed that when he signed a repeal of an Obama rule at a White House ceremony, tears were flowing.

"Strong people, very strong, men and women, and almost all of them were crying," he informed the Economic Club of New York in 2019.

"Half of them were crying," he said in a 2019 speech to the American Farm Bureau Federation.

"People that haven't cried in many years," Trump again told the Farm Bureau in 2020. "Some of them were so tough they never cried, they didn't cry when they were babies, and they were crying."

There's a video of the 2017 signing ceremony available on YouTube. Every eye witnessing the signing is dry.

A RISING TIDE: TRUMP'S FALSE OR MISLEADING CLAIMS

Total number of claims per month

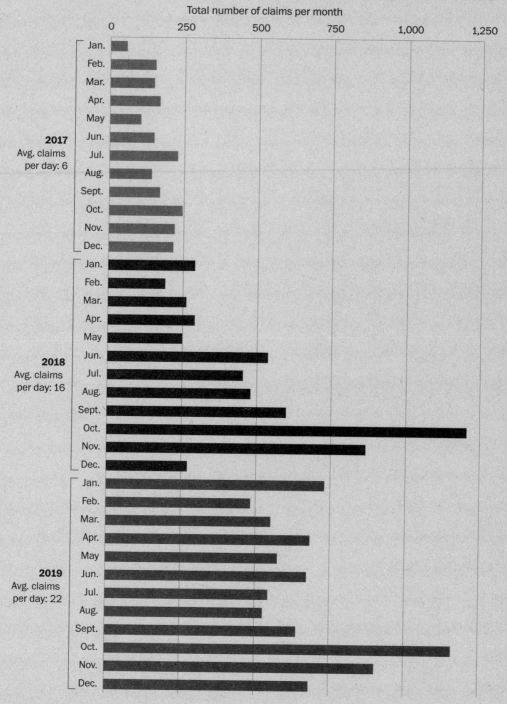

CHAPTER ONE

The Biggest Whoppers:
"Mexico's Paying"

Selecting Trump's Top Ten false or misleading claims is like assembling a year-end list of best songs from an ocean of tunes—thousands of singles and dozens of genres. A pop critic may struggle over whether a list should be filled with critical successes, pop chart darlings or esoteric yet wondrous pieces of music.

That's the challenge The Fact Checker team faced as we tried to select the president's biggest whoppers out of more than 16,000 possibilities. Are the most troubling claims the ones he has repeated most regularly? Or those with the strongest impact on policy or politics? Should the claim be completely, unarguably false, or is it more insidious if the claim is merely misleading, but about a vitally important or sensitive topic? Does it matter when he said it—in the raucous uncertainty of his first months in office, or three years later, after he'd surrounded himself with aides less likely to push back?

Ultimately, we decided that this chapter should collect the most egregious and important false claims, the ones that reveal something essential about Trump's term in office. This list mirrors the most prominent themes in Trump's vision for the country—a strictly controlled immigration system, an economy unleashed

1

from regulations and focused on job creation, a world that respects American strength and allows the United States to go its own way. The list also reveals Trump's fears and peeves, focusing on his enduring sensitivity about being laughed at, disrespected or dismissed.

The claims in this chapter boil down to three types of false statements: "I did it," "It wasn't me," and "They did it."

"I DID IT"

Trump has said that repetition of a claim can lead people to believe it. He has taken that credo to heart. He often takes credit for any act that might be perceived positively. Never mind if a simple Google search can prove these assertions false.

 "Mexico's paying for the wall. You know that. You'll see that. It's all worked out. Mexico's paying."
—Jan. 14, 2020 (campaign rally)

Having Mexico pay for a giant wall along the U.S.-Mexico border was the president's signature campaign line, drawing cheers at every rally.

Trump first made this promise when he announced his candidacy in June 2015. "I would build a great wall, and nobody builds walls better than me, believe me," he told the crowd. "I'll build them very inexpensively, I will build a great, great wall on our southern border. And I will have Mexico pay for that wall."

Spoiler alert: Mexico has not paid for the wall. Nor is there any suggestion that it will. A leaked transcript from Trump's first weeks in office suggests even he wasn't convinced that Mexico would pay. In his first call with then-president Enrique Peña Nieto, Trump told the Mexican leader that they were "both in a little bit of a political bind because I have to have Mexico pay for the wall." The president then bargained with himself, asking Peña Nieto not to outright say "we will not pay." Trump concluded that "I am willing to say that we will work it out, but that means it will come out in the wash and that is okay. But you cannot say anymore that the United States is going to pay for the wall. I am just going to say that we are working it out."

Even if that sounded like a clear acknowledgment that Mexico would not pay for the wall, it did not deter Trump from finding myriad ways to suggest that his seminal campaign promise might yet come to fruition.

Ahead of the 2018 midterm elections, he claimed that his minor reworking of the North American Free Trade Agreement would provide the money to pay for the wall. But that's not how economics works. Countries do not "lose" money on trade deficits, so there is no money to earn; the size of a trade deficit or surplus can be determined by other factors besides trade. Changes in the trade balance with Mexico would not generate cash for the wall.

Trump eventually dropped that talking point only to resurrect an earlier, simpler version. In January 2020, Trump said, "Mexico's paying for the wall. You know that. You'll see that. It's all worked out. Mexico's paying."

There's no evidence for that claim. Trump never won congressional approval for his big concrete wall, but started replacing existing barriers with bollard fencing and, in his fourth year in office, has finally begun to break ground on the border in limited locations where no barrier previously existed. But the current barrier construction is being paid for with billions of dollars appropriated by

Congress for the defense budget and raided by Trump over congressional opposition.

Mexico is still not paying for the wall.

 "Republicans will always protect patients with preexisting conditions. We're doing it."

—Nov. 4, 2018 (campaign rally)

 Donald J. Trump
@realDonaldTrump

"I was the person who saved Pre-Existing Conditions in your Healthcare, you have it now."—Jan. 13, 2020

Trump's biggest domestic defeat of his presidency was his failed drive to repeal the Affordable Care Act. The effort that collapsed in the Senate would have weakened a key tenet of Obamacare: protections for people with preexisting health conditions.

After that defeat, Trump's rhetoric shifted: He falsely asserted nearly 75 times that Republicans had protected people with preexisting conditions.

In 2020, he even tweeted that "I was the person who saved Pre-Existing Conditions in your Healthcare." He didn't.

Obamacare included two provisions designed to make health care accessible regardless of a person's health status: guaranteed issue, which means insurance companies must sell a policy to anyone who wants to buy one, and community rating, which means that people within the same geographic area who buy similar insurance and are the same age will pay similar prices. The two elements together made insurance more affordable for people with ailments

4

that require expensive treatment, such as cancer. Before passage of the ACA, even minor health problems could lead an insurance company to deny coverage because insurers could factor in a person's health status when determining premiums.

On the 2016 campaign trail and throughout his first year in office, Trump fervently opposed Obamacare, promising to repeal and replace it. In theory, the proposed replacement could have strengthened protections for preexisting health conditions, but neither the House nor the Senate GOP plan did so. Either proposal likely would have resulted in higher costs for people with preexisting conditions in some states, according to the Congressional Budget Office. Both proposals would have weakened those protections by letting states seek waivers from the ACA to consider a person's health status when writing insurance policies.

Even after losing his repeal-and-replace effort in Congress, Trump took other steps that could have harmed people with preexisting conditions. The administration refused to defend the ACA against a lawsuit that would declare Obamacare unconstitutional, thereby putting such protections at risk. Then, the administration called for the entire law to be struck down. And it issued new rules that promoted the use of low-quality, short-term insurance plans that had been prohibited under the ACA. (A federal judge ruled that those new rules were legal.) These plans typically allow insurers to deny coverage or charge higher prices to people with existing health conditions.

This is a prime example of where up is down in Trump world. As the president repeatedly takes steps to weaken coverage for people with preexisting health conditions, he falsely claims he "saved" it. Trump had nothing to do with the bill that Obama signed into law in 2010.

"Many [NATO] nations owe vast sums of money from past years, and it is very unfair to the United States. These nations must pay what they owe."

—March 17, 2017 (news conference)

"So when I came in, as you know, NATO was virtually a dead organization. It had no money. Nobody was paying except us. Practically nobody was paying."

—Jan. 10, 2020 (interview)

Throughout the 2016 campaign and his presidency, Trump has demonstrated he has little notion of how the North Atlantic Treaty Organization (NATO) is funded and operates. He repeatedly claimed that other members of the alliance "owed" money to the United States and that they were delinquent in their payments. Then he claimed credit for the money "pouring in" as a result of his jaw-boning, even though much of the increase in those countries' contributions had been set under guidelines arranged during the Obama administration.

There are two types of funding for NATO: direct and indirect. The 29 member countries make direct payments to share the cost of the actual alliance (for example, maintenance and headquarters activity). Trump routinely suggested that the United States paid 70 percent of NATO's costs, but the actual total is far lower: about 22 percent, the largest share of any country. Germany is second, with about 15 percent, though Trump sought an agreement to make the two nations' payments equal.

Indirect spending is what NATO countries spend on their own defense budgets. NATO members are supposed to spend at least 2 percent of their gross domestic product (GDP) on defense spending, but many of them don't reach that level and the commitment is voluntary and not legally binding. After Russia seized Crimea from Ukraine, the Obama administration in 2014 secured an agreement among member nations to increase their spending on defense to the 2 percent guideline within 10 years, by 2024. As Trump became president, NATO members' spending on defense was already on an upward slope and there was wide acknowledgment that the Europeans were not spending as much as they could on defense. None of the increase in defense spending would go to the United States or even necessarily to NATO; this is money that countries would use to bolster their own militaries, effectively supporting the alliance's operations.

Experts say it's virtually impossible to calculate how much of overall U.S. defense spending is devoted to NATO. The mismatch in defense spending occurs in large part because the U.S. military projects its might across the globe, while many other members of the alliance focus more on defending their own homeland.

We wrote many fact checks on this issue, and Trump consistently refused to acknowledge how NATO operates. Trump's aides found this frustrating. *Washington Post* reporters Philip Rucker and Carol Leonnig, in their 2020 book, "A Very Stable Genius," described what happened when top military brass tried to explain the NATO fundamentals.

> Trump proceeded to explain that NATO, too, was worthless. U.S. generals were letting the allied member countries get away with murder, he said, and they owed the United States a lot of money after not living up to their promise of paying their dues.
>
> "They're in arrears," Trump said, reverting to the language of real estate. He lifted both his arms at his sides in frustration. Then he scolded top officials for the untold millions of dollars he believed they had let slip through their fingers by allowing allies to avoid their obligations.

"We're proposing one of the largest tax cuts in history, even larger than that of President Ronald Reagan. Our tax cut is bigger."

—May 1, 2017 (speech)

 "We did pass the largest tax cut in the history of the country, bigger than Ronald Reagan's tax cut."

—Nov. 15, 2019 (interview)

Trump has always had a bit of an obsession with Ronald Reagan, a Republican icon. In May 2017, when the administration's tax plan was still in the planning stages, Trump announced to the Independent Community Bankers Association of America, prompting a wave of applause, that "We're proposing one of the largest tax cuts in history, even larger than that of President Ronald Reagan. Our tax cut is bigger." He reinforced that statement, with similar wording, repeatedly—before the legislation was written, after it passed Congress and two years after it was implemented. After three years in office, Trump had made some variation of this claim 184 times.

Repetition doesn't make it true.

The best way to compare tax cuts over time is to measure them as a percentage of the Gross Domestic Product (GDP), the broadest measure of the U.S. economy. Using a method that the Treasury Department has deployed to compare tax cuts and hikes through the last half-century, we computed that Trump's tax cut amounts to nearly 0.9 percent of GDP, meaning it is far smaller than Reagan's tax cut in 1981, which added up to 2.89 percent of GDP. Trump's tax cut was also smaller than two tax cuts Congress passed under Obama.

Looking back at other tax cuts over the past 100 years, we found that Trump can claim only to have passed the eighth-largest tax cut in the last century—a far cry from the biggest in U.S. history.

Donald J. Trump
@realDonaldTrump

"95% Approval Rating in the Republican Party, A Record. Thank You!"—Jan. 18, 2020

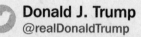

"A recent poll came out: Ninety-five percent approval rating for me in the Republican Party, which is a record. Ronald Reagan was at 87. He was the second."

—Dec. 4, 2019 (remarks)

Donald J. Trump
@realDonaldTrump

"New Poll says Trump, at over 90%, is the most popular Republican in history of the Party. Wow!"—July 10, 2018

Trump's ego is in full flower when he steps away from the details of policy and focuses on his personal success. Few examples illustrate this as clearly as the president's boasts about his own popularity. At least 50 times, he has referred to himself as "the most popular Republican in the history of the Party," noting that Ronald Reagan "was second." As evidence, Trump points to a "90–94 percent approval rating" among Republicans, which, he claims, is an "all-time record."

None of these statements—which are spread across two years—are accurate.

A Gallup poll from June 2018, when Trump first uttered this

boast, found that 90 percent of Republicans approved of Trump's performance. But that didn't make him the "most popular Republican in history." Nor does it mean his support among Republicans was greater than Reagan's. In reality, until he was impeached, Trump was in sixth place among GOP presidents since World War II: George W. Bush maintained an approval rating of close to 99 percent of Republicans during his first term after the Sept. 11 attacks. His father, George H.W. Bush, reached a peak of 97 percent popularity within his own party in 1991, after the successful conclusion of the Persian Gulf War. Ronald Reagan hit a high of 94 percent at the end of 1984, Richard Nixon a high of 91 percent in 1973 and Dwight Eisenhower a high of 95 percent in 1956.

Only Gerald Ford was less popular among Republicans than Trump.

That hasn't stopped Trump from repeating these claims, generally pointing to a 94 or 95 percent approval rating among Republicans. But in early 2020, the impeachment trial rallied Republicans around Trump, and a Gallup poll in January showed him with an approval rating of 92 percent; one poll even had him at 94 percent. That jump moved him up the ranks of GOP presidents, but he still has a long way to go.

Trump at one point acknowledged that he had not topped George W. Bush's record. But he sought to dismiss that detail in a Bloomberg News interview in 2018. "In fact, I guess the Republican poll came out, there's one at 92 and one at 93 and one at 90, and they're the highest numbers that have ever been, with the exception of a tiny period of time with a bullhorn," Trump said, referring to Bush's rallying of the nation after the Sept. 11 attacks. "But that period lasted for about a week."

Ultimately, no matter how you measure it, Trump has never achieved the "all-time record" for approval from Republicans.

"IT WASN'T ME"

If you haven't heard Shaggy's 1999 hit, "It Wasn't Me," put down this book, go listen and come right back. Trust us. The Jamaican reggae singer's anthem about a cheating boyfriend and his girlfriend who "came in and she caught me red-handed, creeping with the girl next door" concludes that the only way to deal with very bad facts is to deny them outright. (Caught on camera? It wasn't me.)

The president seems to have taken a class in exactly this type of denial—getting "caught red-handed" only to say "it wasn't me"—offering plainly baseless responses to unflattering realities. He turned to this strategy when he lied about hush payments to his alleged paramours, when he pretended to have nothing to do with his administration's family separation policy and against the whistleblower claim that led to his impeachment.

No one would call Shaggy's approach anything but "lying," but a political war of words has developed over how to characterize Trump's statements. Many of the president's critics have demanded that his false statements be called "lies." We hesitate to use that term unless we can determine that Trump knew he wasn't telling the truth.

But in one prominent case, we concluded that no other word would be accurate. The president's claim that he knew nothing about hush-money payments to silence women with whom he allegedly had extramarital affairs was obviously false and could not have stemmed from ignorance. We deemed it a lie.

 "No. No. What else? . . . Well, you'll have to ask Michael Cohen. Michael is my attorney. And you'll have to ask Michael Cohen. . . . No, I don't know [about the payment to Stormy Daniels]. No."

—April 5, 2018 (remarks)

 "Later on I knew [about the payments to Stormy Daniels]. Later on."

—Aug. 23, 2018 (interview)

 "I had nothing to do with [Stormy Daniels]. So she can lie and she can do whatever she wants to do."

—Oct. 16, 2018 (interview)

Through most of 2016, the Trump campaign was plagued by rumors about his treatment of women. If Trump's treatment of then–Fox News anchor Megyn Kelly lit the first match, the revelation of a decade-old "Access Hollywood" tape of Trump speaking graphically about kissing and groping women without consent poured lighter fluid on the smoldering fire.

After the tape's release, more than a dozen women came forward to accuse Trump of improper conduct or sexual assault. Many of the women produced witnesses who say they heard about these incidents when they happened—long before Trump's political aspirations were known.

In investigations of sexual abuse allegations, such contemporaneous accounts can help bolster the credibility of the "she said" side of a "he said, she said" standoff. Accounts from people who were told about an incident immediately after it happened don't necessarily prove an allegation, but they can give the news media more confidence about when to report on such allegations. Five of the alleged victims produced at least two witnesses.

In addition to the sexual misconduct allegations, the campaign was plagued by rumors of extramarital affairs and hush-money payments of tens of thousands of dollars aimed at covering up those affairs. Initially, Trump staffers and lawyers brushed off such allegations as tabloid noise or issued flat denials, saying they "had no knowledge of any of this."

When Trump finally weighed in, in response to a question in April 2018 about whether he knew about a $130,000 payment to porn star Stephanie Clifford, who uses the stage name Stormy Daniels, the president delivered a flat "no." He told reporters to ask his attorney, Michael Cohen.

> **Reporter:** "Why did Michael Cohen make [the payment], if there was no truth to her allegations?"
> **Trump:** "You'll have to ask Michael Cohen. Michael is my attorney, and you'll have to ask Michael."
> **Reporter:** "Do you know where he got the money to make that payment?"
> **Trump:** "No. I don't know."

Every answer was false. Trump knew about the payment, he knew Cohen made the payment in an effort to kill damaging stories, and he knew Cohen was reimbursed for laying out the hush money.

Four days after that interview, federal prosecutors raided Cohen's office. Many months later, Cohen's attorney, Lanny Davis, released a recording Cohen had secretly made of his conversation with Trump two months before the election, in which the two discussed an arrangement with the *National Enquirer* to pay $150,000 to *Playboy* model Karen McDougal, another woman who alleged an affair with Trump.

Cohen eventually pleaded guilty to federal charges, telling a judge he had paid off two women to silence them before the 2016 election "at the direction of" a candidate running for federal office, a reference to Trump. Cohen admitted that the payments were illegal.

In an Aug. 22, 2018, interview with Fox News, Trump falsely tried to reframe the issue. He insisted that the payments had not been a "campaign violation." The payments "didn't come out of the campaign," he said. "They came from me."

He knew the payments were made, and he knew why. He lied.

Donald J. Trump
@realDonaldTrump

"Separating families at the Border is the fault of bad legislation passed by the Democrats. Border Security laws should be changed but the Dems can't get their act together!"—June 5, 2018

"President Obama had child separation. Take a look. The press knows it, you know it, we all know it. I didn't have— I'm the one that stopped it. President Obama had child separation. . . . President Obama separated children. They had child separation. I was the one that changed it, okay?"

—April 9, 2019 (remarks)

When outrage over parents being separated from children at the U.S.-Mexico border swept the nation in the summer of 2018, Trump pointed to Democrats and the Obama administration as the culprits.

Trump said he "hated the children being taken away" and "didn't like the sight or the feeling of families being separated." He contended that it had happened in "many administrations" and said Democrats needed to "change their law." Trump even called on Congress to change the laws.

Trump's account is false. The Obama administration rejected a plan for family separations, whereas the Trump administration started testing the idea in mid-July 2017 and then nine months later introduced it across the southern border.

The administration's zero-tolerance policy aimed to prosecute as many border-crossing offenses as possible. The decision to charge illegal border-crossings at an unprecedented rate led directly to family separations because the Justice Department doesn't prosecute children along with their parents. The zero-tolerance policy produced nearly 2,000 separations of immigrant children from their parents during six weeks in April and May 2018, according to the Department of Homeland Security. In total, the department reported that more than 5,400 children were separated from their parents between July 1, 2017, and June 26, 2018.

The Trump administration continues to separate children from parents in special circumstances (when children face danger from a parent, or adults make false claims of parentage, or in human trafficking cases), and the American Civil Liberties Union and others have argued that the administration is abusing those criteria to divide many families for undeserved or arbitrary reasons.

The Trump administration implemented this policy by choice and could end it by choice. No law requires the separations.

 "You had a fake whistleblower that wrote a report that bore no relationship to what was said."

—Jan. 16, 2020 (remarks)

"The fake whistleblower said something about the call—many things that were wrong."

—Nov. 8, 2019 (remarks)

In September 2019, a whistleblower alleged that Trump pushed his Ukrainian counterpart, Volodymyr Zelensky, to investigate his potential 2020 election rival, former vice president Joe Biden—a potential abuse of the presidency for personal gain.

The president replied by calling the whistleblower's facts "so incorrect" and "very inaccurate." Trump said he "didn't know what was on the call." The president made some variation of this statement nearly 90 times over four months in response to the House's impeachment inquiry.

But the whistleblower report is correct on key details about the call between Trump and Zelensky, according to the rough transcript released by the White House. Other details contained in the whistleblower complaint have been largely confirmed, according to The Fact Checker's line-by-line examination of the report.

The rough transcript of the Trump–Zelensky call shows that Trump asked Zelensky to "initiate or continue an investigation" into Joe Biden and to "meet or speak" with Trump's personal lawyer Rudolph W. Giuliani and with Attorney General William Barr. The transcript also shows that the only "corruption cases" discussed involved Biden and the DNC.

Documents, testimony and media reports confirmed other allegations by the whistleblower, including U.S. envoy Kurt Volker's role, Giuliani's behind-the-scenes unofficial diplomacy and Trump's decision to make a phone call or meeting with Zelensky dependent on whether the Ukrainian was willing to "play ball." Media reports and congressional testimony also confirmed that the U.S. ambassador to Ukraine was recalled under "pressure," that Trump suspended all U.S. security assistance to Ukraine in mid-July and that there was official concern about Giuliani's "circumvention" of foreign policy. The whistleblower was also right about the cancellation of Vice President Mike Pence's plans to attend Zelensky's inauguration and the fact that some Ukrainian officials were aware as soon as early August that U.S. aid might be in jeopardy. The White House separately confirmed the whistleblower's assertion that officials intervened to "lock down" records of the call.

The only significant claim in the whistleblower report that could not be confirmed was that Trump suggested that Ukrainian prosecutor Yuriy Lutsenko be retained in his job. The transcript is not clear on this issue, and Volker testified that he believed Trump was referring to Lutsenko's predecessor, Viktor Shokin.

In short, the whistleblower was not "inaccurate"; he had a solid grasp of what had happened. Trump's "it wasn't me" defense failed again.

"THEY DID IT"

At several critical points during the president's first term, he put a twist on that old standby defense. He turned the tables, replacing "it wasn't me" with a pointed "they did it."

Donald J. Trump
@realDonaldTrump

"Terrible! Just found out that Obama had my 'wires tapped' in Trump Tower just before the victory. Nothing found. This is McCarthyism!"—March 4, 2017

"It's spying. It's everything that you can imagine. It's hard to believe in this country that we would have had that. I don't know if you remember a long time ago, very early on, I used the word 'wiretap' and I put it in quotes, meaning surveillance, spying, you can sort of say whatever if you want."

—April 25, 2019 (interview)

Wiretaps. Political rivals. Secret courts. All the makings of a spy thriller. And that is exactly how President Trump makes it sound, but the story, as Trump tells it, is false.

On Sept. 1, 2017, the Justice Department said in a court filing that its National Security Division and the FBI had no evidence to back up Trump's tweets alleging that Obama sought to spy on him. "Both FBI and NSD confirm that they have no records related to wiretaps as described by the March 4, 2017 tweets."

This tale stems from a January 2017 *New York Times* report that investigators were examining intercepted communications and financial transactions as part of the probe into possible links between Russian officials and Trump associates. The headline was dramatic: "Wiretapped Data Used in Inquiry of Trump Aides."

Then, on March 4, Trump tweeted his own allegation: "Terrible! Just found out that Obama had my 'wires tapped' in Trump Tower just before the victory. Nothing found. This is McCarthyism!"

There is no evidence to back up Trump's claims that Obama ordered the tapping of his calls.

The tweet may have been a Trumpian extrapolation based on the president learning that March that the U.S. government had supposedly wiretapped his former campaign chairman Paul Manafort, who had an apartment in Trump Tower. But the White House failed

18

to provide any proof to back up Trump's claim at the time, and the Justice Department later revealed that there had been no such wiretap on Manafort.

What actually happened is more complicated. During its investigation of possible Russian interference in the 2016 election, the FBI obtained a secret surveillance warrant on Trump foreign policy adviser Carter Page. Although Page had left the campaign by the time the warrant was approved, it was renewed three times. The Justice Department's inspector general said in a 2019 report that the FBI made numerous and substantial errors in the application for the warrant and its renewals, but the report found no bias in the FBI's decision-making.

None of this supports Trump's false claim that Obama put a wiretap on him or engaged in any Bond-style "spying."

 "Between 3 million and 5 million illegal votes caused me to lose the popular vote."
—Jan. 23, 2017 (remarks)

Trump only narrowly won the electoral college in 2016 and lost the popular vote by nearly three million votes. He's been exaggerating ever since.

In the United States, the presidency is awarded to the candidate who wins 270 or more of the 538 electoral college votes. The winner of the popular vote gets the equivalent of a participation trophy—nice to have, but it doesn't come with a job.

For three years, Trump has offered several possible (but false) reasons why he lost the popular vote: It's harder for a Republican to win (it's not), he didn't campaign for it (why would he?), and illegal votes kept him from clinching this goal (still no).

The most dangerous of these claims is the idea that millions of people voted illegally. He first broached this topic in a tweet weeks after the election: "In addition to winning the Electoral College in a landslide, I won the popular vote if you deduct the millions of people who voted illegally."

He repeated this claim after he was sworn into office, ahead of the 2018 midterms and, most recently, two and a half years after winning the presidency: "There was much illegal voting. But let me tell you about [the] popular vote. Do you have a second? . . . I think I do better with a popular vote." He finished by hedging, "But I didn't campaign for the popular vote."

There was never any evidence of widespread illegal voting in the 2016 election.

Trump's fixation with this notion apparently began after a few tweets by Gregg Phillips, a self-described conservative voter fraud specialist who started making claims even before data on the 2016 vote was actually available in most jurisdictions. (It had not yet been determined which provisional ballots were valid and would be counted.) Phillips's claims were picked up by such purveyors of false facts as Infowars.com, a conspiracy-minded website, even though Phillips failed to provide any evidence.

After the then-president-elect's first tweet about illegal votes, the Trump transition team scrambled to find proof, but they could only resurrect claims and data that had been previously shown to be irrelevant. None of the information supported Trump's claim of "millions" of illegal votes, just isolated instances of small-scale voting irregularities.

Trump also falsely asserted that undocumented immigrants were skewing the results in elections, apparently basing his claim on a misinterpretation of disputed data. The researcher who produced the data said Trump took his findings out of context. The study concluded that non-citizens do not make a difference in almost any American election.

That didn't stop Trump. He ordered the creation of a commission, officially the Presidential Advisory Commission on Election Integrity, to investigate claims of voter fraud and improper registration. But the commission was disbanded after less than eight months, after a series of adverse legal rulings and fractious disputes among commission members, who could never document Trump's claim.

ONE TERRIBLE, HORRIBLE, NO GOOD, VERY BAD DAY

📖 Claims in interviews: 24   🎤 Claims to media: 2
🐦 Claims in Tweets: 5   👥 Claims in rallies: 108

On Nov. 5, 2018, the day before the midterm elections, President Trump held three rallies, granted four interviews (including to Sean Hannity of Fox News and radio host Mark Levin), spoke with reporters and tweeted during the day. All told, he made 139 false or misleading claims, a personal best for a single day.

Eager to avoid the loss of the House of Representatives, Trump stuck to many of his favorite themes. He told every interviewer—and every rally—that the economy was the best in U.S. history, and he tweeted that as well. He declared he was the most popular Republican president ever and that he was building the wall. At each rally, he made false claims about his crowd size.

Here's how the Trumpiest of all Trump days went, with selected highlights. He started off with a morning tweet that falsely accused CNN of manipulating polls to suppress votes, perhaps to make excuses for bad news at the polls. Then he falsely suggested in a tweet that he had sent specific instructions to monitor polls for illegal voting.

10:18 a.m. tweet: "So funny to see the CNN Fake Suppression Polls and false rhetoric. Watch for real results Tuesday. We are lucky CNN's ratings are so low. Don't fall for the Suppression Game. Go out & VOTE. Remember, we now have perhaps the greatest Economy (JOBS) in the history of our Country!"

10:41 a.m. tweet: "Law Enforcement has been strongly notified to watch closely for any ILLEGAL VOTING which may take place in Tuesday's Election (or Early Voting). Anyone caught will be subject to the Maximum Criminal Penalties allowed by law."

Interviews at White House with Sinclair Broadcasting and Gray Television

"Greatest economy we've ever had. The greatest job numbers we've ever had," he tells Scott Thuman of Sinclair.

"We have the best economy the country has ever had," Trump tells Jacqueline Policastro of Gray Television.

12:40 p.m.: Trump speaks to media at White House before departure. Trump professes ignorance about a campaign commercial that some networks refused to air because of a false claim that Democrats let into the country an illegal immigrant who had killed a police officer. "I don't know about it. I mean, you're telling me something I don't know about. We have a lot of ads. And they certainly are effective, based on the numbers that we're seeing . . . Well, a lot of things are offensive. Your questions are offensive a lot of times—so, you know."

2:45 p.m. rally, Cleveland, Ohio

"You look at this gigantic room and there are many more people outside trying to get in. Should we let them in or not? The problem is we don't have the room to let them in. Thousands of people outside, there is something going on."
(The venue was not filled and thousands were not outside. While Trump was speaking, four people were in front of a TV screen set up outside the venue, according to a photo taken by a Twitter user at the event.)

"We passed a massive tax cut, massive for Ohio workers, and we will soon follow it up with another 10 percent tax cut for the middle class."
(Trump invented a nonexistent plan to cut taxes another 10 percent and his staff had to scramble to pretend the proposal was real.)

"Republicans have created the best economy in the history of our country."

4:18 p.m. tweet: Trump tweets out a campaign ad that alleged that "Democrats let [police killer Luis Bracamontes] into our country . . . Democrats let him stay . . . Who else would Democrats let in?" The reality is that Bracamontes first snuck over the border under a Democratic president. Then he snuck in again under a Republican (George W. Bush) and was deported a second time. He returned yet again when a Republican (Bush) was president. Then he remained in the country through Obama's tenure; a Republican local official dropped the pending case.

4:40 p.m. tweet: "Republicans have created the best economy in the HISTORY of our Country—and the hottest jobs market on planet earth. The Democrat Agenda is a Socialist Nightmare. The Republican Agenda is the AMERICAN DREAM!"

5:15 p.m. arrival, Fort Wayne, Indiana

Speaks to media upon arrival. "There is something going on, okay? I'm just telling you, we all left Ohio together—you never saw crowds like this. Thousands and thousands of people outside. In Indiana, you have to see the crowds." *(Reporters at the Indiana event found no people waiting outside. The Ohio event did not fill the venue.)*

Mark Levin interview: "We have the best economy that there has ever been."

6:05 p.m. rally, Fort Wayne, Indiana

"And you want to see something special? Take a look outside at the thousands and thousands of people that wanted to get inside. You got lucky."
(Reporters at this event found no people waiting outside.)

"Republicans have created the best economy in the history of our country. This is the single best economy in the history of our great country."

Sean Hannity interview

"There is something going on though, Sean. I leave Ohio, thousands and thousands of people can't get into this massive arena. I just left Indiana, thousands and thousands of people outside can't get—there's something going on, there's an electricity that feels like 2016."

"We have the strongest economy we've ever had in the history of our country, and you know that."

9:00 p.m. rally, Cape Girardeau, Missouri

"I'm going to love that debate when I say we have the strongest economy in history."

The next day, Republicans lost control of the House of Representatives.

CHAPTER TWO

Trump on Trump:
"I Call It Truthful Hyperbole"

Trump is always the best, the smartest, the most successful. He excels where others only aspire; he is, in the narrative he has spent a half-century crafting, the richest, "the least racist," the "most transparent." He clamors for notice, for notoriety, for attention of any kind, even as he feigns nonchalance about how he is viewed, portraying himself as "publicity shy."

Yet Trump spent many years posing as his own publicist, adopting fake identities to feed reporters stories about his wealth and sexual prowess, promoting his projects and defending his controversial behaviors.

Ever since the first major profile of Trump appeared in the *New York Times* in 1976, focusing on his "flair" and describing him as "New York's No. 1 real estate promoter of the middle 1970's," Trump has devoted his extraordinary energies to marketing himself as a uniquely powerful, savvy master salesman. That first profile headline was prescient: "Donald Trump, Real Estate Promoter, Builds Image as He Buys Buildings."

Trump has often said that if he could sell Trump, he could sell any Trump-branded product. "The point is that if you are a little different, or a little outrageous, or if you do things that are bold or controversial, the press is going to write about you," Trump said in his 1987 bestseller, "The Art of the Deal." (Caveat: Tony Schwartz, the book's ghostwriter, has said for many years that he wrote the entire book and that Trump made only minor changes, such as deleting criticism of powerful people he no longer wanted to offend.)

But starting soon after he launched his presidential campaign, Trump pledged that he could and would be different in the White House. He would be "presidential." Even three years into his presidency, Trump still contended that he would not "create controversy because [he] hate[s] controversy."

But much of what Trump says about what he's done and what he believes is easily, quickly debunked. Trump does not just nip and tuck details here and there to create an image he finds more pleasing. He edits even the most basic facts—where his parents are from, how well he did in college—and cherry-picks flattering details about his past while excluding or exaggerating the context surrounding them. He glosses over big, unflattering truths—the origin of his wealth, how he used his Trump Foundation—that could jeopardize his carefully crafted narrative. And sometimes, for whatever reason, he just makes things up.

Sorting through the hyperbole of Trump's biography is disorienting at best. Trump makes false assertions about his height, his weight, his worth—anything he sees as a marker of success.

This chapter examines the man (Trump's claims about his background, character and beliefs), the mogul (the myths of Trump Inc., from real estate to reality TV, philanthropy to philosophy) and the president (Trump's transformation from businessman to politician).

THE MAN

 "My father came from Germany."

—Dec. 18, 2019 (campaign rally)

 "My father is from Germany. Both of my parents are from the EU."

—July 12, 2018 (news conference)

This is false. Trump's father, Fred Trump, was born in the Bronx to German immigrants. His mother was born in Scotland. It's unclear why the president continues to suggest otherwise. For whatever reason, Trump has been fudging his ancestry for years. In 1976, Trump told the *New York Times*, "I'm Swedish. . . . Most people think my family is Jewish because we own so many buildings in Brooklyn." Some of Trump's top executives from his early years in New York City real estate have said that he called himself Swedish—he's not—to avoid any ill effect his German heritage might have had on Jewish customers' willingness to rent Trump apartments in those first decades after World War II and the Holocaust.

 "I went to the Wharton School of Finance, I was a very fine student. And I will tell you, one of the great schools in the world, the Wharton School of Finance, one of the hardest schools in the world to get into. I got in—let me tell you, I went there."

—Aug. 4, 2018 (campaign rally)

"I took that test when I got my last physical, and the doctor said that's one of the highest [cognitive] scores we've ever seen."

—Sept. 18, 2018 (interview)

Trump's coyness about his heritage contrasts sharply with his boasts about his intellectual prowess. He's never been shy about what he calls his "super-genius stuff." He tweeted in 2013: "Sorry losers and haters, but my I.Q. is one of the highest—and you all know it! Please don't feel so stupid or insecure, it's not your fault."

His evidence? His undergraduate degree. Trump graduated from the Wharton School, an undergraduate business program at the University of Pennsylvania, an Ivy League college.

Trump often elides the difference between Wharton's more famous MBA graduate program and his own experience in the undergraduate major. He was a transfer student who arrived at Wharton after two years at Fordham University, which *U.S. News & World Report* ranks 74th among national universities. Gwenda Blair, in her 2001 book "The Trumps," reported that Trump's grades at Fordham were just "respectable."

A Penn admissions official told *The Post* that the admissions rate for the year Trump transferred was not available but noted that in 1980, nearly fifteen years later, it was "slightly greater than 40 percent." The admissions rate for Penn's class of 2023, by comparison, was 7.4 percent.

Trump interviewed at Wharton with James Nolan, a close friend of Trump's older brother. Fred Trump Jr. "called me and said, 'You remember my brother Donald?' Which I didn't," Nolan recalled. "'He's at Fordham and he would like to transfer to Wharton. Will you interview him?' I was happy to do that." Admissions officers were likely aware of the Trump family's wealth—though there's no evidence any donation helped grease Trump's acceptance.

For years, Trump claimed to reporters that he graduated first in his class from Wharton, but that's wrong. The 1968 commencement program does not list him as graduating with any honors. In fact, Trump made little impression on campus. Former classmates said he was often back home in New York, working at the family business, and was little seen at Penn, taking part in few campus activities, academic or extracurricular.

Trump often says that he was always more impressed by street smarts than by book learning, arguing in "The Art of the Deal" that "Perhaps the most important thing I learned at Wharton was not to be overly impressed by academic credentials. . . . In my opinion, that degree doesn't prove very much, but a lot of people I do business with take it very seriously, and it's considered very prestigious."

More recently, after being offended by how he was characterized in Bob Woodward's book "Fear," Trump pointed out that he had passed a test known as the Montreal Cognitive Assessment, which tests for "mild cognitive dysfunction." The 10-minute test asks participants to draw a clock, animals and other objects. On a 30-point scale, any score 26 or above is considered normal. Trump scored a 30, as most people would since the test is designed mainly to identify signs of dementia or other cognitive impairment. His score does not indicate any kind of genius.

 "I'll tell you, you know I was [in Cincinnati]—I worked here for a long time."

—Feb. 5, 2018 (remarks)

 "I worked here during a summer. I worked here and I loved it; Cincinnati."

—Aug. 24, 2018 (campaign rally)

"I used to work in Cincinnati, and a place called Swifton Village. You know what that is? Swifton Village."

—Aug. 1, 2019 (campaign rally)

President Trump's emphatic references to his time in Ohio whenever he speaks there seem odd—after all, the Trump name is synonymous with New York. Ohio?

The tale of Trump and Ohio begins at a foreclosure auction in 1964, when Donald Trump was a senior in high school. The president's father purchased the Swifton Village apartment complex, the largest in Cincinnati, for just under $5.7 million—a fraction of what it had cost to build a decade earlier. The 1,168-unit complex had fallen into disrepair.

But Fred Trump liked a challenge. Reports say he took out a mortgage of $5.75 million to cover the purchase and renovations required to entice residents back. On Tuesdays, he would fly to Cincinnati, inspect the week's progress and fly back to New York in time for dinner.

According to "Trump Revealed," by our colleagues Michael Kranish and Marc Fisher, Donald Trump worked at Swifton Village for the summer between high school and college "for a week at a time to take care of menial tasks." Roy Knight, a Swifton maintenance man remembered, "He'd get in there and work with us. He wasn't skilled, but he'd do yard work and clean up—whatever needed to be done." Once he started college, Donald would occasionally join his father on his Tuesday excursions.

The younger Trump may have gotten more involved with the property as he got older, but we found no evidence that he ever lived there or "worked there" with any regularity. When we asked Trump biographer Gwenda Blair about the possibility, she laughed.

"I am the least racist person there is anywhere in the world."

—July 30, 2019 (remarks)

 "I am the least racist person ever to serve in office, okay? I am the least racist person."

—Aug. 21, 2019 (remarks)

Trump vociferously denies holding any racist views. But decades of evidence demonstrate that his attitude toward people of different backgrounds has often been dismissive or derogatory.

The first article about Trump in the *New York Times*, in 1973, was headlined "Major Landlord Accused of Antiblack Bias in City." Trump was quoted saying that the charges that the Justice Department made against Trump Management Inc., his father and him were "absolutely ridiculous." The sides settled, with the Trumps being required to take out ads in New York newspapers telling minorities that they were welcome in Trump apartments. Three years later, the Justice Department charged the family company with continuing discrimination.

When five black and Latino teenagers were implicated in a brutal attack on a white woman jogging in Central Park in 1989, Trump took out full-page newspaper ads calling for the death penalty for "criminals of every age." The suspects were convicted, but they were later exonerated by overwhelming evidence. (The perpetrator, Matias Reyes, later confessed to the crime, and DNA evidence put Reyes at the scene.) The New York district attorney's office recommended in 2002 that all charges and convictions against the five men be vacated, and a court agreed.

Nonetheless, Trump called their wrongful-conviction settlement a "disgrace," arguing that their innocence was unclear because Linda Fairstein, the prosecutor who initially handled the case, has defended her actions. Trump repeated this as recently as 2019, saying, "You have people on both sides of that [the Central Park Five case]. They admitted their guilt. If you look at Linda Fairstein, and if you look at some of the prosecutors, they think that the city should never have settled that case. So we'll leave it at that."

Through the decades, Trump has made numerous remarks—some in public, some behind closed doors—that question blacks' abilities and character.

In the 1991 book "Trumped!," Trump Plaza Hotel and Casino president John R. O'Donnell alleged that Trump once said that "laziness is a trait in blacks." He also claimed Trump said, of his accountants: "Black guys counting my money! I hate it. The only kind of people I want counting my money are little short guys that wear yarmulkes every day." (Trump has called O'Donnell a disgruntled employee, but he has not disputed the remarks. "The stuff O'Donnell wrote about me is probably true," he told *Playboy* in 1997.)

In 1989, Trump said that "a well-educated black has a tremendous advantage over a well-educated white in terms of the job market. . . . If I were starting off today, I would love to be a well-educated black, because I really believe they do have an actual advantage."

When Trump launched his presidential campaign in June 2015, he made a broad-brush accusation against Mexico: "They're sending people that have lots of problems, and they're bringing . . . drugs, they're bringing crime, they're rapists. And some, I assume, are good people."

Speaking at the Republican Jewish Coalition candidate forum in December 2015, Trump made a speech riddled with Jewish stereotypes, such as: "Look, I'm a negotiator like you folks; we're negotiators." And: "I know why you're not going to support me. You're not going to support me because I don't want your money."

In Aug. 2017, Trump failed immediately to denounce the white nationalists behind Charlottesville's Unite the Right rally, where a counterprotester was killed. "We condemn in the strongest possible terms this egregious display of hatred, bigotry and violence," Trump said, before adding, "on many sides, on many sides."

More recently, the president tweeted that four Democratic minority congresswomen—all Americans—should "go back" to where they came from.

The Washington Post's executive editor, Martin Baron, decided that his paper would characterize that statement as "racist." "The 'go back' trope is deeply rooted in the history of racism in the United States," Baron said. "Therefore, we have concluded that 'racist' is the proper term to apply to the language [Trump] used."

"It has not been easy for me. And you know I started off in Brooklyn, my father gave me a small loan of a million dollars."

—Oct. 26, 2015 (remarks)

"He [Marco Rubio] also said I got $200 million from my father. I wish. I wish. I got a very, very small loan from my father many years ago. I built that into a massive empire and I paid my father back that loan. . . . The number is wrong by a factor of hundreds of—I mean, by a fortune. I got a small loan. I started a business."

—Feb. 26, 2016 (news conference)

A small loan. A family business. A self-made empire in New York City. It's the stuff of a Hallmark movie—if it were accurate.

The true story begins in 1978 with the rehabilitation of the Commodore hotel near New York's Grand Central Terminal. Trump's first big deal in Manhattan put him on the map as a developer with an identity distinct from his father's, who had been a prominent builder of middle-class housing in the city's outer boroughs for decades.

As part of the Commodore deal, Donald got a nearly $1 million loan from his father. Fred Trump's Village Construction Corp. provided the loan to help repay draws on a Chase Manhattan Bank credit line that Fred Trump had arranged for his son for the hotel project. But that loan was only a small part of his father's involvement in the deal.

Fred Trump was a vital silent partner in his son's project. In effect, the son was the front man, relying on his father's connections and wealth, while Fred stayed in the background to avoid drawing attention to himself.

After examining more than 100,000 confidential documents, the *New York Times* concluded that Fred's "small loan" was actually $60.7 million, or $140 million in 2018 dollars, much of which was never repaid. The *Times* investigation concluded that Donald Trump had always been highly dependent on his father's wealth: "By age 3, he was earning $200,000 a year in today's dollars from his father's empire. He was a millionaire by age 8. In his 40s and 50s, he was receiving more than $5 million a year." In all, the *Times* found that Trump received the equivalent of at least $413 million in today's dollars from his father's real estate empire.

THE MOGUL

Trump has never liked to lose—anything, anywhere. The myth that everything Trump touches turns to gold began in earnest with that first family-subsidized project. Trump went on through decades in business to use false and flimsy evidence to prove his wealth, influence and power.

 "Look, obviously people know I've been very successful, but I built a truly great company with truly great assets and very little debt, and I don't think that's been recognized to the extent it should."

—Oct. 10, 2017 (interview)

 "By doing this, and taking this particular job [of being president], which I love, it will cost me billions and billions of dollars."

—Sept. 16, 2019 (campaign rally)

Trump got more support from his father than he might like to admit, but a big dose of privilege does not on its own mean that Trump had no hand in building a "truly great company." Many people from well-off backgrounds become successful entrepreneurs in their own right. But Trump's own financial track record raises questions about that narrative.

Did Trump have "very little debt"? No. Only a year before Trump made that claim, he told CBS's Norah O'Donnell, "I'm the king of debt. I'm great with debt. Nobody knows debt better than me. I've made a fortune by using debt, and if things don't work out, I renegotiate the debt. I mean, that's a smart thing, not a stupid thing."

Trump's companies went through bankruptcy six times after he overextended on debt. In 2016, companies Trump owned carried at least $650 million in debt, according to a *New York Times* investigation.

A separate investigation by the *Times* into a decade of Trump tax returns found that from 1985 to 1995, when he was building his brand, the future president reported negative adjusted gross income. That number grew each year after 1988, as new losses piled on top of those from prior years. By the mid-1990s, he reported near billion-dollar losses.

Does he have "great assets"? Yes and no. Shirking tradition, the president has refused to release his tax returns. Consequently, what we know about Trump's finances has been pieced together through leaked documents, Trump's statements, court records and independent analysis.

In 2015, the president said he was worth $10 billion. Most analysts say that is exaggerated. Trump admitted in a legal deposition that he sometimes estimates his financial condition based on his gut feeling about what his name and brand are worth.

Bloomberg News closely studied his 92-page financial disclosure report from 2015 and concluded that he was worth $2.9 billion. Forbes estimated his value at $3.1 billion as of September 2019, about half of it in New York real estate.

Holding about $3 billion in assets certainly makes Trump a very wealthy man, even if many of his ventures—from Trump Shuttle to Trump Vodka, various Trump casinos, Trump Steaks and Trump University—flopped.

As for losing anywhere from $3 billion to $5 billion as president, it is highly unlikely that serving as president could cost him more than his net worth. Indeed, he might well profit from being in the White House because he has refused to divest from his family business and because Trump and his family often blur the line between official actions and private interests.

 "And now guys like Jerry Nadler, who I fought for many years—successfully, I might add—back in New York, in Manhattan. He was a Manhattan congressman. I beat him all the time."

—May 9, 2019 (remarks)

 "I've known Jerry Nadler for a long time. He's opposed many of my jobs. I got them all built—very successfully built in New York."

—Jan. 22, 2020 (news conference)

Trump railed against the Democratic House managers in his impeachment trial. But he had an especially long history with one of them, Rep. Jerry Nadler (D-N.Y.). Trump's beef with Nadler is personal as well as political, stretching back decades to a New York City real estate deal along Manhattan's West Side.

The feud began in 1985, when Trump purchased a railroad yard along the Hudson River in Nadler's state assembly district and proposed to turn it into Television City, a mini-city of residential towers, TV studios and retail outlets. Trump faced fierce community opposition to his plan and found no support from Nadler, who sided with his constituents. But Trump would not relent. He lobbied the assemblyman to support a key aspect of the project, the submerging of part of the West Side Highway.

But Nadler was not swayed—if anything, he was emboldened to quash Trump's ambitions. When Nadler was elected to Congress in 1992, he made clear he did not want Trump to see a dime of federal funding to move the highway.

"It is outrageous, at a time of deep budget cuts, that Mr. Trump would seek a down payment from working Americans for his luxury high-rise development in Manhattan," Nadler said in 1995. "Why should taxpayers be asked to chip in for this massive and wasteful boondoggle?"

In the end, neither man got what he wanted. Trump could not get the highway moved, though Nadler never got him to abandon the project entirely—only to scale it back significantly in height and density. Not exactly a case of "beating" the congressman.

Trump ultimately sold the property for $1.8 billion in 2005. And between 2016 and 2019, the condo boards that managed the six Trump-branded apartment buildings on Manhattan's West Side voted to strip the family name off their facades.

 "We have the all-time record in the history of *Time* magazine. . . . I've been on it for 15 times this year."
—Jan. 21, 2017 (remarks)

With 55, Richard Nixon—not Trump—holds the record for *Time* magazine covers.

The president is, however, gaining ground. The July 1, 2019, issue marked the 29th time he has graced the magazine's cover. But at the time he made this claim, in 2017, Trump had only been on the cover of *Time* 11 times in his life—not 15 times in one year. (That count does not include a fake *Time* cover featuring Trump's face that hung in Trump golf clubs around the country.)

"I had 'The Apprentice.' It was one of the top shows on television. No matter what I did—before that, I was a businessman."

—Sept. 7, 2018 (news conference)

 "NBC, I made a lot of money for NBC with 'The Apprentice,' right? A lot of money, a lot. Plus, we had the number one show a lot, and they had nothing in the top 10, except for a thing called 'The Apprentice,' and they treat me so bad."

—Dec. 18, 2019 (campaign rally)

Trump's reality-television show was a hit at first. It debuted with a big splash in the 2003–2004 season, and immediately ranked seventh among primetime shows, averaging almost 21 million viewers a week. But that was the show's only year in the top 10. After its second season, neither "The Apprentice" nor its successor, "The Celebrity Apprentice," cracked the top 20 again. Four years into its run, roughly half as many people watched as had when the show debuted.

Trump was obsessed with the ratings, unwilling to believe the show's decline. Jim Dowd, the publicity manager for "The Apprentice," said in 2016 that "There's about 10 people who cover ratings in terms of the publications that matter most. And [Trump] would want to make sure I called all those 10 people and told them, 'Number one show on television, won its time slot,' and I'm looking at the numbers and at that point, say season five, for example, we were number 72. . . . He became kind of a monster when it came to these ratings."

Donald J. Trump
@realDonaldTrump

"The sleazy New York Democrats, and their now disgraced (and run out of town) A.G. Eric Schneiderman,

are doing everything they can to sue me on a foundation that took in $18,800,000 and gave out to char-
ity more money than it took in, $19,200,000. I won't
settle this case! Schneiderman, who ran the Clinton
campaign in New York, never had the guts to bring
this ridiculous case, which lingered in their office for
almost 2 years. Now he resigned his office in disgrace, and his disciples brought it when we would not
settle."—June 14, 2018

New York state started investigating the Trump Foundation following a *Washington Post* investigation that documented how Trump
used the charity's money to pay legal settlements for his private business and to buy art for one of his clubs. The New York attorney general said the foundation's board had not met since 1999, and without
outside supervision, the foundation had come to serve Trump's
spending needs—and those of his 2016 campaign.

In a civil complaint filed in 2018, then–Attorney General Barbara D. Underwood charged that the now-defunct Donald J. Trump
Foundation had violated a federal law that bars charities from
supporting candidates for office. Trump's campaign "extensively
directed and coordinated the Foundation's activities in connection
with a nationally televised charity fundraiser," Underwood charged.

The fundraiser was billed as an effort to "raise funds for veterans' organizations," but the Trump campaign commandeered nearly
$2.8 million in donations and "dictated the manner in which the
Foundation would disburse those proceeds, directing the timing,
amounts and recipients of the grants," the lawsuit said. Despite his
pledge never to settle lawsuits, Trump settled and shut down the
foundation.

THE PRESIDENT

Politicians aren't especially known for their honesty, and Trump's new role as politician has only amplified his lifelong propensity for hyperbole. Through Twitter, rallies and shouted volleys with reporters on the White House lawn, Trump almost daily gives Americans the opportunity to see how he perceives himself as candidate, president and master of all media.

Let's start with Trump's trademark campaign slogan, Make America Great Again. (Hint: It wasn't his.)

 "Ronald Reagan had a small thing called 'Let's Make America Great.' That was good. I don't like it as much."
—April 2, 2019 (prepared speech)

Trump takes great pride in his skill as a consummate marketer. But in this case, he is an editor at best and a copycat at worst. Reagan's slogan was "Let's Make America Great Again." Trump's 2016 campaign slogan was virtually the same. He just dropped the "let's."

 "I am a politician, I guess, but I accomplished more than I promised, and I'm doing it for you."
—April 28, 2018 (campaign rally)

"But now, I've completed more promises than I've made. I mean, I've actually completed more than I've made, right?"
—Jan. 9, 2020 (campaign rally)

41

Trump made more than 280 promises during the 2016 campaign. Many were contradictory or uttered just once at a campaign event, making it tough to know if he meant them or if they were crowd-pleasing whims of the moment.

In October 2016, Trump issued his "Contract with the American Voter," listing 60 promises, some of which he said he would fulfill on the day he took the oath of office. Others would be implemented in his first 100 days.

Of course, no one expected him to meet those ambitious timelines, but the document served as a marker of his intentions. It featured major campaign themes such as withdrawing from the Trans-Pacific Partnership trade agreement and growing the economy at 4 percent a year. Trump signed the document with his distinctive bold signature.

Three years in, contrary to what he tells his fans, Trump has broken more of these promises than he has kept. Here's the scorecard: Trump broke 25 promises, kept 21 and compromised on seven. The remaining seven are in process—Trump has proposed a bill or issued an executive order in an effort to move forward.

In this way, Trump turned out to be an ordinary politician—complete with broken promises.

Donald J. Trump
@realDonaldTrump

"The media was able to get my work schedule, something very easy to do, but it should have been reported as a positive, not negative. When the term Executive Time is used, I am generally working, not relaxing. In fact, I probably work more hours than almost any past President."—Feb. 10, 2019

Donald J. Trump
@realDonaldTrump

"No president ever worked harder than me (cleaning up the mess I inherited)!"—Feb. 11, 2019

 "Believe it or not, even when I'm in Washington and New York, I do not watch much television."

—Nov. 11, 2017 (remarks)

Don't believe it.

There is no evidence that Trump has worked harder than any other president. In fact, his schedule, with its ample hours devoted to "executive time," suggests he works less than many recent presidents. During these long blocks of unstructured time every day, Trump tweets, watches TV and gets on the phone with friends and advisers. Judging by his Twitter feed, it's safe to say he watches a lot of TV, no matter what city he is in.

 "I'm the most transparent president in history."

—Nov. 15, 2019 (remarks)

Although Trump frequently entertains shouted questions on his way to the Marine One helicopter, he has been one of the least transparent presidents. The White House ended the tradition of releasing visitor logs. His administration has largely ended press briefings at the White House, the State Department and the Pentagon. The White House has refused to answer oversight inquiries from House Democrats or to allow testimony by key administration officials.

Unlike George W. Bush and Bill Clinton, Trump refused to sit for an interview with the special counsel investigating executive branch actions. He responded to written questions only, answering many with a curt "I do not recall." Trump has also refused to release his tax returns, unlike every other president since Gerald Ford.

In short, he is no picture of transparency.

> "I'm going to tell you about the Nobel Peace Prize. I'll tell you about that. I made a deal. I saved a country, and I just heard that the head of that country is now getting the Nobel Peace Prize for saving the country. I said, 'What—did I have something to do with it?' Yeah, but you know, that's the way it is."
>
> —Jan. 9, 2020 (campaign rally)

Where to start with this one?

The Norwegian Nobel Committee awarded the 2019 Nobel Peace Prize to Ethiopian Prime Minister Abiy Ahmed for his pursuit of democratic reforms and "his decisive initiative to resolve the border conflict with neighboring Eritrea." (The award was announced on Oct. 11, 2019, yet Trump said three months later that he had "just heard" about it.)

The peace deal had not yet led to the resumption of normal relations, but the pact "unfroze diplomatic relations, reopened telephone lines and has allowed some travel between the two countries," said William Davison, an Ethiopia analyst with the International Crisis Group. Still, border disputes remained unresolved.

Where does Trump figure in all of this? Nowhere. He had nothing to do with the peace negotiations. Trump did offer to help negotiate an agreement between Ethiopia's and Egypt's prime ministers over a dam on the Nile. But those are two different countries, and that's a different story.

"Because nobody's done more than me—I mean nobody."

—Jan. 10, 2020 (interview)

"We've achieved more in this month alone than almost any President has achieved in eight years in office, if you think about it—if you think what we've done."

—Dec. 21, 2019 (speech)

Trump, unlike many presidents in their first three years, signed relatively few major pieces of legislation. The whirlwind of change under presidents such as Franklin D. Roosevelt, Lyndon B. Johnson and Ronald Reagan exceeded Trump's efforts.

As of Jan. 19, 2020, his 1,095th day in office, Trump had signed 548 bills, most of which were minor. Trump signed more bills and joint resolutions than Obama, but he was still behind every other president since Eisenhower, according to a calculation provided to The Fact Checker by Joshua Tauberer of GovTrack.

Trump signed the bulk of those bills during his first two years, when Republicans controlled both chambers of Congress. But Tauberer noted that much of what Trump accomplished involved "increasing the size of the federal government in Democrat-led legislation," thereby going against "the regulation-cutting and swamp-draining philosophy that he and the Republican Party campaigned on."

"I don't want to go quickly and just make a statement for the sake of making a political statement. I want to know the facts. . . . Before I make a statement, I need the facts. So I don't want to rush into a statement."

—Aug. 15, 2017 (news conference)

"I'm the only one that tells you the facts."

—Nov. 3, 2018 (campaign rally)

The idea that Trump is "the only one that tells you the facts" is preposterous, and Trump at some level knows it. After all, this is the same man who said in "The Art of the Deal" that "I play to people's fantasies. People may not always think big themselves, but they can still get very excited by those who do. That's why a little hyperbole never hurts. People want to believe that something is the biggest and the greatest and the most spectacular. I call it truthful hyperbole. It's an innocent form of exaggeration—and a very effective form of promotion."

The president often makes statements without knowing or checking the facts. Indeed, if President Trump stuck to the facts, this book would not exist.

TRUMP'S ATTACKS ON DEMOCRATIC CITIES: "RAT-INFESTED MESS"

President Trump often disparages cities and states where Democrats are in power, painting them as dark, dysfunctional, violent scars, visions of a country going to hell.

 "Our policemen that are on the beat are getting sick. They're actually sick. They're going to the hospital. . . . Hundreds and hundreds of tents and people living at the entrance to their office building [in San Francisco]."

—Sept. 17, 2019 (remarks)

California is disproportionately responsible for the nationwide increase in the homeless population. But the claim that police are getting sick is based on a single incident—and one that is in dispute. A police union said three Los Angeles officers contracted a staph infection after attending to a homeless person. But Dr. Brad Spellberg, chief medical officer at LAC+USC Medical Center, told a local CBS station, "You wouldn't be able to say that it came from one person or another. It's everywhere around us."

 "There's tremendous pollution being put into the ocean [from San Francisco], because they're going through what's called a storm sewer. That's for rainwater. And we have tremendous things that we don't have to discuss pouring into the ocean. There are needles, there are other things."

—Sept. 18, 2019 (remarks)

All of the city's solids get filtered out at the Southeast Treatment Plant in the Bayview neighborhood or the Oceanside Treatment Plant near the zoo, according to San Francisco city officials and environmentalists.

Donald J. Trump
@realDonaldTrump

"Cumming [*sic*] District is a disgusting, rat and rodent infested mess."—July 27, 2019

Donald J. Trump
@realDonaldTrump

"The Radical Left Dems went after me for using the words 'drug-infested' concerning Baltimore."—July 31, 2019

Rep. Elijah Cummings, a Democrat who died in 2019, was chairman of a House committee actively investigating the Trump administration. Trump called Baltimore a "rat and rodent infested mess," then falsely stated he was being attacked for calling the city "drug-infested."

"All over the world, they're talking about Chicago. Afghanistan is a safe place by comparison. It's true."

—Oct. 28, 2019 (speech)

Chicago's police superintendent skipped a Trump speech because "it just doesn't line up with our city's core values." Trump responded by depicting Chicago as a war-torn crime zone.

A State Department advisory says that "Travel to all areas of Afghanistan is unsafe because of critical levels of kidnappings, hostage taking, suicide bombings, widespread military combat operations, landmines, and terrorist and insurgent attacks." Chicago has one of the highest homicide rates among U.S. cities, but Afghanistan has been at war for more than 40 years. Since 2001, about 157,000 people have been killed in the Afghanistan war, including more than 43,000 civilians. In Chicago in the same period, just under 10,000 people were murdered.

CHAPTER THREE

Trump and His Enemies: "I Call Them Animals"

Donald Trump had no rational reason to believe that Barack Obama was born in Kenya, but Trump persisted with the "birther" lie for years. Ted Cruz's father played no role in the JFK assassination, but that didn't steer Trump away from a crackpot conspiracy theory in the *National Enquirer*. When he became president, Trump referred to African nations as "shithole countries," to Rep. Adam Schiff as "Adam Schitt" and to his own attorney general, Jeff Sessions, as a bumbling "Mr. Magoo."

Fact-checking the Trump presidency often means watching an erstwhile real estate mogul and reality-TV star fire insults and smears like a schoolyard bully. Democrats, Republicans, men, women, the young and the old, previous and current Cabinet officials—all have faced Trump's slashing, sneering and slippery calumnies. Many a true word is said in jest. But not so much when Trump is in the picture. He lobs insults filled with falsehoods. He changes history to denigrate opponents. He fabricates tall tales about his foes out of whole cloth. He gaslights. In one case, he falsely accused a Democrat of killing a newborn.

This side of Trump gets especially frothy when the legal stakes are high. He accused Robert Mueller of a series of nonexistent conflicts of interest as part of his PR warfare against the special counsel's Russia investigation. Trump falsely accused ex–FBI director James Comey of leaking classified information. He sometimes indulges in a strange, ever-morphing rant about a Democratic senator who is suing him over his business dealings with foreign governments.

This chapter sets the record straight on some of the most venomous personal attacks in Trump's repertoire.

Sen. Richard Blumenthal (D-Conn.)

 "Look at Blumenthal. He lied about Vietnam. He didn't just say, 'Hey, I went to Vietnam.' No, no. For 15 years, he said he was a war hero, he fought in Da Nang province. We call him Da Nang Richard. Da Nang—that's his nickname. Da Nang. He never went to Vietnam. And he's up there saying, 'We need honesty and we need integrity.' This guy lied when he was the attorney general of Connecticut. He lied. I don't mean a little bit. And then, when he got out . . . and when he apologized, he was crying. The tears were all over the place. And now he acts like, 'How dare you?'"

—Oct. 1, 2018 (remarks)

Few foes get under Trump's skin like Sen. Richard Blumenthal of Connecticut. Both men were born to privilege in New York City in 1946. Both went to Ivy League schools, and both managed to get five deferments to avoid the Vietnam War.

After his fifth deferment, however, Blumenthal enlisted in the Marine Corps Reserve in 1970 and served for six years, based in the United States. Trump's fifth deferment (he was diagnosed with bone spurs in his heels after graduating from college in 1968) exempted him from all military service. He said on Howard Stern's radio show in 1998 that avoiding sexually transmitted diseases stateside was his own, personal Vietnam.

The "Da Nang Richard" story is a richly detailed but false smear that Trump repeats whenever Blumenthal crosses him. When Blumenthal first ran for Senate in 2010, the New York Times published an article that called him out for saying he had gone to war in Vietnam.

"We have learned something important since the days that I served in Vietnam," Blumenthal, then Connecticut's attorney general, said in 2008. He also praised a group of military families in 2003 by saying, "When we returned [from Vietnam], we saw nothing like this."

The day after the Times article was published, Blumenthal said at a news conference, "On a few occasions, I have misspoken about my service, and I regret that, and I take full responsibility. But I will not allow anyone to take a few misplaced words and impugn my record of service to our country."

A few days later, Blumenthal apologized for mischaracterizing his military record.

Trump took those facts and spun a tangled web of falsehoods.

"For 15 years, he said he was a war hero, he fought in Da Nang province," Trump said. "We call him Da Nang Richard. Da Nang— that's his nickname."

Blumenthal never described himself as a war hero or claimed to have fought in Da Nang. His misleading remarks came during events in 2003 and 2008, not over 15 years.

"And then, when he got out . . . and when he apologized, he was crying," Trump said. "The tears were all over the place."

He appeared to be referring to Blumenthal's news conference the day after the *Times* article. Blumenthal did not apologize, drop out or cry at this event, as the video makes plain. He apologized days later in a written statement, but written statements don't have tear glands.

Rep. Ilhan Omar (D-Minn.)

"I look at Omar. I don't know. I never met her. I hear the way she talks about al-Qaeda. Al-Qaeda has killed many Americans. She said . . . 'When I think of al-Qaeda, I can hold my chest out.' . . . A politician that hears somebody, where we're at war with al-Qaeda, and sees somebody talking about how great al-Qaeda is. Pick out her statement. That was Omar. 'How great al-Qaeda is.' . . . And we're losing great soldiers to al-Qaeda."

—July 15, 2019 (remarks)

The president falsely accused Rep. Ilhan Omar of Minnesota of supporting the terrorist group behind the 9/11 attacks.

A Somali American and practicing Muslim, Omar won a House seat in 2018. She's an unabashed Trump critic. She's a naturalized U.S. citizen. She's the first lawmaker to wear a hijab in Congress. And she's not a terrorist sympathizer.

In 2019, Trump tweeted that Omar and three other Democratic congresswomen of color should "go back" to their countries. Asked about those racist comments the next day, Trump claimed Omar had voiced support for al-Qaeda: "'When I think of al-Qaeda, I can hold my chest out,'" he quoted her as saying.

Omar appeared as a guest on "BelAhdan," a Twin Cities PBS show about Middle East issues, in 2013. She did not voice approval for al-Qaeda and in fact condemned terrorist acts as "evil" and "heinous."

She said the Muslim community should not be held accountable for the acts of Islamic terrorists. "I think the general population needs to understand that there is a difference between the people that are carrying on the evil acts—because it is an evil act, and we do have evil people in this world—and then the normal people who carry on, the normal people, regular citizens who carry on their life," she said.

The discussion later turned to English speakers who say Arabic words in scary tones.

"I remember when I was in college, I took a terrorism class. . . . We learned the ideology," Omar recalled. "The thing that was interesting in the class was, every time the professor said 'al-Qaeda,' he sort of, like, his shoulders went up, and you know. 'Al-Qaeda.' You know, 'Hezbollah.' . . . You don't say 'America' with an intensity. You don't say 'England' with an intensity. You don't say 'the Army' with an intensity. But you say these names because you want that word to carry weight. You want it to leave something with the person that's hearing. . . . It's said with a deeper voice."

Rather than proudly proclaiming support for al-Qaeda, as Trump insinuated, Omar recounted how her college professor would arch his shoulders and accentuate the name of the terrorist group for effect.

Former president Barack Obama

 "The toughest calls I have to make are the calls where this happens, soldiers are killed. It's a very difficult thing. . . . If you look at President Obama and other presidents, most of them didn't make calls. A lot of them didn't make calls. I like to call when it's appropriate."

—Oct. 16, 2017 (remarks)

Trump appeared to forget the name of a fallen Army sergeant, La David Johnson, while offering condolences to his widow over the phone. Days later, he falsely claimed that Obama never even called the families of fallen soldiers.

The president maligns Obama with false claims on a near-daily basis, but this one is especially revealing. Nothing is out-of-bounds when it comes to Trump's falsehoods, not even the deaths of U.S. service members.

In reality, Obama often consoled the families of the fallen.

After a military helicopter was shot down over Afghanistan in 2011, Obama comforted the families of all those killed, according to Jeremy Bash, a top Pentagon official at the time. The White House photographer for Obama, Pete Souza, said in an Instagram post that he "photographed him meeting with hundreds of wounded soldiers, and family members of those killed in action."

Former FBI director James Comey

 Donald J. Trump
@realDonaldTrump

"James Comey is a proven LEAKER & LIAR. . . . He leaked CLASSIFIED information, for which he should be prosecuted."—April 13, 2018

No evidence shows that Comey leaked classified information. The Justice Department inspector general issued a report that cleared Comey and his attorneys of this smear.

Before Trump sacked him, Comey wrote a series of memos about his interactions with the president in early 2017. Trump had just taken office. The FBI had launched an investigation into his campaign and its contacts with Russians. At an Oval Office meeting on Valentine's Day, the president asked Comey to cease looking into Michael Flynn, who had resigned a day earlier from his position as national security adviser because of undisclosed contacts with Russians.

"I hope you can see your way clear to letting this go, to letting Flynn go," Trump told Comey, according to Comey's unclassified memo of the Feb. 14 conversation. "He is a good guy. I hope you can let this go."

How did this conversation wind up on the front page of the *New York Times* three months later?

As FBI director, Comey was in the unusual position of deciding which of his memos were classified. He was sure that his memo describing the Feb. 14 meeting with Trump contained no classified information. He sent the memo to a law professor friend, who then read its contents to a *Times* reporter.

"A private citizen may legally share unclassified details of a conversation with the president with the press, or include that information in a book," Comey wrote in his own book, "A Higher Loyalty."

In 2018, the Comey memo was released to the public with no redactions. In 2019, the Justice Department inspector general issued a report that criticized Comey over several matters but cleared him of leaking secrets. "We found no evidence that Comey or his attorneys released any of the classified information contained in any of the memos to members of the media," the report said.

Former special counsel Robert S. Mueller III

Donald J. Trump
@realDonaldTrump

"Is Robert Mueller ever going to release his conflicts of interest with respect to President Trump, including the fact that we had a very nasty & contentious business relationship, I turned him down to head the FBI (one day before appointment as S.C.) & Comey is his close friend. Also, why is Mueller only appointing Angry Dems, some of whom have worked for Crooked Hillary, others, including himself, have worked for Obama?"—July 29, 2018

These are false claims about imaginary conflicts of interest.

Career ethics officials in the Justice Department cleared Mueller, a Republican, to investigate Trump in May 2017. He was appointed special counsel by a Trump appointee, Rod Rosenstein. Although they worked together for years, Comey and Mueller both hesitate to describe themselves as close friends.

At a congressional hearing, Mueller said under oath that Trump did not interview him for the FBI director job, which he had held for 12 years. Rather, Mueller took the meeting with Trump to offer his views on the organization. "It was about the job and not about me applying for the job," Mueller said. Former White House chief strategist Stephen K. Bannon told investigators that the purpose of the meeting was not a job interview but to have Mueller "offer a perspective on the institution of the FBI," according to the special counsel's report.

"Although the White House thought about beseeching Mueller to become Director again, he did not come in looking for the job," Bannon said.

The Washington Post reported that when the question came up of whether Mueller might be interested in retaking the top FBI job, he said he could not do so unless the law limiting tenure in that position was changed. Mueller had already served a full ten-year term as FBI director, and Congress in July 2011 passed legislation allowing him to serve an additional two years.

It's misleading to say Mueller "worked for Obama." The FBI is an independent agency. Mueller was appointed FBI director by President George W. Bush and was extended in office under a bipartisan law.

The "angry" Democrats, according to Trump, are the lawyers who worked on Mueller's team. Eleven of the 16 attorneys on Mueller's team contributed to Democrats, including Hillary Clinton and Obama. The other five have no record of political contributions. One attorney who donated the maximum amount represented the Clinton Foundation in a 2015 lawsuit. Another attorney without a record of political donations represented a Clinton aide at one point. Both of those lawyers worked for WilmerHale, a firm that also represented Trump's former campaign manager Paul Manafort, as well as Ivanka Trump and Jared Kushner. Regardless, under federal law, Mueller was not allowed to consider the political leanings of his staff during the hiring process.

Finally, the Mueller report sharply disputes Trump's character-ization of a "nasty & contentious business relationship." Instead, it portrays a man seeking a refund.

"In October 2011, Mueller resigned his family's membership from Trump National Golf Club in Sterling, Virginia, in a letter that noted that 'we live in the District and find that we are unable to make full use of the Club' and that inquired 'whether we would be entitled to a refund of a portion of our initial membership fee,' which was paid in 1994," the Mueller report says in a footnote. "About two weeks later, the controller of the club responded that the Muel-lers' resignation would be effective October 31, 2011, and that they would be 'placed on a waitlist to be refunded on a first resigned / first refunded basis' in accordance with the club's legal documents. . . . The Muellers have not had further contact with the club."

Bannon, according to the Mueller report, "told the President that the golf course dispute did not rise to the level of a conflict and claiming one was 'ridiculous and petty.'"

House Speaker Nancy Pelosi (D-Calif.)

"Just the other day, Nancy Pelosi came out in favor of MS-13. That's the first time I've heard that. She wants them to be treated with respect, as do other Democrats."

—May 22, 2018 (speech)

"The Democrat Party supports—totally, they love them—sanctuary cities where crime pours in . . . that unleash violent predators like MS-13 into American communities, leaving innocent Americans at the mercy of really, by the way, really ruthless animals, really ruthless animals. Nancy Pelosi said, 'How dare he call a human being an animal?' I'm sorry, Nancy."

—Sept. 29, 2018 (campaign rally)

"I call them animals and Nancy Pelosi said, 'They're not animals; they're human beings.'"

—Jan. 9, 2020 (campaign rally)

On May 16, 2018, Trump appeared to suggest that undocumented immigrants were "animals" during a meeting with California law enforcement officials.

"We have people coming into the country or trying to come in—and we're stopping a lot of them—but we're taking people out of the country," Trump said. "You wouldn't believe how bad these people are. These aren't people. These are animals. And we're taking them out of the country at a level and at a rate that's never happened before."

The next day, May 17, Pelosi said, "When the president of the United States says about undocumented immigrants, 'These are not people, these are animals," you have to wonder, does he not believe in the spark of divinity? In the dignity and worth of every person?" She continued, saying that "calling people animals is not a good thing" and defending "undocumented immigrants."

The following day, May 18, Trump tweeted a clarification: "I referred to MS 13 Gang Members as 'Animals,' a big difference—and so true."

This smear works like a shell game: Pelosi had referred to "undocumented immigrants"—not to MS-13 gang members, on the day before Trump posted his clarification. Two years later, he was still repeating the attack on Pelosi.

The late Sen. John McCain (R-Ariz.)

Donald J. Trump
@realDonaldTrump

"So it was indeed (just proven in court papers) 'last in his class' (Annapolis) John McCain that sent the Fake Dossier to the FBI and Media hoping to have it printed BEFORE the Election."—March 17, 2019

"John McCain campaigned for years to repeal and replace Obamacare—for years, in Arizona. . . . When he finally had the chance to do it, he voted against 'repeal and replace.' He voted against, at two o'clock in the morning."

—March 20, 2019 (speech)

"I disagree with John McCain on the way he handled the vets, because I said you got to get Choice. He was never able to get Choice. I got Choice."

—May 30, 2019 (remarks)

Trump often fumed at Sen. John McCain of Arizona when he was alive. But these fumes all came after the senator died in 2018.

McCain only learned of the existence of the Steele dossier, a private intelligence memo containing uncorroborated allegations of contacts between the Trump campaign and Russia, after the election, at a conference in Canada.

In late November 2016, McCain dispatched David J. Kramer, a senior director of the McCain Institute, to London to meet with Christopher Steele, the former British spy who wrote the report. Kramer returned with a copy of the dossier, which McCain gave to the FBI. The FBI already had a copy.

McCain was not last in his class at the United States Naval Academy, though he was near the bottom.

Trump often claims McCain's "no" vote in the Senate was the only impediment to a bill that would have repealed and replaced the Affordable Care Act. That's not the case.

The House in 2017 narrowly passed the American Health Care Act, 217 to 213. An earlier version of the bill had failed, but some amendments won over conservatives who had balked. The Senate was not happy with the House proposal and crafted its own repeal-and-replace legislation, the Better Care Reconciliation Act. McCain voted for that bill, but it failed to get enough support in the Senate. As a last-ditch effort, Republicans put up a bare-bones bill (the "skinny repeal") that would have kicked some of the hardest policy decisions to a conference between the House and the Senate.

McCain and two other Republicans, Susan Collins of Maine and Lisa Murkowski of Alaska, voted against the skinny repeal. The differences between the House and Senate positions had proven to be huge and intractable through months of negotiations. There was no guarantee that a conference committee would have hammered out an agreement.

Finally, Trump often takes credit for reforms enacted years before he took office. In response to a 2014 scandal over wait times and patient care at Veterans Affairs in Phoenix and other locations, a bipartisan group of lawmakers led by McCain and Sen. Bernie Sanders (I-Vt.) created the VA Choice program. Obama signed it into law. Trump in 2018 signed the MISSION Act, an expansion and update of the Choice program that is named after McCain. But he falsely takes credit for the whole effort while erasing McCain's role, even at one point saying, "McCain didn't get the job done for our great vets. I got it done."

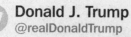

Donald J. Trump
@realDonaldTrump

"The New York Times and a third rate reporter named Maggie Haberman, known as a Crooked H flunkie who I don't speak to and have nothing to do with, are going out of their way to destroy Michael Cohen and his relationship with me in the hope that he will 'flip.'"—April 21, 2018

Donald J. Trump
@realDonaldTrump

"The writer of the story, Maggie Haberman, a Hillary flunky, knows nothing about me and is not given access."—March 11, 2018

A picture is sometimes worth a thousand fact checks.

New York Times reporter Maggie Haberman (interviewing Trump)

Attorney George Conway

Donald J. Trump
@realDonaldTrump

"George Conway, often referred to as Mr. Kellyanne Conway by those who know him, is VERY jealous of his wife's success & angry that I, with her help, didn't give him the job he so desperately wanted. I barely know him but just take a look, a stone cold LOSER & husband from hell!"—March 20, 2019

"I barely know him" is not the most credible sentence coming from Trump, who knows George Conway well. Not only is Conway married to one of Trump's top advisers, but the president once considered him for a top Justice Department post, leading the civil division.

Things didn't work out. ("The administration is like a shitshow in a dumpster fire," Conway explained, shortly after tweeting claims that Trump suffers from malignant narcissistic personality disorder.)

Up until Trump's presidency, the two men had been on somewhat-friendly terms, as evidenced by a 2006 letter from Trump to Conway:

Dear George: I wanted to thank you for your wonderful assistance in ridding Trump World Tower of some very bad people. What I was most impressed with was how quickly you were able to comprehend a very bad situation. In any event, the building has now been normalized, and the employees are no longer doing menial tasks, etc. for our former Board Members. . . . PS—And, you have a truly great voice, certainly not a bad asset for a top trial lawyer!

The Washington Post reported that shortly after they were married in 2001, Kellyanne and George Conway moved into an apartment in Trump World Tower in Manhattan. A few years later, George Conway impressed the future president by arguing at a condominium board meeting that Trump's name should not be removed from the building.

Conway detailed sundry other interactions: at a fundraiser with Trump in Alpine, N.J.; during a shared SUV ride to a costume party; on a plane ride to an inaugural ball in Washington. He said the president called to pick his brain about a lawsuit alleging violations of the foreign emoluments clause; Trump also called Conway, a prominent conservative lawyer, for his opinion on lawyers the president was considering hiring as his outside counsel in the Russia investigation.

Gov. Ralph Northam (D-Va.)

 "The governor of Virginia executed a baby, remember that whole thing? After birth, after birth. Some people never heard of it."

—Nov. 1, 2019 (campaign rally)

Gov. Ralph Northam of Virginia, a pediatrician, did not execute a newborn.

Northam, a Democrat, was asked on a radio show whether he supported a bill in the state legislature to loosen abortion requirements. He did not take a position on the bill and instead discussed late-term abortion procedures in general terms:

The first thing I would say is, this is why decisions such as this should be made by providers, physicians, and the mothers and fathers that are involved. There are—you know, when we talk about third-trimester abortions, these are done with the consent of, obviously, the mother, with the consent of the physicians, more than one physician, by the way. And it's done in cases where there may be severe deformities, there may be a fetus that's non-viable. So in this particular example, if a mother is in labor, I can tell you exactly what would happen. The infant would be delivered, the infant would be kept comfortable, the infant would be resuscitated if that's what the mother and the family desired, and then a discussion would ensue between the physicians and the mother.

This is a clinical explanation of circumstances that might lead to a late-term abortion. Northam did not perform such an abortion, nor did he endorse them as a policy matter, nor was he advocating for the bill to ease abortion requirements in Virginia.

Former FBI officials Lisa Page and Peter Strzok

 "Strzok and Page were talking about the insurance policy, right? The insurance policy—just in case Hillary Clinton lost, they wanted an insurance policy against me. And what we were playing out until just recently was the insurance policy."

—March 27, 2019 (interview)

 " 'If for any reason, she loses, Peter, we've got to have an insurance policy, we have to do it, because we're going to go out'—and that's what's been happening for the last two and a half years, okay? It was their phony insurance policy. So, FBI lawyer Lisa Page, so in love that she didn't know what the hell was happening. . . . Peter Strzok, likewise, so in love he couldn't see straight. This poor guy. Did I hear he needed a restraining order after this whole thing to keep him away from Lisa? That's what I heard. I don't know if it's true, the fake news will never report it, but it could be true. No, that's what I heard. I don't know, I mean, who could believe a thing like that? No, I heard that Peter Strzok needed a restraining order to keep him away from his once-lover."

—Dec. 10, 2019 (campaign rally)

 "We learned about Lisa Page and her wonderful lover, Peter Strzok. I love you, Lisa. I love you more than anybody in the world. I love you more than anybody in the world. Causes problems with the wife, but we won't talk about that. . . . I've never loved anyone like you. He's going to lose one hundred million to one, Peter, right? That's right. He's going to lose one hundred million to

one. But there's no bias. How about the insurance policy?"

—Dec. 18, 2019 (campaign rally)

This is what happens when Trump's imagination runs wild. He invents conversations between former FBI officials Lisa Page and Peter Strzok and acts out both parts for his audience. Trump's impersonation shtick at one campaign rally featured crude gestures and what Page called "sickening . . . fake orgasm" noises.

Behind the lurid facade, Trump is also accusing them of an undemocratic plot: leveraging the FBI machinery to help Hillary Clinton win. It's an unsupported accusation, still devoid of evidence after years of investigating the investigators.

The Justice Department inspector general criticized anti-Trump text messages between Page and Strzok but found that bias did not taint FBI officials' decisions in the investigation of Trump's campaign and Russia. ("These judgment calls were not unreasonable," the inspector general's report says.)

Trump often mentions an "insurance policy" at the FBI targeting him in case he won. But Strzok has insisted that the reference to an insurance policy in a text message he sent to Page did not mean he or fellow agents were targeting Trump. Instead, Strzok said, the phrase was bureau shorthand for a difficult question involving intelligence-gathering.

"That text represented a debate on information that we had received from an extraordinarily sensitive source and method, and that typically when something is that sensitive, if you take action on it, you put it at risk," Strzok publicly testified in July 2018.

The crux of the issue was whether an important source could be burned. "Given that Clinton was the 'prohibitive favorite' to win, Strzok said that they discussed whether it made sense to compromise sensitive sources and methods to 'bring things to some sort of precipitative conclusion and understanding,'" the inspector general said in a report.

Trump, out of the blue, also claimed that Page got a restraining order on Strzok. "This is a lie," Page tweeted in response. "Nothing like this ever happened. I wish we had a president who knew how to act like one."

"I'M PRETTY GOOD
AT ESTIMATING CROWD SIZES"

President Trump's term began with a surreal national debate over how many people attended his inauguration. Photographs from the National Park Service contradicted his wild boasts, yet Trump and the White House insisted that he had attracted the largest crowd ever to witness a president's swearing-in.

Trump's obsession with crowd size was nothing new—and it would become a constant of his presidency. There's no question Trump can draw supporters by the thousands, but his crowd-size estimates are often so inflated that they are easily disproven.

For example, Trump claimed 50,000 people were outside a rally in Houston because they couldn't get in, but the city police chief said the number was much lower—3,000. In Cleveland, Trump claimed thousands of people had been left outside because the venue was packed. Twitter users at the event posted evidence that Trump didn't even fill the space inside and that only a handful of people were milling around in the parking lot. At a Tampa rally, Trump claimed thousands of people who couldn't get in were watching outside on a "tremendous movie screen," which didn't exist.

These Trumpian boasts are easily debunked, because there are local officials, fire marshals, police officers, venue managers and others on the ground whose job it is to count the attendees. Their counts almost invariably come in way lower than the president's exaggerated guesswork.

We did some scouring. For nine rallies leading up to the 2018 midterm elections, the president's aggregate estimate of attendance came to 352,600 people. Our review of local officials' counts and news reports showed the number was much lower: 101,000.

Here's a taste:

Air Force One at a 2018 Trump campaign rally in Georgia

 "I went and did a rally, and the real number was probably 55,000 people, 'cause, you know, were you there in Georgia? . . . Because we had a hangar, another hangar holding 18,000 at the top of the hangar. These are massive, like 747 hangars."

—Nov. 14, 2018 (interview)

Trump said he filled two airport hangars; there was only one. The Bibb County Sheriff's Office estimated 12,500 people inside and nearly 6,000 outside, a far cry from the 55,000 Trump claimed.

 "In Erie, Pennsylvania, the other night with 25,000 people outside of a 12,000-seat arena. It's been amazing."

—Oct. 12, 2018 (interview)

Police estimated 3,000 people outside a 9,000-seat venue.

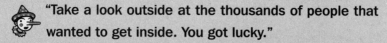 **"Take a look outside at the thousands of people that wanted to get inside. You got lucky."**

—Nov. 15, 2018 (rally in Indiana)

Reporters looked outside. There was no one.

CHAPTER FOUR

Boasts to the Base:
"You're the Super-Elite!"

President Trump says his supporters are unmatched, tougher and "more elite" than Washington insiders and coastal liberals. "We do better than they do, we're smarter than them, we make more money, we have better houses—we have better everything—and then they say 'the elite,'" Trump said at a 2019 campaign rally in New Mexico. "That means you're the super-elite!"

Trump routinely makes statements that seem intended to coddle and deceive his core supporters. Hundreds of times, Trump has claimed falsely that he "decimated" the Affordable Care Act, that he's far along in building the wall he promised on the southern border or that he sparked a blue-collar jobs boom in the swing states where he could win or lose reelection.

In this rosy version of reality, new auto plants, steel mills and coal mines are cropping up all over the country (mostly false); Apple and other corporations are rushing manufacturing jobs back to America after decades of outsourcing (greatly exaggerated); and Trump's deregulatory moves have turned the United States into the world's top energy producer (that happened, but under Barack Obama).

These feel-good lines get debunked each time Trump utters

them, yet he keeps repeating them and supporters keep cheering. In this sense, Trump's presidency reflects the nation's divided realities, separate news sources and polarized politics. How many Trump supporters are true believers, and how many simply like the show and Trump's achievements, even if they know his facts aren't always up to snuff? Hard to say. Researchers have found that people experience a dopamine rush from information, true or not, that echoes what they already believe. Trump, for his part, basks in delivering entertaining, provocative, outrageous monologues that portray his presidency as far more historic and consequential than it has been.

Here are some of the biggest deceptions that Trump seems to have tailored for his base.

"WE DID IT"

 "Obamacare is a disaster. It's virtually dead."
—Oct. 17, 2017 (remarks)

 "Essentially, we are getting rid of Obamacare. Some people would say, essentially, we got rid of it. But you no longer have the individual mandate."
—April 28, 2018 (campaign rally)

 "We've decimated Obamacare."
—Nov. 2, 2018 (campaign rally)

Trump promised to repeal the Affordable Care Act, a longtime target for conservatives, but most of the law remains intact. He has neither "decimated" nor virtually eliminated Obamacare, not by any stretch.

Obama's signature legislative accomplishment has survived years of Republican attempts to undo it. Trump and GOP lawmakers did reduce to zero the individual mandate, a financial penalty levied on people who don't purchase health insurance, but Obamacare is a complex piece of legislation with multiple remaining parts.

One portion of the law established health insurance marketplaces, or exchanges, where individual consumers may shop for coverage plans. The exchanges are still available, as are Obamacare's subsidies for millions of participating buyers. Another part of the act prevents insurers from denying coverage to patients with preexisting health conditions. That guarantee is still the law, though as described in Chapter One, the Trump administration is in court arguing for its repeal. One of the biggest components of Obamacare is an expansion of Medicaid in participating states. Thirty-six states and the District of Columbia had accepted the Medicaid expansion as of early 2020.

According to the Centers for Disease Control and Prevention, nearly 20 million fewer people were uninsured in 2018 compared with 2010, the year before Obamacare was enacted.

"We're building the wall."

—Nov. 12, 2019 (speech)

"We've built almost 100 miles already. It's going up rapidly, and it's the real deal."

—Dec. 21, 2019 (speech)

By our count, Trump claimed 242 times in three years that the border wall, his signature campaign promise, was under construction. The reality is Trump failed to get Congress to fund a massive concrete wall, even when Republicans controlled both chambers during his first two years in office.

Without congressionally-allocated money, the Trump administration instead grabbed billions of dollars in military funds that had been earmarked for Puerto Rico's rebuilding following Hurricane Maria and for schools serving the children of service members, among other programs, and redirected the money toward building a fortified system of roads, sensors, vehicle barriers and pedestrian fencing along the U.S-Mexican border.

Trump personally selected a see-through fence made of hollow steel bars partially filled with concrete. *The Washington Post* reported that a modified power saw can cut through the fence's beams. Portions of the fence lie along flood-prone areas, so the barrier is equipped with sluice gates that must be opened during certain seasons, providing easy access for undocumented immigrants. Near El Paso, U.S. immigration officials say, smugglers have been selling inexpensive ladders that blend in with the bollard fence's rust-brown color. (The *El Paso Times* reported that the border "is littered with the rusted rebar ladders at the base on both sides—ladders lying in wait on the Mexican side, ladders pulled down by border agents or abandoned by smugglers on the U.S. side.")

An impenetrable concrete bulwark it ain't. But many Trump supporters, along with some critics who oppose the bulked-up fence, have taken to calling it a "wall."

In his first run for president, Trump envisioned a 1,000-mile-long wall made of precast concrete slabs, rising 35 to 40 feet. Once he was in office, prototypes were built. Trump traveled to California to see them. He asked Congress for $25 billion to cover the wall's cost in 2018, but Congress refused. Nonetheless, Trump ordered the fence built, and he began claiming that the wall was finally under construction.

Trump says that 100 miles of fence have been completed. But it's all replacement fencing, none of which went up in open areas of the border, though some of the barriers that got replaced were quite dilapidated. When the project is finished, administration officials say, the 500 miles of new fencing would include only about 100 miles of barriers where none previously existed.

 "We got rid of the Johnson Amendment."
                                            —May 2, 2019 (remarks)

The Johnson Amendment—named for President Lyndon B. Johnson—prohibits religious organizations and many nonprofits from endorsing or opposing political candidates. Trump's claim that he got rid of the law is false. In fact, the New York attorney general alleged that Trump violated the Johnson Amendment during the 2016 campaign, and the president, in response, dissolved his own charitable foundation and settled the lawsuit.

Section 501(c)3 of the U.S. tax code covers nonprofit groups such as charities, universities and religious organizations. As a condition of their tax-exempt status, these groups "are absolutely prohibited from directly or indirectly participating in, or intervening in, any political campaign on behalf of (or in opposition to) any candidate for elective public office," according to the IRS. However, the prohibition is seldom enforced by the IRS, and some clergy simply disregard the law. In their personal capacities, leaders of 501(c)3 organizations remain free to support or oppose candidates. They also may speak about political issues on behalf of their organizations, short of endorsing or opposing candidates.

Trump's claim that he "got rid" of the Johnson Amendment and that religious organizations are now free to embrace political candidates usually wins applause from his evangelical supporters. But the amendment is still on the books. Congress has not repealed it; the courts have not struck it down.

Trump signed an executive order in May 2017 with the stated purpose of giving religious groups more leeway in political speech. But executive orders cannot overwrite the laws passed by Congress.

Using somewhat-circular logic, Trump's order says the Treasury Department should not treat speech "about moral or political issues from a religious perspective" as a sign of support for or opposition to a candidate if similar language, in the past, has not ordinarily been treated that way. In other words, the order changes nothing. "The Order does not exempt religious organizations from the restrictions on political campaign activity applicable to all tax-exempt organizations," according to a Justice Department filing submitted in August 2017 as part of a court case.

 "We did well in the '18 election. . . . I wasn't able to go out and work for the House members because I had to win the Senate. And we picked up two seats and nobody talks—we picked up two Senate seats, we got up to 53, and nobody ever talks about that."
—Dec. 21, 2019 (prepared speech)

"We had a great election in North Carolina recently. Two great congressmen got elected you don't hear about. When they win, you don't ever hear about it. . . . They got elected because I wanted at the end—you don't talk about the fact that you have sanctuary cities and they had some horrible crimes happening from those sanctuary cities. As soon as

I mentioned that, boom, they went up like rocket ships and they won their elections."

—Dec. 18, 2019 (campaign rally)

 "I raised them up almost to victory and they had no chance. . . . I've won virtually every race that I've participated in."

—Dec. 3, 2019 (remarks)

Republicans lost the House to Democrats in 2018. Defying reality, Trump called it a "very close to complete victory" for his side.

The truth is he barnstormed the country with dozens of rallies and endorsements for House candidates in tight races, only to see more than 30 of them lose. Republicans already controlled the Senate and gained one seat over the 2016 outcome, not two, a result that was expected and widely reported at the time.

Contrary to his boasts, Trump's overall endorsement record is spotty. While he picks plenty of winners, he has endorsed a fair share of clunkers, too. Ten candidates with Trump endorsements lost their Senate races in 2018. In 2019, the president threw his support behind Republican candidates for governor in Kentucky and Louisiana; they lost. In 2017, Trump backed Luther Strange in the Republican Senate primary in Alabama; he lost. Then he endorsed Roy Moore in the general election; he lost, too. Then Trump said Moore never had a chance. "I was right!" Trump tweeted. "Roy worked hard but the deck was stacked against him!"

North Carolina held a special election for two congressional seats in 2019. Both districts were held by Republicans, only one race was considered close, and the GOP candidate had been ahead in every poll. The races did not turn on Trump's comments about sanctuary cities. The candidates did not go up "like rocket ships."

"WE BROUGHT SO MANY THINGS BACK"

 "This is a blue-collar boom. Everybody is booming, frankly, but it's a blue-collar boom"
—Jan. 19, 2020 (prepared speech)

Toward the end of Trump's third year in office, the jobs picture had grown bleaker for many blue-collar workers. But that didn't stop Trump from powering past bad news with claims of a "blue-collar boom."

The manufacturing sector was in a technical recession when Trump declared the boom. Only 9,000 jobs in that sector were gained in the second half of 2019, compared with 460,000 in the first two and a half years of Trump's presidency. Job growth had slowed or reversed in many blue-collar sectors such as steelmaking, construction and mining.

 "The head of U.S. Steel called me the other day, and he said, 'We're opening up six major facilities and expanding facilities that have never been expanded.' They haven't been opened in many, many years."
—June 20, 2018 (remarks)

 "U.S. Steel is now building seven plants."
—Nov. 1, 2018 (campaign rally)

 "U.S. Steel is opening up eight plants."
—Oct. 9, 2018 (remarks)

The number is closer to zero. As a publicly-traded company, U.S. Steel is required to disclose materially-important information to investors and regulators. The opening of six, seven or eight new plants and the expansion of even more would be huge news. Trump said the head of U.S. Steel slipped him this market-moving information, but the company declined to confirm his implausible account.

What U.S. Steel had announced when Trump made these remarks was a restart of two blast furnaces and production facilities at its Granite City Works integrated plant in Illinois, which the company said would add about 800 jobs. The following year, U.S. Steel announced it would idle other blast furnaces due to slumping demand, laying off thousands of workers, including more than 1,500 in the Detroit area.

Labor data for primary metal manufacturing, the category that includes the steel industry, shows a net gain of 6,000 jobs in Trump's first three years in office, an increase of less than 2 percent.

 "Pennsylvania has never done this well. We've got steel back, we brought coal back, we brought so many things back, and the state now is doing better than it's ever done. . . . Miners are going back to work that never thought they'd see that job again."
—May 20, 2019 (interview)

These boasts sound like campaign gold, but they crumble like pyrite. The number of coal-mining jobs nationwide hardly changed during Trump's first three years as president; in Pennsylvania, the number declined from 5,000 to 4,800 by the end of 2019, according to Bureau of Labor Statistics data.

Pennsylvania, a swing state in the 2020 presidential election, had experienced a sharp drop in steel-manufacturing jobs during the Obama administration. The state recorded a modest gain of about 500 such jobs in Trump's first three years, reaching an estimated 11,800.

 "We took historic and dramatic action to save the American auto industry and to defend American autoworkers right here in Michigan. . . . And just in the last very short period of time, we have added another 6,000 vehicle-manufacturing and auto-parts jobs in Michigan alone and prevented thousands more from being shipped overseas and from going to Mexico."

—March 28, 2019 (campaign rally)

The Bush and Obama administrations bailed out the U.S. auto industry during the 2008–2009 financial crisis. Trump's claim about "historic and dramatic action to save the American auto industry" refers to his imposition of tariffs and his reworked version of NAFTA, which had not been approved by Congress at the time.

When Trump made this claim about job gains in Michigan's auto industry, his 6,000 figure was accurate. But by two months later, one-third of that growth had vanished.

Looking at Trump's term more comprehensively, auto-manufacturing jobs in Michigan remained flat at 42,000 between February 2017 and December 2019. Employers in the state added nearly 2,000 auto-parts manufacturing jobs over the same period, for a total of 132,000.

"Our automobile industry is pouring back into our country. . . . Everyone's coming back in. Toyota's coming in. Honda's coming in. Many, many car companies. General Motors today just announced three big plants, 450 workers, $700 million. . . . With all of the companies pouring into Michigan, all of the companies pouring into Florida, North Carolina, South Carolina, Ohio, everywhere with all of these companies."

—May 8, 2019 (campaign rally)

 "Toyota's coming in with $14 billion. Many, many companies are coming in. And they're coming in, frankly, to Michigan, they're coming back, they want to be back to Ohio, to Pennsylvania, to North Carolina, South Carolina, Florida and what's the name of this special place? It's called Wisconsin."

—April 27, 2019 (campaign rally)

What a coincidence. Trump's list of places that reaped the benefits of an auto-manufacturing revival included five key swing states. But his claims don't add up.

GM announced a $700 million investment and plans to create nearly 450 manufacturing jobs in Ohio, as Trump said. Toyota has a $13 billion investment in the works for its U.S. plants, which would add 600 jobs, though the first $10 billion was announced in the days before Trump took office.

Automakers indeed have announced new plants or expansions in Ohio, Michigan and South Carolina since Trump took office. But no new car plants or expansions have been announced in Florida, North Carolina, Pennsylvania or Wisconsin.

Mercedes-Benz and Volvo both opened plants in South Carolina in 2018, but the projects broke ground in 2015, before Trump was elected. And a Volvo executive said that the company was considering shifting some production to India because of the Trump administration's trade policies.

According to the Center for Automotive Research (CAR), BMW and Volvo each announced a $600 million investment in South Carolina in 2017. BMW said it would expand its 25-year-old plant in the state. Volvo said it was doubling a $500 million investment it had announced in 2015.

The expansions in Florida, Pennsylvania, North Carolina and Wisconsin came entirely from companies that supply car manufacturers; such businesses have announced more than $2.8 billion in investments since 2017, according to CAR's "Book of Deals" database.

"The other four states are really automaker supplier states," said Kristin Dziczek, CAR's vice president of industry, labor and economics. "The one automaker investment in Pennsylvania, for example, represents Spartan Motors—a relatively small specialty chassis and vehicle design, manufacturing, and assembly firm."

 "We've brought a lot of car companies into Ohio, you know that. A lot of them coming in, a lot of them have already been brought in. They're coming in from Japan. They're coming in from all over the world. This is where they want to be. They want to be in the United States. That's where the action is. They're all coming back."

—Jan. 9, 2020 (campaign rally)

"Many other investments we've gotten from Japanese companies, car companies and other companies, but they're all coming in and a lot of them are coming to Michigan."

—Dec. 18, 2019 (campaign rally)

More swing-state spin. No car companies have come to Ohio during Trump's presidency, and jobs in the state's motor vehicle manufacturing sector have decreased by about 1,000 since February 2017, Trump's first full month in office.

Some automobile industry investments have been announced in Michigan, but not by Japanese companies.

"THE GOOD NEWS KEEPS ROLLING IN"

 "Apple, by the way, is spending $350 billion in this country, bringing back $230 billion from offshore, only because of our tax cuts."

—Oct. 24, 2018 (campaign rally)

Trump never gets this right. The Tax Cuts and Jobs Act he signed near the end of 2017 slashed the corporate tax rate from 35 percent to 21 percent, among other provisions favoring multinational corporations.

In quick order, in January 2018, Apple announced a five-year investment plan that adds up to nearly $350 billion. That includes roughly $275 billion in spending with U.S. suppliers and manufacturers, $30 billion in capital expenditures and $4 billion for a fund to promote innovation among its manufacturers of product parts.

Apple plans to build a new campus and hire 20,000 employees. But the tech giant did not directly attribute any of those moves to Trump's tax overhaul.

Apple chief executive, Tim Cook, told ABC News that "there are large parts of this that are a result of the tax reform, and there's large parts of this that we would have done in any situation."

We asked Apple to break down how much of its new spending stemmed from the tax changes and how much had been in the pipeline, but Apple did not provide an answer. That leaves us with only one component of Apple's plan specifically linked to Trump's tax overhaul: a $38 billion payment to repatriate overseas profit.

 "Because of our tax cuts . . . ExxonMobil, in addition to many others, just announced that they are investing $50 billion in the United States. So the good news just keeps on rolling in."

—Feb. 1, 2018 (remarks)

Exxon's chairman and chief executive wrote a blog post weeks after Trump's tax cuts were signed into law, announcing an investment of "billions of dollars to increase oil production in the Permian Basin in West Texas and New Mexico, expand existing operations, improve infrastructure and build new manufacturing sites."

Missing from Trump's commentary: Exxon added that the investment was only partly due to the tax changes (again, the company didn't specify how much). A company spokesman later clarified that the new investment over five years totaled $35 billion—not $50 billion—because $15 billion worth of projects already had been announced.

"GM Korea company announced today that it will cease production and close its Gunsan plant in May of 2018, and they're going to move back to Detroit. You don't hear these things, except for the fact that Trump became president."

—Feb. 13, 2018 (remarks)

At a White House meeting to discuss international trade, Trump said four times that GM was closing a plant in South Korea and moving it to Detroit. "I just think that General Motors moving back into Detroit is just a fantastic thing," he said.

But GM announced only that it was closing a plant in Gunsan, South Korea. There was no word that it would move those operations to Detroit or anywhere else in the United States. In fact, GM said it expected to take charges of $850 million from closing the plant.

"The Gunsan facility has been increasingly underutilized, running at about 20 percent of capacity over the past three years, making continued operations unsustainable," according to a GM news release at the time. The White House did not respond to a request for comment on this issue. Were we missing anything? "Our announcement was strictly about the Gunsan plant," a GM spokesman told us.

 "We ended the last administration's war on American energy. The United States is now the number one producer of oil and natural gas anywhere in the world."

—Nov. 26, 2019 (campaign rally)

"We're an exporter of energy for the first time in our history, really."

—Dec. 6, 2019 (remarks)

 "We are now the number one producer of oil and natural gas anywhere in the world. We are independent, and we do not need Middle East oil."

—Jan. 8, 2020 (remarks)

These statements may sound plausible to casual observers, and they often slip past the scrutiny of fact-checkers, swamped by more spectacular falsehoods. It is yet another house of cards. Trump frequently takes credit for a boom in the U.S. energy sector that began during the Obama administration, and almost none of what he says on this topic is accurate.

The decade-long boom in domestic oil and gas production is mainly the result of new drilling techniques—most notably, hydraulic fracturing, also known as fracking.

Since at least 2014, the United States has been the world's top energy producer. Americans have led in natural gas production since 2009. Crude oil production has been increasing rapidly since 2010, and the United States was the leading crude oil producer in 2013, according to the U.S. Energy Information Administration (EIA).

The United States was exporting energy long before Trump took office. Trump pledged during his campaign to turn the country into a net energy exporter, meaning one that sells more energy to other countries than it buys from them. But that hasn't happened. The U.S. became a net exporter of natural gas for the first time in 2017, and exports of crude oil and petroleum products more than doubled from 2010 to 2016. For one week in November 2018, the U.S. was a net exporter of crude oil. It bears mentioning that the United States lifted restrictions on exporting crude oil in December 2015, while Obama was in office.

Trump's claim that the United States is now energy-independent and does "not need Middle East oil" is wrong and misleading. "In 2018, the United States imported about 9.94 million barrels per day of petroleum from nearly 90 countries," according to an EIA report, with 43 percent coming from Canada and 16 percent from Persian Gulf countries.

 "I was able to get ANWR in Alaska. It could be the largest site in the world for oil and gas. I was able to get ANWR approved. Ronald Reagan wasn't able to do it. Nobody was able to do it. They've been trying to do it since before Ronald Reagan. I got it approved."

—Aug. 26, 2019 (news conference)

Sometimes Trump speaks about Reagan as if the two are in competition for some imaginary prize for conservative accomplishment. The president seems to chafe at Reagan's revered status among Republicans and often tries to even the score with false claims, such as the notion that Reagan comes in second, after him, in polls measuring GOP support for presidents. Trump also fibs that his 2017 tax cuts were bigger than Reagan's.

"We all like Ronald Reagan. I liked him. I thought he was a great guy. But if he came to Pennsylvania for a rally, you know, if he had a thousand people in a ballroom or something," Trump said at a 2019 campaign rally with nearly 10,000 attendees. In fact, Reagan drew 10 times as many people in 1984 to an event in Doylestown, Pa., where he spoke out against an "America divided by envy."

The Trump administration is seeking to open the entire coastal plain of the Arctic National Wildlife Refuge to oil and gas exploration, picking the most aggressive development option for an area long closed to drilling.

The U.S. Geological Survey projected that anywhere from 5.7 billion to 16 billion barrels of oil could be drilled from this land. That doesn't even make it the biggest drilling site in Alaska. Its average estimated oil reserves fall below Prudhoe Bay's 13.6 billion barrels but are similar to the National Petroleum Reserve in Alaska's 10.6 billion barrels. The Ghawar field in Saudi Arabia, which has been producing oil since the 1950s, has 70 million barrels left in reserves.

SHARPIEGATE

Donald J. Trump
@realDonaldTrump

"In addition to Florida—South Carolina, North Carolina, Georgia, and Alabama, will most likely be hit (much) harder than anticipated. Looking like one of the largest hurricanes ever. Already category 5. BE CAREFUL! GOD BLESS EVERYONE!"—Sept. 1, 2019

Trump instinctively understands that when extreme weather takes lives and destroys property hit hard, Americans expect the federal government to come to the rescue. The president takes an active role, akin to a mayor who shows up at every major fire, whenever a hurricane approaches U.S. shores. Trump canceled a trip to Poland to monitor Hurricane Dorian in 2019. He's even mused about using nuclear weapons to stop approaching storms.

But Trump's role as weatherman-in-chief backfired when he declared that Alabama was in Dorian's path. Nervous residents contacted the National Weather Service's Birmingham office, which, apparently unaware of Trump's tweet, issued its own tweet contradicting Trump: "Alabama will NOT see any impacts from #Dorian. We repeat, no impacts from Hurricane #Dorian will be felt across Alabama. The system will remain too far east."

But Trump is never wrong. He doubled down.

He repeated to reporters that Alabama *was* in the storm's path. And a few days later, he called reporters into the Oval Office and displayed the National Hurricane Center's August 29 diagram of Dorian's projected track. A Sharpie—Trump's favorite writing instrument—had been used to extend Dorian's cone of uncertainty, the area that might feel the impact, into Alabama.

Trump initially claimed to reporters that he did not know how the map came to be modified, but *The Washington Post* reported he had done it himself. Trump falsely declared that forecasters "actually gave a 95 percent chance probability" that Alabama could be hit. Actually, an advisory issued two days before Trump's tweet said Montgomery, Ala., had an 11 percent chance of high winds, but that likelihood quickly dwindled.

Watch the path of the Sharpie

The president's handcrafted map sparked ridicule. Memes spread across Twitter mocking the doctored map—Sharpie extensions of Trump's legendarily short fingers, Sharpie renditions of a new wall along the Mexican border and so on.

Trump, naturally, tripled down. He told his staff that the National Oceanic and Atmospheric Administration (NOAA) had to correct the Birmingham weather office and announce that the president had been right. Commerce Secretary Wilbur Ross ordered NOAA to comply or else people would be fired.

On Sept. 6, NOAA issued an unsigned statement admonishing the Birmingham office and supporting Trump's false claim, saying that the information NOAA had provided to the president indeed "demonstrated that tropical-storm-force winds from Hurricane Dorian could impact Alabama."

But NOAA's acting chief scientist said the statement appeared to violate the agency's scientific integrity policy and would damage the agency's ability to protect Americans from danger to public health and safety: "If the public cannot trust our information, or we debase our forecaster's warnings and products, that specific danger arises."

From Trump's perspective, though, all was right: The U.S. government finally had officially declared his improvised warning to be correct.

CHAPTER FIVE

The Twitter Presidency: "He Needs to Tweet Like We Need to Eat"

No matter what has happened during Trump's presidency, there has almost always been a tweet for the occasion, a morsel in which the Trump of the past contradicts or predicts the Trump of the present. Since he joined Twitter in 2009, Trump has amassed more than 70 million followers and has posted more than 46,000 tweets, creating a nine-million-word archive of grievances, rants, insults, policy pronouncements, likes and dislikes.

Before he announced he would run for president, Trump's Twitter feed read like a dog's breakfast of complaints and suggestions. He slammed celebrities, opined on the hot gossip of the day, took aim at policy moves and public relations decisions, dished out leadership advice and critiqued everything from the timing of Obama's vacations to the quality of his chiefs of staff. His political tweets added up to a manifesto of 140-character snippets on how to run the most powerful nation in the world.

Things are different when you are doing the job. The Trump who confidently nitpicked Obama's moves now feels as though he is con-

101

stantly under siege. And when he's under pressure, he tweets on average 13 times per day, or once every other hour for a total of 14,296 times in his first three years in office—4,001 retweets, 10,295 original tweets and 521 deleted tweets. "He needs to tweet like we need to eat," his White House counselor Kellyanne Conway told the *New York Times*. Trump tweeted twice as much in 2019 as in 2018, spinning false narratives of accomplishment, conspiracy and exoneration to his 72.7 million followers. (The Fact Checker generally does not fact-check Trump's retweets of other people's commentaries.)

More than a third of the president's 3,083 false or misleading tweets focus on either the investigation into his campaign's connection to Russian interference in the 2016 election or to the impeachment inquiry into the president's attempt to pressure the government of Ukraine into investigating Joe and Hunter Biden.

"Twitter is a way that I can get out the word," Trump said in 2019. "Because our media is so dishonest—a lot of it—the mainstream. A lot of it. They don't report the facts." But Trump is not especially judicious about the accuracy of what he shares. Nor is he particular about the sources of his retweets. His feed is a motherlode of misinformation.

This is the story of the president and his platform of choice. We look at how Trump's tweets reveal his comfort with contradicting himself, and we offer a chronological survey of the various ways the president counterpunches with his itchy Twitter fingers—digitally shouting out conspiracy theories, railing against investigations, Democrats, former staff and any and all he believes to be "against Trump."

THERE'S ALWAYS A TWEET

Donald J. Trump
@realDonaldTrump

"The real scandal here is that classified information is illegally given out by 'intelligence' like candy. Very un-American!"—Feb. 15, 2017

Donald J. Trump
@realDonaldTrump

"Huma calls it a 'MESS,' the rest of us call it CORRUPT! WikiLeaks catches Crooked in the act—again. #DrainTheSwamp"—Oct. 21, 2016

This is a flip-flop. Before becoming president, Trump heartily endorsed WikiLeaks and the release of classified information, particularly about his then-rival Hillary Clinton. During a July 2016 news conference, Trump even called on Russia to hack Clinton's email account.

Just four months later, facing leaks out of his own new administration (including information that led to the resignation of national security adviser Michael Flynn), Trump decided that the unauthorized revelation of classified material was now a bad thing.

Donald J. Trump
@realDonaldTrump

"With only a very small majority, the Republicans in the House & Senate need more victories next year since Dems totally obstruct, no votes!"—July 18, 2017

Donald J. Trump
@realDonaldTrump

"Obama's complaints about Republicans stopping his agenda are BS since he had full control for two years. He can never take responsibility."—Sept. 26, 2012

The Republicans controlled both the House of Representatives and the Senate during Trump's first two years in office, just as Democrats did during Obama's. Trump passed his signature tax cut but failed to push through any other major legislation; Obama in his first year managed to pass both the Affordable Care Act and an $800 billion economic stimulus bill.

Now, Trump rails against the "Do Nothing Dems" in the House of Representatives—which flipped to Democratic control in 2019—much as Obama complained about the Republican-led Senate.

Donald J. Trump
@realDonaldTrump

"Russia vows to shoot down any and all missiles fired at Syria. Get ready Russia, because they will be coming, nice and new and 'smart!' You shouldn't be partners with a Gas Killing Animal who kills his people and enjoys it!"—April 11, 2018

Donald J. Trump
@realDonaldTrump

"What other country tells the enemy when we are going to attack like Obama is doing with ISIS. Whatever happened to the element of surprise?"—Aug. 8, 2014

During the 2016 campaign, and before, Trump vehemently argued that revealing any aspect of military strategy—whether timetable or weaponry—was a mistake. In office, Trump regularly tweets details of military operations that are either in the planning stages or have just been completed. He even foreshadowed the official announcement of the targeted killing of ISIS leader Abu Bakr al-Baghdadi, tweeting, "Something very big has just happened!"

Donald J. Trump
@realDonaldTrump

"I am pleased to announce that Mick Mulvaney, Director of the Office of Management & Budget, will be named Acting White House Chief of Staff, replacing General John Kelly, who has served our Country with distinction."—Dec. 14, 2018

Donald J. Trump
@realDonaldTrump

"3 Chief of Staffs in less than 3 years of being President: Part of the reason why @BarackObama can't manage to pass his agenda."—Jan. 10, 2012

Rahm Emanuel and Bill Daley each served as chief of staff during Obama's first three years. Pete Rouse served as acting chief of staff for 100 days between the two men.

President Trump's three-year track record looks remarkably similar, as Reince Priebus and John F. Kelly served in the role. After Kelly was fired in early 2019, the position of chief of staff remained technically vacant while Mick Mulvaney served in an acting capacity. In early 2020, Trump chose then-Rep. Mark Meadows as his fourth chief of staff.

Donald J. Trump
@realDonaldTrump

"Mitch, use the Nuclear Option and get it done! Our Country is counting on you!"—Dec. 21, 2018

Donald J. Trump
@realDonaldTrump

"Thomas Jefferson wrote the Senate filibuster rule. Harry Reid & Obama killed it yesterday. Rule was in effect for over 200 years."—Nov. 22, 2013

This is a flip-flop. Trump was appalled at the 2013 rule change that allowed federal judges to be appointed without a two-thirds majority vote in the Senate. But once in office, Trump and Senate Majority Leader Mitch McConnell (R-Ky.) followed the same playbook, changing how many votes are needed to end debate on Supreme Court nominees. Trump's 2018 tweet encouraging McConnell to "use the Nuclear Option" is aimed at defanging the filibuster entirely, allowing legislation to pass the Senate with a simple majority rather than a two-thirds vote.

Donald J. Trump
@realDonaldTrump

"We got A Pluses for our recent hurricane work in Texas and Florida (and did an unappreciated great job in Puerto Rico, even though an inaccessible island with very poor electricity and a totally incompetent Mayor of San Juan). We are ready for the big one that is coming!"—Sept. 12, 2018

Donald J. Trump
@realDonaldTrump

"The federal gov. has handled Sandy worse than Katrina. There is no excuse why people don't have electricity or fuel yet."—Nov. 6, 2012

During Hurricane Sandy in 2012, 285 people died. It took 13 days for New York to restore power to 95 percent of customers after the storm; in New Jersey, it took 11 days. When Hurricane Katrina and a second storm hit in 2005, more than 1,800 people died. Louisiana took 23 days to restore power to three-quarters of customers.

Those death tolls pale in comparison to the damage Hurricane Maria inflicted on Puerto Rico in 2017. A study by George Washington University estimated the death toll at between 2,658 and 3,290. Puerto Rico adopted the midpoint number, 2,975, as its official statistic. Full power was not restored to Puerto Rico for 11 months.

Donald J. Trump
@realDonaldTrump

"Negotiating [*sic*] are proceeding well in Afghanistan after 18 years of fighting."—Jan. 30, 2019

Donald J. Trump
@realDonaldTrump

"While @BarackObama is slashing the military, he is also negotiating with our sworn enemy the Tailiban— who facilitated 9/11."—Jan. 13, 2012

Trump criticized Obama for engaging in talks with the Islamist rebels in Afghanistan in 2012. Seven years later, he struck a different chord. Though the president wavered on the negotiations, stopping and starting them at different points during his administration, the two sides said in February 2020 that they had agreed to a deal in which the United States would withdraw all troops within 14 months if the Taliban rebels cut their ties with al-Qaeda and other terrorist groups and began talks with Afghanistan's government. Trump even spoke with the Taliban leader in March. But the future of the peace deal remained very much in doubt in early 2020.

Donald J. Trump
@realDonaldTrump

"Campaigning for the Popular Vote is much easier & different than campaigning for the Electoral College. It's like training for the 100 yard dash vs. a marathon. The brilliance of the Electoral College is that you must go to many States to win. . . . I used to like the idea of the Popular Vote, but now realize the Electoral College is far better for the U.S.A."
—March 19, 2019

Donald J. Trump
@realDonaldTrump

"The electoral college is a disaster for a democracy."
—Nov. 6, 2012

Something—victory, perhaps?—changed Trump's mind. Losing the popular vote and winning the electoral college gave the president a new perspective.

Trump claims that the "brilliance of the Electoral College is that you must go to many States to win." That is indeed one reason the electoral college has maintained strong support through the years; it does force candidates to focus on the whole country rather than a few highly populated states. But it doesn't always result in candidates campaigning in most of the country: According to data on nearly 400 campaign trips Trump made from July 1, 2016, until Election Day, he made no visits to 29 states. The data, compiled by National Journal, showed that 20 states received no visits from any major-party presidential or vice-presidential candidates during the fall 2016 campaign.

Donald J. Trump
@realDonaldTrump

"With our wonderfully low inflation, we could be setting major records &, at the same time, make our National Debt start to look small!"—April 30, 2019

Donald J. Trump
@realDonaldTrump

"Our $17T national debt and $1T yearly budget deficits are a national security risk of the highest order."—Nov. 13, 2012

By nearly every measure, the national debt doubled under Obama. Although Trump once promised to eliminate the national debt in eight years, the size of the debt is projected to double again by 2024 under Trump, growing faster than it has under any previous president.

Donald J. Trump
@realDonaldTrump

"When the World watches @CNN, it gets a false picture of USA. Sad!"—June 3, 2019

Donald J. Trump
@realDonaldTrump

"Up 13 in IA according to respected CNN."—Dec. 11, 2015

How did CNN go from "respected" to giving a "false picture" in four years? Trump has for many years blasted news organizations when they report stories he doesn't like, yet he has turned around and praised those same outlets as "respected" when they deliver good news about him.

Donald J. Trump
@realDonaldTrump

"I think you might want to listen [if a foreign power offered dirt on a political opponent]. There's nothing wrong with listening. . . . If somebody called from a country—Norway—[and said,] 'We have information on your opponent.' Oh, I think I'd want to hear it."
—June 13, 2019

Donald J. Trump
@realDonaldTrump

"It's Thursday and only 26 days until the election. How many illegal donations from China and Saudi Arabia did Obama collect today?"—Oct. 11, 2012

Requesting foreign assistance in U.S. elections is a crime. Barack Obama's 2012 reelection campaign unknowingly received approximately $1.87 million in foreign contributions as a result of a criminal conspiracy to funnel illegal donations to the campaign and conceal their origin. There's no evidence that the campaign was aware of the scheme.

In Trump's case, much of the Mueller investigation centered on whether Trump or his campaign knowingly coordinated with Russia to interfere in the 2016 election—which could have constituted an illegal in-kind campaign contribution. Trump seemed to be approving that kind of coordination in his 2019 interview with ABC News. Months later, he was impeached for asking Ukraine to investigate a political rival.

Donald J. Trump
@realDonaldTrump

"I played a very fast round of golf yesterday. Many Pols exercise for hours, or travel for weeks. Me, I run through one of my courses (very inexpensive). President Obama would fly to Hawaii."—Sept. 3, 2019

Donald J. Trump
@realDonaldTrump

"Can you believe that, with all of the problems and difficulties facing the U.S., President Obama spent the day playing golf. Worse than Carter."—Oct. 13, 2014

Both presidents hit the golf course regularly. Obama flew to Hawaii to go on vacation, not just to play a round of golf. When in Washington, Obama would play golf nearby.

Trump generally tees off at one of his own courses. He

played 113 confirmed games of golf in three years, according to trumpgolfcount.com. In the same time period, Obama played 92 games, according to obamagolfcounter.com.

Trump regularly critiqued the timing of Obama's golf games, but since taking office, he has done some high-stakes multitasking. He played golf ahead of a surprise trip to Afghanistan, while monitoring hurricanes and as tension escalated with Iran.

 Donald J. Trump
@realDonaldTrump

"The LameStream Media had a very bad week. They pushed numerous phony stories and got caught, especially The Failing New York Times, which has lost more money over the last 10 years than any paper in history, and The Amazon Washington Post. They are The Enemy of the People!"—Sept. 21, 2019

Donald J. Trump
@realDonaldTrump

"I commend Roger Ailes for publicly supporting @FoxNews' employees against the Obama administration's intimidation of its reporters."—May 28, 2013

Trump supports reporters of a cable news channel when he sees "the Obama administration's intimidation." In his own White House, however, Trump has waged war on the press, taking aim at mainstream media outlets—including the *New York Times* and *The Washington Post*—on a regular basis. Calling news outlets and their reporters "the enemy of the people" is, according to Fox News anchor Bret Baier, "a problem" because media organizations are "just trying to call balls and strikes."

Donald J. Trump
@realDonaldTrump

"Something very big has just happened!"—Oct. 26, 2019

Donald J. Trump
@realDonaldTrump

"Stop congratulating Obama for killing Bin Laden. The Navy Seals killed Bin Laden."—Oct. 22, 2012

Trump complained about Obama being congratulated for the death of Osama bin Laden. Yet when U.S. special forces killed ISIS leader Abu Bakr al-Baghdadi, Trump teased the announcement on Twitter, added the accomplishment to his stump speech and falsely lamented, "[The press] wrote very little about it, relatively speaking." The story was front-page news for days.

Donald J. Trump
@realDonaldTrump

"Heading back to The Southern White House (Mar-a-Lago!). Updates throughout the day."—Dec. 31, 2019

Donald J. Trump
@realDonaldTrump

"Pres. Obama is about to embark on a 17 day vacation in his 'native' Hawaii, putting Secret Service away from families on Christmas. Aloha!"—Dec. 19, 2013

Trump attacked Obama for taking Secret Service agents away from their families during the holidays, but then he did the same thing. Trump spent 11 days at his Mar-a-Lago resort over the holidays in 2017 and more than two weeks there in 2019. (He canceled his 2018 trip because of the government shutdown, but his family and their respective Secret Service details still made the journey.) Moreover, Trump spent nearly a third of his first three years in office at a Trump-branded property, according to a *Washington Post* analysis.

 Donald J. Trump
@realDonaldTrump

"Leadership: Whatever happens, you're responsible. If it doesn't happen, you're responsible."—Nov. 8, 2013

As a private citizen, Trump argued that a leader is responsible for everything that takes place under his or her authority. But in 2020, when he was confronted as president with a question about whether he shouldered any responsibility for the government's inability to scale up testing for the coronavirus, Trump immediately rejected the premise. "I don't take responsibility at all because we were given a set of circumstances, and we were given rules, regulations, and specifications from a different time," he said at a March 13 news conference.

SPIES, LIES AND BAD GUYS

Donald J. Trump
@realDonaldTrump

"Russia has never tried to use leverage over me. I HAVE NOTHING TO DO WITH RUSSIA—NO DEALS, NO LOANS, NO NOTHING!"—Jan. 11, 2017

No deals? Not for lack of trying. Trump actively pursued real estate deals in Russia and has relied on Russian investors for decades—even while he was running for president. Trump started talks on building a Trump Tower in Moscow in 1987, and he personally signed a letter of intent to license his name to a Moscow skyscraper in October 2015. Conversations continued about the project through June 2016, according to a sentencing memorandum in the case of Trump's former personal attorney, Michael Cohen. Wealthy Russians bought many of Trump's condos via shell companies without a mortgage, an indication of money-laundering.

Donald J. Trump
@realDonaldTrump

"I don't know Putin, have no deals in Russia, and the haters are going crazy."—Feb. 7, 2017

Didn't know Putin? He sure wished he did. Trump hosted the Miss Universe pageant in Moscow in 2013, ahead of which he publicly wondered, "Do you think Putin will be going to The Miss Universe Pageant in November in Moscow—if so, will he become my new best friend?" Putin didn't show up to the pageant. But Trump worked to arrange a meeting with the Russian leader and was cagey in 2016 interviews about whether the two men had met.

Donald J. Trump
@realDonaldTrump

"I hereby demand a second investigation, after Schumer, of Pelosi for her close ties to Russia, and lying about it."—March 3, 2017

This is Trumpian misdirection at its worst. Two days before this tweet, it was revealed that Attorney General Jeff Sessions had met Russia's ambassador to Washington, Sergey Kislyak, during the 2016 presidential campaign. Sessions, who at the time was a senator from Alabama, failed to disclose these meetings in his application to the FBI for a security clearance or to Congress during his confirmation hearing. A day after the news broke about his meeting with the Russian ambassador, Sessions abruptly recused himself from any involvement in the investigation of Russian interference in the 2016 election.

Trump here tries to turn the tables, highlighting meetings that senior Democrats had had with Russian officials years earlier. But they didn't lie about it—and they were not facing a confirmation hearing. Sessions, in contrast, had not revealed the Kislyak encounters even when asked directly, under oath, about contact with Russian government officials.

Donald J. Trump
@realDonaldTrump

"122 vicious prisoners, released by the Obama Administration from Gitmo, have returned to the battlefield. Just another terrible decision!"—March 7, 2017

This is false. Only eight former Guantanamo Bay detainees who were later "confirmed of reengaging" in terrorist or insurgent activities were released under Obama; 113 were released under George W. Bush. Although this @realDonaldTrump tweet, sent at 7:04 a.m., was immediately called out as false on Twitter, Trump repeated it on the @POTUS account at 8:03 a.m. the same day.

Donald J. Trump
@realDonaldTrump

"Why isn't the House Intelligence Committee looking into the Bill & Hillary deal that allowed big Uranium to go to Russia, Russian speech."—March 27, 2017

Trump is imagining scandal where there is none. The Obama administration approved Russia's nuclear energy agency acquiring a controlling stake in Uranium One, a Canadian company that had mining operations in Wyoming. Uranium One wasn't a "Bill & Hillary deal." In 2010, the Committee on Foreign Investment in the United States approved the sale of the majority of the company's shares to the Russians. The State Department was one of nine agencies on the committee that approved the deal. The deal was also separately approved by the Nuclear Regulatory Commission. There is no evidence that Clinton got involved in the deal personally, and it is highly questionable that this deal ever reached the office of the secretary of state.

Donald J. Trump
@realDonaldTrump

"Is Fake News Washington Post being used as a lobbyist weapon against Congress to keep Politicians

from looking into Amazon no-tax monopoly?"
—July 24, 2017

The Washington Post is owned by Jeffrey P. Bezos, the founder of Amazon. Amazon does not own *The Post*, nor does *The Post* report "fake news." (The president tends to use this label for any critical reporting.) In addition, the president's claims about "no-tax" Amazon were out-of-date. Amazon used to lobby to keep Internet sales free from state taxes, but no more. Starting in March 2017, Amazon collected taxes on purchases in every state that levies sales taxes.

As for federal taxes, Amazon has come under fire, especially from the left, for allegedly paying little or no taxes even though it is owned by the world's richest man. The company's tax returns are private, so the answer is elusive, but some experts say it does pay taxes. "Amazon for many years reinvested all its profits into expansion, with the result that it paid little or no taxes because taxes are calculated based on profits," said Joseph Bishop-Henchman, executive vice president of the Tax Foundation, in 2018. "However, in the last few years, it has expanded its warehouse footprint and now pays considerable federal taxes as well as state income and property taxes."

Trump's signature legislative achievement, the Tax Cuts and Jobs Act, lowered the corporate tax rate from 35 percent to 21 percent and gave Amazon a $789 million windfall in 2017.

Donald J. Trump
@realDonaldTrump

"Most politicians would have gone to a meeting like the one Don jr attended in order to get info on an opponent. That's politics!"—July 17, 2017

Ethics lawyers and campaign veterans say the sort of encounter between Donald Trump Jr. and a Russian attorney he believed would provide damaging information about Hillary Clinton was highly unusual.

Donald J. Trump
@realDonaldTrump

"@FoxNews—FBI's Andrew McCabe, 'in addition to his wife getting all of this money from M (Clinton Puppet), he was using, allegedly, his FBI Official Email Account to promote her campaign. You obviously cannot do this. These were the people who were investigating Hillary Clinton.'"—Dec. 24, 2017

Former FBI deputy director Andrew McCabe became part of the investigation of Clinton's emails long after his wife, Jill McCabe, ran unsuccessfully for a Virginia State Senate seat. The political action committee of then–Virginia Gov. Terry McAuliffe (D) gave $452,500 to Jill McCabe, and the state Democratic Party gave her campaign an additional $207,788. That was about one-third of the $1.8 million her campaign received in donations. McAuliffe is close to Clinton, but there is no evidence she knew of the contributions. Moreover, Trump's conspiracy theory supposes that McAuliffe somehow knew that the husband of someone he was supporting in a Virginia legislative race would be promoted months later to a position of authority in the email investigation.

Donald J. Trump
@realDonaldTrump

"The Mueller probe should never have been started in that there was no collusion and there was no crime."—March 17, 2018

Special counsel Robert S. Mueller III was appointed because Trump fired Comey and then went on television and suggested that he'd done so because of the Russia probe. That left the Justice Department little choice but to appoint the special prosecutor. (Attorney General Jeff Sessions recused himself from that decision because he'd played a prominent role in the Trump campaign. It fell, therefore, to Deputy Attorney General Rod J. Rosenstein to appoint the special counsel.) Mueller's investigation yielded concrete evidence of Russian interference, including the indictments of Russian individuals and entities.

Donald J. Trump
@realDonaldTrump

"It was based on fraudulent activities and a Fake Dossier paid for by Crooked Hillary and the DNC."
—March 17, 2018

The investigation did not start with the dossier written by former British intelligence officer Christopher Steele. (Steele was working for the political research firm Fusion GPS, which had a contract with a law firm that worked for the Clinton campaign and the Democratic National Committee.) Rather, the tip that sparked the investigation came from the Australian government, which notified U.S. authorities about a conversation between a Trump campaign aide, George Papadopoulos, and an Australian diplomat, in which Papadopoulos claimed to know that the Russians had damaging material on Clinton and were prepared to use it. The information in the dossier came to the FBI's attention later.

Donald J. Trump
@realDonaldTrump

"We now know there was Russian collusion, with Russians and the Democrats."—June 2, 2018

Trump falsely says the Democrats colluded with Russia even though it was the Democratic Party that fell victim to a hacking attack by Russia as part of their attempt to influence the election in Trump's favor. Moreover, the special counsel detailed significant criminal activity by some of Trump's campaign advisers and by Russian individuals and entities. The investigation concluded that Russian government actors successfully hacked into computers and obtained emails from people associated with the Clinton campaign and from Democratic party organizations. The Russians then publicly disseminated those materials through various intermediaries, including WikiLeaks.

Donald J. Trump
@realDonaldTrump

"Our Justice Department must not let Awan & Debbie Wasserman Schultz off the hook. The Democrat I.T. scandal is a key to much of the corruption we see today. They want to make a 'plea deal' to hide what is on their Server. Where is Server? Really bad!"
—June 7, 2018

In 2018, Imran Awan, a technology worker for Democrats in the House of Representatives, pleaded guilty to making false statements on a home equity loan application, but before that he had been the subject of feverish speculation in the right-wing media.

Conservatives suggested he was engaged in something much worse, intimating that Awan, a U.S. citizen who was born in Pakistan, had stolen government secrets for Pakistan. An internal review found that rather than any nefarious political motive, Awan and his colleagues had bent the rules on computer network access so they could share their work duties. Federal prosecutors debunked several conspiracy theories fanned by right-wing websites about Awan's work in Congress, but those notions still found their way to the president's Twitter feed.

Donald J. Trump
@realDonaldTrump

"If anyone is looking for a good lawyer, I would strongly suggest that you don't retain the services of Michael Cohen!"—Aug. 22, 2018

Funny how time and guilty pleas can change Trump's opinion of a person. Just four months earlier, Trump had tweeted that "Michael [Cohen] is a businessman for his own account/lawyer who I have always liked & respected. Most people will flip if the Government lets them out of trouble, even if it means lying or making up stories. Sorry, I don't see Michael doing that despite the horrible Witch Hunt and the dishonest media!"

Donald J. Trump
@realDonaldTrump

"Bob Woodward is a liar who is like a Dem operative prior to the Midterms. He was caught cold, even by NBC."—Sept. 10, 2018

Washington Post associate editor Bob Woodward is tough, but regularly wins extensive cooperation from both Republican and

Democratic sources who consider his reporting fair and accurate. He has written about the inner workings of both Democratic and Republican administrations since the 1970s. In 2013, Trump criticized the Obama White House's negative response to Woodward's reporting, tweeting that "only the Obama WH can get away with attacking Bob Woodward." But Trump balked when he became the object of Woodward's attention. "Fear," Woodward's book about the Trump administration, describes a White House in disarray. In his reporting, Woodward relied on many sources who were not named, as is his longstanding practice; he keeps hundreds of hours of taped interviews with sources who have direct knowledge of events described in his books. Reporting by major media outlets largely corroborated his account.

Donald J. Trump
@realDonaldTrump

"Rex Tillerson, didn't have the mental capacity needed [to be Secretary of State]. He was dumb as a rock and I couldn't get rid of him fast enough. He was lazy as hell. Now it is a whole new ballgame, great spirit at State!"—Dec. 7, 2018

What a difference two years makes. After appointing Tillerson, Trump lavished praise on the former chief executive of ExxonMobil, calling him "a world-class player" whose "tenacity, broad experience and deep understanding of geopolitics make him an excellent choice for secretary of state." The "dumb as a rock" comment clearly qualifies as a flip-flop. (Tillerson, for his part, did not think much of the president either, reportedly calling him a "fucking moron" in the months before he was fired.)

Donald J. Trump
@realDonaldTrump

"So Democrats and others can illegally fabricate a crime, try pinning it on a very innocent President, and when he fights back against this illegal and treasonous attack on our Country, they call It Obstruction? Wrong! Why didn't Robert Mueller investigate the investigators?"—July 24, 2019

Democrats didn't "illegally fabricate a crime." Mueller's report concluded that there was significant evidence that Trump obstructed justice. Mueller said he declined to reach a decision on whether to file obstruction charges against Trump in part because of a Justice Department policy against indicting a sitting president and in part because he didn't want to get in the way of a potential impeachment process in Congress.

Donald J. Trump
@realDonaldTrump

"NO COLLUSION, NO OBSTRUCTION, TOTAL EXONERATION. DEMOCRAT WITCH HUNT!"—July 27, 2019

Trump's snappy summary of Mueller's findings erases critical details. Even Attorney General William Barr's summary of the special counsel's report stated, "While this report does not conclude that the President committed a crime, it also does not exonerate him." The special counsel's report, released in April 2019, concluded that the Trump campaign welcomed assistance from Russia even if it did not coordinate with it. The report also stated, "If we had confidence after a thorough investigation of the facts that the President clearly did not commit obstruction of justice, we would so state. Based on the facts and the applicable legal standards, however, we are unable to reach that judgment."

Donald J. Trump
@realDonaldTrump

"Paul Manafort was with me for a short period of time. He did a good job. I was, you know, very happy with the job he did."—Sept. 19, 2019 (remarks)

Paul Manafort, a longtime Republican operative who was sentenced to seven and a half years in prison after his convictions for fraud, conspiracy and obstruction of justice, worked on Trump's 2016 campaign for five months during a crucial period. He was hired on March 28, 2016, to manage the campaign's delegate-wrangling efforts. He was promoted to campaign chairman and chief strategist on May 19, 2016. (Some reports say he took over on April 7.) He continued to serve in that capacity through Aug. 19, when he resigned from the campaign. Far from being just "with me for a short period," Manafort was an instrumental figure in Trump's 2016 election effort.

Donald J. Trump
@realDonaldTrump

"So Crooked Hillary Clinton can delete and acid wash 33,000 emails AFTER getting a Subpoena from the United States Congress, but I can't make one totally appropriate telephone call to the President of Ukraine? Witch Hunt!"—Oct. 5, 2019

Clinton's staff had asked for the emails to be deleted months before the subpoena, according to the FBI's August 2016 report. There's no evidence that Clinton deleted the emails in anticipation of the subpoena, and FBI director James B. Comey has said that his agency's investigation found no evidence that any work-related emails were "intentionally deleted in an effort to conceal them."

Donald J. Trump
@realDonaldTrump

"Do not believe any article or story you read or see that uses 'anonymous sources' having to do with trade or any other subject. Only accept information if it has an actual living name on it. The Fake News Media makes up many 'sources say' stories. Do not believe them!"—Dec. 6, 2019

The White House, the State Department and the Pentagon often provide background briefings to reporters on the condition that officials' names not be disclosed. Trump himself famously has insisted to reporters that he be described in news stories as an unnamed source. He has also tweeted about information he received from unidentified sources.

Donald J. Trump
@realDonaldTrump

"The Impeachment Hoax, just a continuation of the Witch Hunt which started even before I won the Election, must end quickly. . . . It is a con game by the Dems to help with the Election!"—Jan. 6, 2020

The issues raised by Trump's phone call with the Ukrainian president were so serious that they led the House of Representatives to pass two articles of impeachment. The Russia probe separately documented serious potential cases of obstruction of justice. Special Counsel Robert Mueller III declined to prosecute Trump in part because of longstanding Department of Justice policy against charging a sitting president. He did not exonerate Trump.

Donald J. Trump
@realDonaldTrump

"They are taking the Democrat Nomination away from Crazy Bernie, just like last time. Some things never change!"—Jan. 18, 2020

There is no evidence that Democrats "rigged" the election against Sen. Bernie Sanders. He just happened to be the opponent Trump most wanted to run against. In response to an earlier tweet along these lines, Sanders said: "Let's be clear about who is rigging what: It is Donald Trump's action to use the power of the federal government for his own political benefit that is the cause of the impeachment trial. His transparent attempts to divide Democrats will not work." Unless, of course, they do.

TRUMP TILTING AT WINDMILLS

 "Try dropping a windmill someplace close to your house. Try selling your house. They make noise. They kill all the birds. The energy is intermittent. If you happen to be watching the Democrat debate and the wind isn't blowing, you're not going to see the debate. 'Charlie, what the hell happened to this debate?' He says, 'Darling, the wind isn't blowing. The goddamn windmill stopped. That windmill stopped.'"

—Sept. 12, 2019 (speech)

Trump has made no secret of his hatred of wind power. He fought a losing battle with the Scottish government to prevent an offshore wind farm from being built in view of his golf courses along Scotland's coast.

But he often gets his facts wrong. He's said that the proximity of a windmill devalues the price of a house by 50 percent; the London School of Economics says prices decline by about 5 to 6 percent when a wind farm is visible within 2 kilometers. Trump claims they kill "all the birds" and that every windmill is a "bird graveyard." But a 2019 study said about three birds are lost for every turbine within 1,000 feet of a bird habitat. Cats kill about 16,000 times more birds a year in the United States than do wind turbines. Windmills produce a noise level of about 45 decibels, akin to the hum of a refrigerator.

But Trump's strangest claim is that the power shuts off when turbines stop turning. The power grid is designed to handle this variability, which Trump might have learned if he had checked the Department of Energy website.

"People are flushing toilets 10 times, 15 times, as opposed to once. They end up using more water."
—Dec. 6, 2019 (remarks)

Under a law President George H.W. Bush signed in 1994, manufacturers needed to find water-saving designs. Older toilets used as much as six gallons per flush, while low-flow toilets now use 1.28 gallon or less.

But nothing supports Trump's claim that people are flushing as much as he says. He seems stuck in a time warp. The first-generation low-flush toilets, introduced in the 1990s, often worked poorly. But manufacturers said the new efficiency standards have led them to build products that use less water and power, but with no noticeable decline in performance.

"We're even bringing back the old lightbulb. You heard about that, right? The old lightbulb, which is better. . . . The new light, they're terrible. You look terrible. They cost you many, many times more, like four or five times more. And you know, they're considered hazardous waste."
—Dec. 18, 2019 (campaign rally)

A law signed by George W. Bush and implemented by Barack Obama led to efficiency standards that would have phased out incandescent bulbs. The Trump administration rejected those standards, allowing incandescent bulbs to remain on the market.

But again, Trump seems stuck in a time warp. Many consumers rebelled against the early version of more efficient lightbulbs—compact fluorescent, or CFL, bulbs. CFLs contain mercury, take time to gain full intensity and tend to have harsher color quality. But CFLs now account for only about 4 percent of all sales of classic pear-shaped bulbs, according to the National Electrical Manufacturers Association.

Light-emitting diode, or LED, bulbs make up more than 70 percent of sales. They're safer and, contrary to Trump's claim, are not "four or five times" more expensive. LEDs have now achieved colors similar to those in incandescent bulbs, though they have not yet reached the perfect "warm" 100 on the color-rendering index. At Home Depot, 60-watt incandescent bulbs costs 97 cents a bulb, compared to $1.24 for an equivalent LED. But LED bulbs will last ten years, at an energy cost of $1.08 a year, compared to $5.18 for the incandescent bulb—which Home Depot says dies after less than a year.

CHAPTER SIX

Trump on Immigration: "They're Bringing Crime"

The Trump presidency has been a long, counterfactual excoriation of immigrants, especially those from Central America and Mexico. President Trump has called them violent criminals, terrorists, drug mules and scofflaws. This barrage of anti-immigrant statements sets the tone for an administration that regularly finds ways to curb immigration—legal and illegal alike—to the United States.

It's no surprise that Trump would start an immigration crackdown. The border wall was his biggest campaign promise, and he made his first big splash in politics by kicking off his candidacy in 2015 saying, "When Mexico sends its people, they're not sending their best. . . . They're bringing . . . drugs, they're bringing crime, they're rapists. And some, I assume, are good people."

What may be surprising is that Trump has continued to distort and deceive on this issue even as his administration has real skin in the game: Trump has hardened the nation's barriers to entry with new regulations that sent illegal border crossings plummeting and sharply diminished legal migration as well—even as congressional investigations and major court rulings pushed back. Yet

Trump undercuts his whole project with a stream of false, misleading, unsupported, absurd and easily debunked statements.

Immigration is the top category of false and misleading claims in our Trump database, accounting for 15 percent of the total 16,241 statements we fact-checked in the first three years of Trump's presidency.

But the parade of horribles Trump associates with immigrants flies against the facts, creating a warped view of reality. In this chapter, we will unwarp it.

IMMIGRANTS CAUSE CRIME

 "The Democrats are really looking at something that is very dangerous for our country. . . . They want to have illegal immigrants pouring into our country, bringing with them crime, tremendous amounts of crime."

—Dec. 6, 2017 (remarks)

Do immigrants bring crime? Trump says so, but all the research contradicts him.

The U.S. violent crime rate was cut by nearly half between 1990 and 2013, while the number of unauthorized immigrants in the United States more than tripled, rising to 11.2 million, according to the nonpartisan American Immigration Council.

"FBI data indicate that the violent crime rate declined 48 percent—which included falling rates of aggravated assault, robbery, rape, and murder. Likewise, the property crime rate fell 41 percent, including declining rates of motor vehicle theft, larceny/robbery, and burglary," the group said.

According to a 2015 peer-reviewed study of how immigrants have integrated into American society, the perception that they bring crime with them has been popular for nearly a century and is perpetuated by proponents of restrictionist immigration policies. "Far from immigration increasing crime rates, studies demonstrate that immigrants and immigration are associated inversely with crime," the National Academy of Sciences study concluded. "Immigrants are less likely than the native-born to commit crimes, and neighborhoods with greater concentrations of immigrants have much lower rates of crime and violence than comparable non-immigrant neighborhoods. However, crime rates rise among the second and later generations, perhaps a negative consequence of adaptation to American society."

Immigrants are proportionately less likely to be incarcerated than natives, according to a 2017 study by the libertarian Cato Institute, which also found that "even illegal immigrants are less likely to be incarcerated than native-born Americans."

Some experts say such studies should be taken with a grain of salt because they rely on statistical modeling (which introduces a margin of error) or on self-reporting to the Census Bureau (some immigrants may not disclose that they are undocumented for fear of reprisals). Nonetheless, every peer-reviewed study that has delved into this question has reached the same conclusion: no link between immigration and higher crime rates.

 "I'm very much opposed to sanctuary cities. They breed crime. There's a lot of problems."

—Feb. 5, 2017 (interview)

 "Far-left politicians support deadly sanctuary cities, demonstrating their sneering contempt, scorn

and disdain for everyday Americans. These jurisdictions deliberately release dangerous, violent criminal aliens out of their jails and directly onto your streets, where they are free to offend, where they are free to kill, where they are free to rape, where they are free to beat up people."

—Dec. 10, 2019 (campaign rally)

Trump often spotlights a few gruesome crime cases involving immigrants who were released from custody in U.S. jurisdictions that have declared themselves sanctuaries for undocumented immigrants.

Every demographic group includes criminals. But Trump's correlation between sanctuary cities and crime is unfounded.

There's no official definition of a "sanctuary," but it generally refers to rules restricting state or local governments from alerting federal authorities about immigrants who may be undocumented. Immigration enforcement is a federal responsibility, but state and local law enforcement decide how much to cooperate with federal authorities.

Researchers have identified hundreds of local and state governments with sanctuary policies, though there's no official count. These jurisdictions vary widely in their approach. Some don't cooperate at all, while others do so only in civil investigations, for felony convictions or for offenders otherwise deemed to be a public safety threat.

In a 2016 study of roughly 80 jurisdictions, researchers at the University of California at Riverside and Highline College used FBI data to measure how crime rates changed after sanctuary policies were adopted. Then they compared each sanctuary city to a similarly situated non-sanctuary city, based on Census data and other variables. They found that "a sanctuary policy itself has no statistically meaningful effect on crime."

University of California at San Diego professor Tom Wong looked at 608 sanctuary counties and found lower rates of crime in those counties than in non-sanctuary counties. Other studies showed that in some jurisdictions, immigrant-friendly policies led to a decrease in crime.

 "Last month alone, 100,000 illegal immigrants arrived at our borders, placing a massive strain on communities and schools and hospitals and public resources like nobody's ever seen before. Now we're sending many of them to sanctuary cities, thank you very much. They're not too happy about it. I'm proud to tell you that was actually my sick idea, by the way. No. Hey, hey, what did they say? 'We want them.' I said: 'We'll give them to you. Thank you.' They said, 'We don't want them.'"

—April 27, 2019 (campaign rally)

 "We're releasing them into sanctuary cities almost exclusively. You know, sanctuary cities want them. But once we started releasing them, they didn't want them. So, you know, they want them, they talk—they talk a good game. But once you start saying: 'Okay. Congratulations. Here are some.' And they don't want them. And they fight very hard. So, the whole sanctuary city thing is a big scam."

—April 29, 2019 (interview)

First at a campaign rally and then in an interview, Trump claimed twice in one week that undocumented immigrants were being released into sanctuary cities—and that the cities weren't taking them.

He appears to have made up the whole thing.

The White House had floated a proposal along these lines to U.S. Immigration and Customs Enforcement, aiming to retaliate against President Trump's political adversaries. Democratic strongholds such as Chicago, San Francisco and New York City have adopted sanctuary status.

But ICE's legal department "rejected the idea as inappropriate," and that was the end of that, *The Washington Post* reported, based on Department of Homeland Security officials and email messages. Homeland Security never announced it would implement Trump's plan. A DHS spokesman declined to comment for our fact check and referred us to the White House, which did not respond to our questions. We also sent questions to ICE and did not receive a response.

Which took us back to Trump.

At a campaign rally in Green Bay and in a Fox Business interview, the president claimed that immigrants were being released into sanctuary cities "almost exclusively," that "now we're sending many of them to sanctuary cities," that it was his "sick idea" and that the cities in question (none of which he named) were turning back migrants rather than receiving them.

We asked several of the biggest sanctuary jurisdictions whether the Trump administration had released undocumented immigrants in their cities. "We have not seen any sort of uptick to warrant this claim," a spokesman for then–Chicago Mayor Rahm Emanuel (D) told us. "But if we did, and as the mayor has indicated, we'd welcome it." A spokesman for New York Mayor Bill de Blasio (D) told us, "We have seen nothing to indicate such actions from the Trump administration, and we are certainly not turning anyone away."

One sanctuary city that had been on Trump's mind was Oakland,

Calif. The president didn't mention it at the rally or in the interview, but he had feuded with Mayor Libby Schaaf (D) in the past and criticized her again in a 2019 tweet: "So interesting to see the Mayor of Oakland and other Sanctuary Cities NOT WANT our currently 'detained immigrants' after release."

In fact, Schaaf had said the opposite. "My job as a mayor is to welcome people," Schaaf told NPR the same day as Trump's tweet. "I don't build walls. It's our job to welcome everyone into our city, ensure their safety, ensure that their families can thrive. And that is my job no matter where those people came from or how they got there."

There's no evidence that the Trump administration had begun to release immigrants into Oakland.

Donald J. Trump
@realDonaldTrump

"New report from DOJ & DHS shows that nearly 3 in 4 individuals convicted of terrorism-related charges are foreign-born. . . . [W]e need to keep America safe, including moving away from a random chain migration and lottery system, to one that is merit-based."—Jan. 16, 2018

Making the case for tighter immigration controls, Trump cited a flawed report from the Homeland Security and Justice departments that said foreign-born people accounted for 73 percent of convictions for international terrorism and related offenses between the 9/11 attacks and 2016.

We gave the president Four Pinocchios when he claimed in a speech to Congress in 2017 that "the vast majority of individuals convicted of terrorism and terrorism-related offenses since 9/11 came here from outside of our country." Almost a year later, the DHS/DOJ report appeared to back up Trump's claim—but only where *international* terrorism is concerned. For some reason, the president did not include that word in his tweets. The report does not include people convicted of domestic terrorism.

The Justice Department's National Security Division keeps a list of people convicted in federal court of international terrorism and related charges since the 9/11 attacks. The list predates the Trump administration and for years has been the subject of inquiry and debate.

When Trump posted these tweets, the roster listed 549 international terrorism convictions between Sept. 11, 2001, and Dec. 31, 2016. Homeland Security determined that 402 of them (73 percent) were not born in the United States: 254 were foreigners and 148 were naturalized U.S. citizens. The remaining 147 were U.S. citizens by birth.

But researchers at Lawfare analyzed Justice Department data released under the Freedom of Information Act and found that 100 people on the list of convicted terrorists had been transported to the United States to be prosecuted. Another researcher, Karen Greenberg, the director of Fordham University's Center on National Security, told *The Post* that there were 80 such cases.

In either event, a significant number of the terrorists on the list were not immigrants, but had been brought to the United States solely to face prosecution. Trump's 73 percent statistic would be lower if those cases had been excluded. Lawfare's analysis found that if you included domestic terrorism cases and excluded international terrorists who had been transported to the United States, immigrants would account for only 18 to 21 percent of all terrorism convictions.

U.S. LAWS ARE FLAWED

 "I hate the children being taken away. The Democrats have to change their law. That's their law."

—June 15, 2018 (remarks)

 "We have the worst immigration laws in the entire world. Nobody has such sad, such bad and, actually, in many cases, such horrible and tough—you see about child separation, you see what's going on there."

—June 18, 2018 (remarks)

Trump's family separations in 2018 caused a national uproar. U.S. immigration officials separated thousands of Central American migrant children from their parents, sending the kids off to shelters or relatives while their parents were prosecuted and put on track to be deported.

The Trump administration's messaging seemed at times Orwellian. Top government officials claimed there was no family-separation policy. The president falsely asserted that existing laws were forcing his hand. But the real reason for the separations was Trump's own zero-tolerance policy.

In spring of 2018, the Homeland Security and Justice departments began to prosecute all adults who had been detained for illegal entry, regardless of whether they crossed the border alone or with children. The Justice Department doesn't prosecute children, so the natural result of the zero-tolerance policy was widespread family separations.

The government has limited resources and cannot litigate every crime, so prosecutors make choices and set priorities. The Trump administration used its prosecutorial discretion to focus on cases of illegal entry to the United States, which is a misdemeanor for first-time offenders.

Contrary to Trump's claims, no law or court ruling required that migrant families be separated. In fact, during its first 15 months, the Trump administration released nearly 100,000 migrants who had been apprehended at the U.S.-Mexico border, including more than 37,500 unaccompanied minors and more than 61,000 members of family units. The legal landscape did not change between the time the Trump administration released those families and the time the zero-tolerance policy took effect.

What changed was the administration's handling of such cases. Undocumented migrant families seeking asylum previously had been released into the country while they awaited immigration hearings, but under zero tolerance, parents were detained and sent to criminal courts while their kids were resettled in the United States as though they had arrived as unaccompanied minors.

Which laws did Trump claim were forcing his hand? We asked his immigration adviser, Stephen Miller, who pointed to a 1997 federal consent decree requiring the government to release rather than detain minors who are apprehended while crossing the border. The *Flores* decree covers only children and not their parents. But nothing in the agreement requires family separations or forbids the government from releasing parents alongside their kids. Miller also mentioned two other statutes, but neither of them requires family separations.

After he put a stop to the separations, Trump began to minimize the damage they had done by falsely claiming that Obama had done the same thing.

The Obama administration actually rejected a plan for family separations, according to Cecilia Muñoz, Obama's top adviser for immigration. The Trump administration, by contrast, operated a pilot program for family separations in the El Paso area beginning in mid-2017, then expanded it to the entire border in 2018.

That zero-tolerance approach is worlds apart from the Obama and George W. Bush policies of separating children from adults at the border in limited circumstances, such as when officials suspected human trafficking or other danger to the child, or when false claims of parentage were made.

Trump did not end that policy, which remains in effect. He issued an executive order on June 20, 2018, to end his own, much broader policy of systematic family separations.

Between 2010 and 2016, the Department of Homeland Security referred for prosecution an average of 21 percent of "amenable adults" who were detained crossing the border illegally. It's unclear how many of those adults had children in tow. Regardless, prosecuting 21 percent is elementally different from prosecuting 100 percent. That's what Trump's zero-tolerance policy called for, because it applied to all adults.

Donald J. Trump
@realDonaldTrump

"Border Patrol Agents are not allowed to properly do their job at the Border because of ridiculous liberal (Democrat) laws like Catch & Release. Getting more dangerous."—April 1, 2018

"President Obama made changes that basically created no border. It's called catch and release."

—April 3, 2018 (remarks)

The phrase "catch and release" usually serves as shorthand for U.S. immigration authorities' practice of releasing undocumented migrants into the country while they await immigration hearings, rather than keeping them in custody. With some exceptions, only children and asylum seekers are eligible for this kind of release.

Trump described "catch and release" as a liberal Democratic law, but it's actually a collection of policies, court precedents, executive actions and federal statutes spanning more than 20 years, cobbled together throughout Democratic and Republican administrations.

"Catch and release" entered the political lexicon during George W. Bush's presidency. Immigration surged from 2000 to 2010, as 14 million new legal and undocumented migrants settled in the United States, according to Census Bureau data. The federal government did not have enough space to house all the migrants being apprehended, so the Bush administration released many of them under their own recognizance, and many then failed to report for their immigration hearings.

In 2014, the Obama administration issued deportation guidelines that prioritized gang members, felons and people who posed security threats. This led to a renewed catch-and-release regime, although some argue that the Bush-era policy had never ended. Upon taking office, Trump rolled back the Obama guidelines.

But the same arithmetic that confronted Bush—lots of migrants arriving at the border, not enough space to house them pending hearings—has continued under Obama and Trump.

Trump administration officials argue that catch and release is a purely Democratic creation, citing the Obama guidelines and the *Flores* settlement agreement dating to the Clinton administration.

But Trump officials also cite the Trafficking Victims Protection Reauthorization Act, which Bush, a Republican, signed in 2008. The practice of mass-releasing immigrants began when Bush was in the

White House, not out of ideological conviction so much as practical necessity.

"We've ended catch and release. We've ended it."
—Dec. 18, 2019 (campaign rally)

The Trump administration has not ended the practice of releasing migrants into the country while they await immigration hearings; rather, it has launched policies to whittle away at catch and release.

The Department of Homeland Security announced that migrants could petition for asylum in the United States from their home countries in Central America and that those who showed up at the border to apply in-person would be sent to Mexico to wait for a ruling.

The latter program, which the Trump administration calls the Migrant Protection Protocols, or "Remain in Mexico," has been the subject of numerous legal challenges and remains tied up in the courts. A federal judge in California issued a nationwide injunction blocking the program in September 2019, and an appeals court upheld that ruling in March 2020.

International laws recognized by the United States prohibit what's known as "refoulement," or returning refugees to places where they face threats or persecution. The group Physicians for Human Rights, which had doctors in Tijuana, Mexico, evaluated 18 asylum seekers who they said provided credible accounts and corroborating evidence showing that they had indeed fled persecution and suffered physical trauma. "The recent murder and dismemberment of [an] asylum seeker in Tijuana is just one extreme example of how the 'Remain in Mexico' policy compounds the trauma these migrants seek to escape and renders them highly vulnerable to grave new dangers," the group concluded.

"Most border crossers never show up in court. They never come. About 3 percent show up. Nobody even knows why they show up. But only 3 percent show up."

—July 1, 2019 (remarks)

Because immigration court records are secret, the government's statistics are difficult to verify. Adding to the haziness, the Justice Department reports several different figures for immigration court appearances—and the numbers vary widely.

Trump's claim is false no matter how you count.

There are some oddities to the Justice Department's no-show statistics. They don't credit migrants for showing up to court if their hearings were postponed, which happens often because of a huge backlog of hundreds of thousands of cases. But the department does count all migrants who fail to appear for their hearings. Still, the data show that immigrants overwhelmingly attend their hearings. Judges ordered in absentia deportations in 14 percent of cases in fiscal 2013, a rate that rose to 25 percent in fiscal 2018. Flip the numbers, and that means 75 percent to 86 percent of migrants did show up for court.

Justice Department officials say that since migrants who are in detention always attend their hearings—they have no choice—the right way to measure whether migrants show up in court is to look only at those who were never held in detention facilities. Using that measure, 59 percent showed up for immigration hearings in 2018.

But researchers at the Transactional Records Access Clearinghouse (TRAC) at Syracuse University studied the question and came up with a much higher number: 81 percent of migrant families attended all their court hearings. Susan B. Long, co-director of TRAC and a managerial statistics professor, said the higher number results from counting court appearances in all ongoing cases, not just in already-completed cases.

TRAC looked at 46,743 families over a nine-month period and found that 85.5 percent of them attended their initial hearing and 81 percent attended all their hearings.

 "We actually have lottery systems where you go to countries and they do lotteries for who comes into the United States. Now, you know they are not going to have their best people in the lottery, because they're not going to put their best people in a lottery. They don't want to have their good people to leave. . . . We want people based on merit, not based on the fact they are thrown into a bin, and many of those people are not the people you want in the country, believe me."

—Feb. 24, 2018 (interview)

Trump consistently mischaracterizes the Diversity Immigrant Visa Program, claiming absurdly that foreign countries raffle off green cards granting legal residence in the United States.

In fact, a computer program managed by a State Department office in Williamsburg, Ky., randomly selects up to 50,000 immigrant visa applications per year—out of nearly 15 million in 2017—from countries with low rates of immigration. This means people from nearly 20 countries—such as Brazil, Canada, China, India, Mexico, Nigeria, Pakistan, South Korea, the United Kingdom (except North Ireland) and Vietnam—are out of luck because more than 50,000 people from these countries were admitted to the United States through other programs over the past five years.

The diversity visas are apportioned among six regions around the world, with a maximum of 7 percent available to any one country. The odds of being selected are under 1 percent—and winning that lottery gets you only an invitation to apply for a green card. (In 2017, the State Department notified nearly 116,000 people that they could apply, but the program ends after 50,000 people are accepted. Each person selected gets a number on the list, so people in the bottom half have a high chance of being cut off before they even start the process.)

Applicants must have at least a high school diploma (or its equivalent) or two years' work experience of a type specified by the State Department. Then they undergo a background check, an interview and medical tests before entering the United States. Some applicants face an additional in-depth review if they are considered a possible security risk.

No foreign country submits applicants for the diversity visa lottery; applicants select themselves.

 "He is a man that through chain migration brought in his mother, his father, his uncles, his brothers, his sisters. They think it's probably 22 people came on and into this country because of this guy, who killed eight people and so gravely wounded and injured so many more. It's a disgrace."

—Nov. 1, 2018 (campaign rally)

Sayfullo Saipov, a native of Uzbekistan, allegedly killed eight people and injured a dozen others in 2017 by driving a pickup truck down a bicycle path near the World Trade Center in Manhattan. Trump immediately blamed the diversity visa program, which had given Saipov a green card.

The president also made the startling claim—which he often repeats—that Saipov was the "point of contact" for "22 people" or "23 people that came in or potentially came in with him" through "chain migration."

Chain migration refers to immigrants who bring their close relatives to the United States, such as parents, siblings or children. U.S. law gives preferential treatment to the relatives of migrants already living in the country. That's how first lady Melania Trump's parents, born in Austria and Slovenia, became naturalized U.S. citizens in 2018.

And it's how Akayed Ullah, who was sentenced to life in prison for setting off a pipe bomb in Manhattan in 2017, came to the United States from Bangladesh in 2011, according to the Department of Homeland Security. He obtained a green card as the nephew of a U.S. citizen.

Saipov, however, arrived in 2010 through the diversity visa lottery. He is not a U.S. citizen; he just has legal permanent residence. The rules are stricter for green-card holders: they can petition only for a spouse or unmarried children.

Saipov's wife (also Uzbek) was already in the United States when they met and then married in Ohio. Her parents live in Brooklyn. Saipov and his wife have three young children, all of whom are U.S. citizens because they were born in the United States.

That adds up to zero people brought in by Saipov.

 Jonathan Swan, Axios reporter: "On immigration, some legal scholars believe you can get rid of birthright citizenship without changing the Constitution."
President Trump: "With an executive order."
Swan: "Have you thought about that?"

Trump: "Yes. . . . It was always told to me that you needed a constitutional amendment. Guess what? You don't. . . . You can definitely do it with an act of Congress. But now they're saying I can do it just with an executive order. Now, how ridiculous—we're the only country in the world where a person comes in, has a baby and the baby is essentially a citizen of the United States for 85 years, with all of those benefits."

—Oct. 30, 2018 (interview)

The 14th Amendment grants citizenship to people born in the United States. Trump can't change that with an executive order (and he quickly discarded this claim). He falsely said no other country offers birthright citizenship, when more than 30 do so.

The Supreme Court ruled in 1898 that the 14th Amendment's birthright citizenship guarantee covered Wong Kim Ark, who was born in San Francisco to Chinese nationals legally residing in the United States.

The court did not say whether the same right extended to the children of undocumented immigrants. However, the justices said the constitutional amendment was broadly worded, and they listed only a few exceptions to birthright citizenship, such as the children of foreign diplomats or hostile enemies occupying U.S. territory.

"The Fourteenth Amendment affirms the ancient and funda-mental rule of citizenship by birth within the territory, in the alle-giance and under the protection of the country," Justice Horace Gray wrote for the court. That right covers "all children here born of res-ident aliens, with the exceptions or qualifications (as old as the rule itself) of children of foreign sovereigns or their ministers, or born on foreign public ships, or of enemies within and during a hostile occupation of part of our territory, and with the single additional exception of children of members of the Indian tribes owing direct allegiance to their several tribes.

"The Amendment, in clear words and in manifest intent, includes the children born, within the territory of the United States, of all other persons, of whatever race or color, domiciled within the United States."

Then, in *Plyler v. Doe* in 1982, the court said Texas could not exclude children of undocumented immigrants from public schools. The justices added that "no plausible distinction with respect to 14th Amendment 'jurisdiction' can be drawn between resident aliens whose entry into the United States was lawful, and resident aliens whose entry was unlawful."

In 1995, the Justice Department's Office of Legal Counsel rejected the idea that Congress could restrict birthright citizenship through legislation (never mind an executive order). Birthright citizenship is in the Constitution, so the only way to change it is by constitutional amendment, then–Assistant Attorney General Walter Dellinger wrote. That policy remains in effect and is binding on the executive branch.

 "Think of it this way: A general who's on an opposing army, and we're at war, comes into the United States. They have a baby. He's not here. They have a baby. The baby's a citizen of the United States, and yet the father is the enemy of our country? It's ridiculous."

—Oct. 31, 2018 (interview)

 "You're an enemy of our country. You're a general with war on your mind. You're a dictator who we hate and who's against us. And that dictator and his wife have a baby on American soil. Congratulations. Your son or daughter is now an American citizen. Does anybody think this makes sense? Does anybody think it makes sense? Congratulations, General, you have a United States citizen as your daughter. It's crazy. It's crazy. But we're getting it all worked out."

—Nov. 1, 2018 (campaign rally)

Trump could have picked literally any other imaginary threat during these riffs on birthright citizenship. But he somehow landed on enemy generals and foreign rulers, whose children are specifically made exceptions to birthright citizenship under a 120-year-old decision by the Supreme Court in the *Wong Kim Ark* case.

Even if a dictator or hostile foreign general during wartime managed to have a child in the United States (improbable at best), the court's ruling covers this situation and contradicts the president's version.

"As a practical matter, I've never heard of such a situation arising anyway," said Stephen H. Legomsky, a law professor at Washington University in St. Louis and former chief counsel of U.S. Citizenship and Immigration Services during the Obama administration. "I don't know where he's getting that from."

THE U.S.-MEXICO BORDER

 "Mexico, as you know, as of yesterday, has been starting to apprehend a lot of people at their southern border coming in from Honduras and Guatemala and El Salvador. And they've—they're really apprehending thousands of people. And it's the first time, really, in decades that this has taken place. And it should have taken place a long time ago. You know, Mexico has the strongest immigration laws in the world. There's nobody who has stronger. I guess some have the same, but you can't get any stronger than what Mexico has."

—April 2, 2019 (remarks)

Donald J. Trump
@realDonaldTrump

"After many years (decades), Mexico is apprehending large numbers of people at their Southern Border, mostly from Guatemala, Honduras and El Salvador."
—April 2, 2019

Trump threatened to close down the southern border unless Mexico detained the waves of migrants headed from Central America to the United States. Days later, he canceled his plans to close the U.S.-Mexico border and said his threats had forced Mexico to detain migrants by the thousands for the first time in decades.

The claim is nonsense. Mexican immigration authorities had 886,640 encounters with Guatemalans, Hondurans and Salvadorans from 2011 through February 2019, according to data from Mexico's Department of the Interior. Fifty-three percent of these encounters happened at the four Mexican states that border Central America.

The statistics also show that over the last two decades, Mexico deported 2.15 million people who came from El Salvador, Guatemala and Honduras, the three countries driving the Central American migration phenomenon. In fact, from 2013 to 2018, Mexico deported more people from those three countries than the United States did. The numbers were huge: Mexico: 692,199; U.S.: 550,186.

Trump's threat in April 2019 had no bearing on the deportations. In the first two months of that year—before Trump's threat—Mexican immigration authorities had already returned 13,281 people to those three Central American countries, according to Mexican government data.

Trump also claimed Mexico has the strongest immigration laws in the world. Experts sharply disagreed. Mexico imposes penalties for immigration violations, but it decriminalized the act of crossing the border in 2011. Contrast that with the United States—where unauthorized entry is a misdemeanor for first-time offenders and a felony for repeat offenders—and Trump's claim falls apart.

We gave these claims Four Pinocchios. The president so disliked our fact check that he responded on Twitter (with the same falsehood): "The Crazed and Dishonest Washington Post again purposely got it wrong. Mexico, for the first time in decades, is meaningfully apprehending illegals at THEIR Southern Border, before the long march up to the U.S."

> "That wall is also going to help us, very importantly, with the drug problem, and the massive amounts of drugs that are pouring across the southern border."
>
> —Aug. 22, 2017 (campaign rally)

Would a wall stop the flow of drugs across the southern border? Not likely.

The Drug Enforcement Administration in a 2016 report found that the six main Mexican cartels smuggle "multi-ton quantities" of heroin, methamphetamines, cocaine and marijuana into the United

States, most of it through legal ports of entry. Traffickers conceal the drugs in hidden compartments within passenger cars or hide them alongside other legal cargo in tractor trailers.

In 2016, U.S. Customs and Border Protection seized 1.29 million pounds of marijuana and 4,184 pounds of cocaine at nine ports of entry along the border. Yet millions of pounds still make it through.

Many drugs are smuggled through elaborately built tunnels that start in Mexico and end inside stash houses in the United States, according to the DEA. Between 1990 and 2016, authorities discovered 224 tunnels along the southwest border. Some tunnels were up to 70 feet below the surface, far beneath the foundations of any border barrier. Traffickers are also using advanced technology and flying drugs over the border using drones.

 "They [Democrats] wanted that caravan, and there are those that say that caravan didn't just happen, it didn't just happen."

—Oct. 18, 2018 (campaign rally)

 "Do you know how the caravan started? Does everybody know what this means? I think the Democrats had something to do with it."

—Oct. 22, 2018 (campaign rally)

In the run-up to the 2018 midterm elections, Trump made frequent false or misleading claims about a caravan of Central American migrants traveling en masse to the United States.

There's no evidence that Democrats organized, funded or in any way aided the caravan. But conspiracy theories ran amok inside the Trump administration and among Republicans. Vice President Pence claimed that Venezuela funded the caravan. Then–U.N. ambassador Nikki Haley said Cuba egged on the caravanners. Rep. Matt Gaetz (R-Fla.), a Trump ally, speculated that billionaire investor George Soros, a donor to liberal causes and a frequent subject of right-wing conspiracy theories, was paying the migrants.

Washington Post reporters who spent time with the caravan found that many migrants had wanted to leave for months or years, and then saw pictures of the growing caravan in a Facebook post, on TV or in a WhatsApp group, and decided to join in.

"Right away, I knew I would go," said Irma Rosales, 37, from Santa Ana, El Salvador, who saw the caravan on television and bought a bus ticket to meet the group in Guatemala.

"I had been waiting for a way to get north, and then I heard about the caravan," said Ediberto Fuentes, 30, who had fled Honduras for southern Mexico but was stranded for months, without money to pay a smuggler for help getting to the United States.

"I packed my bag in 30 minutes," said Jose Mejia, 16, from Ocotepeque, Honduras, who heard about the caravan when his friend knocked on his door at 4 a.m. and said simply, "We're going."

IT'S ALL GOOD: TRUMP'S FLIPS ON BORDER ARRESTS

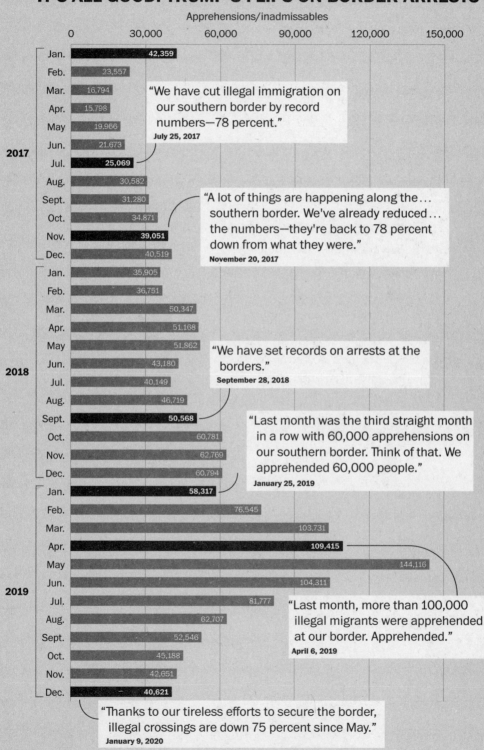

Apprehensions/inadmissables

2017 Jan.	42,359
Feb.	23,557
Mar.	16,794
Apr.	15,798
May	19,966
Jun.	21,673
Jul.	25,069
Aug.	30,582
Sept.	31,280
Oct.	34,871
Nov.	39,051
Dec.	40,519

"We have cut illegal immigration on our southern border by record numbers—78 percent."
July 25, 2017

"A lot of things are happening along the... southern border. We've already reduced... the numbers—they're back to 78 percent down from what they were."
November 20, 2017

2018 Jan.	35,905
Feb.	36,751
Mar.	50,347
Apr.	51,168
May	51,862
Jun.	43,180
Jul.	40,149
Aug.	46,719
Sept.	50,568
Oct.	60,781
Nov.	62,769
Dec.	60,794

"We have set records on arrests at the borders."
September 28, 2018

"Last month was the third straight month in a row with 60,000 apprehensions on our southern border. Think of that. We apprehended 60,000 people."
January 25, 2019

2019 Jan.	58,317
Feb.	76,545
Mar.	103,731
Apr.	109,415
May	144,116
Jun.	104,311
Jul.	81,777
Aug.	62,707
Sept.	52,546
Oct.	45,188
Nov.	42,651
Dec.	40,621

"Last month, more than 100,000 illegal migrants were apprehended at our border. Apprehended."
April 6, 2019

"Thanks to our tireless efforts to secure the border, illegal crossings are down 75 percent since May."
January 9, 2020

CHAPTER SEVEN

Trump on Economics and Trade: "The Best Economy Ever!"

Trump pitched himself to voters as a businessman who could return the country to prosperity. The Great Recession had officially ended six months after Barack Obama took office, but the recovery started out slowly and unevenly. By 2016, the post-recession expansion was one of the longest post–World War II booms on record; the unemployment rate dropped below the historical norm and nearly 12 million jobs were added. But during his campaign, Trump described the economy as a disaster and promised annual economic growth of 4 percent (a stretch, according to many economists). He even falsely claimed in his announcement speech that the gross domestic product was "below zero." (Literally that meant the U.S. economy was smaller than Tuvalu's GDP of $38 million, but presumably he meant negative economic growth. That was still false.)

At The Fact Checker, we take a skeptical view of claims that any president's actions greatly influence the course of the economy, at least in the short term. That's because the U.S. economy is complex, and the decisions of companies and consumers often loom larger than the acts of government. Nevertheless, all presidents are eager to claim credit for good economic news on their watch. Obama repeat-

159

edly touted a slowdown in the rise of health-care costs, attributing the trend to passage of the Affordable Care Act. But health-care costs around the world slowed in the wake of the Great Recession, so either that also was a major factor or Obamacare magically affected costs around the globe.

Trump is noteworthy both for the exaggerated nature of his claims and for how his view of the economy turned on a dime after he was elected.

Trump quickly claimed credit for an improving economy while insisting it was a mess before he was president. The unemployment rate kept falling, jobs kept getting created, the stock market kept climbing—all along roughly the same trend line as under Obama. But, in Trump's telling, this was all his doing—even before his policies took effect. There's little doubt that some of his policies provided a jolt to the economy, such as the tax cut he signed into law in 2017 and the anti-regulatory approach he championed. Before Trump was elected, the Congressional Budget Office had predicted a slowdown in job growth as the expansion ran its course; instead, job numbers kept rising at almost the pace as under Obama. (Some economists argue that higher budget deficits and a dirtier environment stemming from Trump's decisions were not worth the trade-off in the near-term and will burden future generations.) Another favorite Trump metric is the performance of the U.S. stock market, but there, too, Obama has an edge.

Similarly, on trade, Trump marks a sharp dividing line—everything before him was awful, and now everything under him is fantastic, even if the big changes he touts in his trade deals amount to relatively minor adjustments. Making trade deals is a singular focus of the president, even if he does consistently get his numbers wrong.

Trump's economic claims fall into five basic arguments—that

he took over a mess, transformed the American economy, is saving Americans money, is protecting us from rapacious foreigners, and is making great trade deals.

"I INHERITED A BAD ECONOMY"

 "It was going bad. If you look at the numbers from the end of the Obama [administration], it was crashing. It was crashing."

—June 20, 2019 (interview)

 "You remember how bad we were doing when I first took over. There was a big difference. And we were going down. This country was going economically down."

—Dec. 14, 2017 (remarks)

 "It was very important to a lot of people, because our country was going to hell and now our country is on a path that we haven't seen in decades and decades."

—Jan. 16, 2020 (remarks)

 Donald J. Trump
@realDonaldTrump

"We have accomplished an economic turnaround of historic proportions."—July 27, 2018

These quotes are surely going to puzzle future historians when they examine trend lines such as employment and job growth. Trump often speaks as if he took office in the middle of the Great Recession when in fact he inherited a pretty good economy. The U.S. added more than 250,000 jobs each month in 2014 and 227,000 a month in 2015; it added 193,000 a month in 2016, as Trump barnstormed the country saying the economy was in crisis. In 2017, Trump's first year in office, monthly job growth slowed to 179,000 per month. It jumped to 223,000 a month in 2018—lower than under Obama in 2014 and 2015—and fell back to 175,000 a month in 2019.

When Trump proclaimed, twice in the same day, "an economic turnaround of historic proportions," the United States had been adding jobs for 94 straight months, of which 18 were under Trump's leadership.

 "Let me just tell you a little secret, if Crooked Hillary would have won, your economy would have crashed."

—Dec. 18, 2019 (campaign rally)

 "You know, if the other administration had continued, our economy would have crashed, our country would have crashed. We would have been in a depression, because the regulations made it impossible. . . . And they like to say, 'Well, Obama helped.' He didn't help. We were going down, folks. We were going down. We were going down. We were going down."

—Nov. 3, 2018 (campaign rally)

 "And let me tell you, if for some reason I wouldn't have won the election, these markets would have crashed and that will happen even more so in 2020."

—Aug. 15, 2019 (campaign rally)

At times, Trump seems to acknowledge that the economy was doing okay when he was elected but claims it was headed for a big crash. There is little evidence to support this argument. The stock market had been going gangbusters under Obama, so it's unclear why a Clinton victory would have been a letdown. (Certainly, however, Wall Street investors were happy with the election of a business-friendly Republican.)

Rising stock-market prices under Obama were a problem for Trump during the campaign, so he blamed low interest rates for artificially propping up the markets. During his first debate with Clinton, in September 2016, Trump said: "We are in a big, fat, ugly bubble. . . . The only thing that looks good is the stock market. But if you raise interest rates even a little bit, that's going to come crashing down." And, while campaigning in Ohio that same month, Trump said: "We have a very false economy. . . . The only thing that is strong is the artificial stock market."

Trump repeatedly argued that as soon as the Federal Reserve raised interest rates, the market would crash. The Fed did begin boosting interest rates a month after Trump was elected—and the market kept going up.

"MY ECONOMY IS THE BEST EVER"

 "Nobody in the White House has ever had the greatest economy in the history of our country."

—Nov. 5, 2018 (campaign rally)

 "I have the greatest economy in the history of this country."

—Dec. 18, 2019 (campaign rally)

"We have never had an economy like this in history."

—Jan. 16, 2020 (remarks)

It started, as ever, with a tweet. On June 4, 2018, the president wrote: "In many ways this is the greatest economy in the HISTORY of America."

By Jan. 19, 2020, about a year and half later, Trump had declared that the U.S. economy was the greatest, the best or the strongest in U.S. history almost 260 times, according to our database. That's a rate of nearly every two days.

This type of presidential braggadocio left us with a conundrum. One could dismiss it as merely overheated rhetoric, as one historian suggested to The Fact Checker. (Another joked, "You should put these questions to a rabbi, not an economic historian.") But we decided there is a point at which the statement threatens to become its own form of truth through consistent repetition. In fact, the president said it so often that he began to quote himself: "It's said now that our economy is the strongest it's ever been in the history of our country."

Until the coronavirus crisis tanked the stock market and led to millions of layoffs and furloughs, the president could certainly brag about the state of the economy, but he ran into trouble when he repeatedly made a play for the history books. There are several metrics one could look at, but the economy during the Trump administration's first three years did not perform at historic levels, according to experts we consulted. The unemployment rate reached a low of 3.5 percent under Trump, but it was as low as 2.5 percent in 1953. Trump has never achieved an annual growth rate above 3 percent, but in 1997, 1998 and 1999, the gross domestic product grew 4.5 percent, 4.5 percent and 4.7 percent, respectively. Even that period paled when compared to the 1950s and 1960s. Growth between 1962 and 1966 ranged from 4.4 percent to 6.6 percent. In 1950 and 1951, it was 8.7 and 8 percent, respectively. Higher economic growth was probably achieved in the 1870s, when Ulysses S. Grant was president, though 19th-century data isn't as precise as post–World War II calculations.

By just about any important measure, the economy under Trump was not doing as well before the coronavirus crisis as it did under presidents Dwight D. Eisenhower, Lyndon B. Johnson and Bill Clinton—not to mention Grant.

Yet Trump keeps making this false claim.

 "America now has the hottest economy anywhere on earth and there's no place close."

—Jan. 19, 2020 (speech)

This is a variation of his "greatest economy" claim, but in this case he compares the United States to the rest of the world. (He has not limited himself to earth. He once tweeted that the U.S. economy was the best in the "universe." Residents of Tralfamadore may beg to differ.)

Trump has uttered some variation of this statement more than 70 times. Trump first started saying this when the U.S. economy expanded at an annual rate of 3.5 percent in the third quarter of 2018. Many other countries had faster growth rates at that time, including China, India, Latvia, Poland and Greece. The U.S. economy started to slow in the next quarter, down to 2.2 percent, compared to 4.2 percent in the second quarter.

This is a case where Trump's lack of precision gets him into trouble. He would have a better point if he had specified that he was comparing the United States to other highly advanced economies, rather than all countries in the world. Since he started making this claim, the United States has had the fastest growth of any of the Group of Seven (G7) industrialized countries. Some members of the broader G20 group, such as China, India and Indonesia, continue to have faster growth.

"Yesterday, we had the strongest dollar in the history of our country. . . . We had literally the strongest dollar in the history of our country."

—Aug. 21, 2019 (remarks)

Trump made a variation of this claim five times in the space of a couple of weeks. The reason is a mystery, but the facts are clear: The dollar was at peak historical strength in 1985, according to the U.S. Dollar Index. The index is based on a weighted average of U.S. exchange rates with six currencies: the euro, the Japanese yen, the British pound, the Canadian dollar, the Swedish krona, and the Swiss franc.

Compared to individual currencies such as the euro, yen and Chinese yuan, the dollar was nowhere near historical highs. The dollar was strongest against the euro in 1985, strongest against the yen in 1971 and strongest against the yuan in 1994.

At the time of Trump's first tweet, the dollar had hit its highest level of 2019. Characteristically, he took an annual figure and tried to turn it into a historical record.

"We have more people working in the United States today—almost 160 million people—than at any time in the history of our country."

—October 9, 2019 (remarks)

Trump loves this claim—he's said it nearly 130 times—but it's pretty silly. Of course, there are more Americans working. That's because there are more Americans today than ever before. This is a claim President Obama could have made in 2014, 2015 and 2016 as people regained jobs following the recession, but we contacted a top aide for the former president, who confirmed that Obama never made such a claim. This is another example of Trump's willingness to push the limits of fact.

More meaningful measures of the health of the job market take population into consideration. The unemployment rate, or the share of people who don't have jobs, has never reached a record low in Trump's presidency.

An even better measure is one that addresses employment status as a ratio of the population. For starters, let's look at the labor force participation rate for people ages 25 to 54, which counts the number of people who are either employed or unemployed as a share of the U.S. population. (There is an overall labor force participation rate, which includes all Americans ages 16 and up, but this metric is less useful because it lumps in people who might be unemployed while in school as well as people aging out of the labor force.)

Economists often use the participation rate as an indicator of the health of the job market. The higher the number, the healthier the market. In late 2019, the labor force participation rate for people ages 25 to 54 hovered around 83 percent but it peaked in 1997 at 84.5 percent.

Another telling stat is the employment-to-population rate for Americans ages 25 to 54. This rate measures the number of people who are working or looking for work as a share of the population. The rate in August 2019 exceeded the pre-recession level, but as of January 2020, it had yet to top its 2000 peak.

"Our unemployment numbers are the best we've ever had."

—Dec. 24, 2019 (remarks)

False. The unemployment rate has declined but not achieved record lows under Trump. Moreover, prior to the mass layoffs caused by the coronavirus crisis, the labor force participation rate was below levels seen in the 1990s and 2000s.

 "We've added 12,000 brand new factories and many more are coming in."

—Jan. 9, 2020 (campaign rally)

Trump began making this claim after reports that the manufacturing sector was entering a recession, but it is misleading. "Factories" conjures up images of smokestacks and production lines, but this is typical Trumpian hype. The data set Trump cited is not really about factories, though the number he uses is correct.

Trump is using a Bureau of Labor Statistics database set known as the Quarterly Census of Employment and Wages. Sure enough, the data shows that the United States gained almost 10,000 additional "manufacturing establishments" from the first quarter of 2017 through the first quarter of 2019; the number increased to above 12,000 in the second quarter of 2019. (There was also a gain of 10,000 in Obama's second term.) But more than 80 percent of these "manufacturing establishments" employ five or fewer people. If those sound like pretty small factories, that's because many are not "factories." The BLS counts any establishment "engaged in the mechanical, physical, or chemical transformation of materials, substances, or components into new products," so that also includes businesses "that transform materials or substances into new products by hand or in the worker's home and those engaged in selling to the general public products made on the same premises from which they are sold, such as bakeries, candy stores, and custom tailors."

 "My daughter has created millions of jobs. I don't know if anyone knows that, but she's created millions of jobs."

—Feb. 25, 2019 (remarks)

 "She [Ivanka] has done, really, a fantastic job for women and also for jobs. Thirteen million additional jobs."

—Sept. 27, 2019 (remarks)

Trump rarely credits anyone other than himself, but on more than a dozen occasions, he has celebrated his daughter Ivanka's creation of millions of jobs. By January 2020, Trump bragged she had created 15 million jobs. That's a neat trick, since official government statistics show the economy had gained fewer than 7 million jobs in the first three years of Trump's presidency.

So what is Trump talking about? His daughter co-chairs a workforce policy advisory board that encourages companies to pledge training opportunities to workers over the next five years. That's right—training *opportunities*. It turned out that many of these companies and organizations were already planning to offer such retraining programs, but as part of a publicity effort, the White House got them to sign a public pledge.

Ivanka Trump can certainly be congratulated for getting so many companies to put their names in writing and pledge to train workers. Yet these are not new jobs; they are training opportunities. Moreover, the numbers reflect pledges over a five-year period, not something already achieved, as the president consistently frames it.

> "The African American youth unemployment, this was so important to me. You remember how high, it was 60, 70%, has now reached the lowest number ever recorded in the history of our country."
>
> —Nov. 8, 2019 (prepared speech)

This is an example of how Trump sometimes reaches back to a bogus figure he cited in the 2016 campaign, and then favorably compares it to a real number today.

The African American youth (ages 16 to 24) unemployment rate did fall to the lowest level since these employment numbers started to be calculated in 1972. But notice how he claims it had been 60 to 70 percent. During the campaign, Trump had claimed it was 58 percent, but that was the result of some very fuzzy math. The Trump campaign came up with the number by calculating the number of people classified as "unemployed" and "not in the labor force" as a percentage of the total civilian population.

"Unemployed" refers to people who are available for work and actively looking for a job, but don't have one. "Not in the labor force" refers to people who are not looking for jobs because they have given up looking or are not interested—such as students.

The result of these manipulations? They basically tripled the official black youth unemployment rate in 2016 of 19.2 percent. If we applied Trump's campaign math to the 2019 numbers—which show an official rate of 13.8 percent, a steep decline from 2016—the rate for African Americans ages 16 to 24 would be 55 percent, barely changed from his similarly inflated numbers for 2016.

 "While every Democrat running for President wants to shut down our coal mines, we are putting our miners back to work."

—Jan. 9, 2020 (campaign rally)

From the start of his administration, Trump has told coal miners that he's getting them their jobs back. This is mostly baloney. The U.S. total of 51,000 coal-mining jobs has barely budged in the three years since Trump took office, according to the Bureau of Labor Statistics. The addition of a few hundred jobs is a drop in the bucket measured against the 125,000-job loss the industry suffered since 1985, or the 36,000-job decline since 2012. U.S. coal consumption in 2018 was at its lowest level in 39 years, according to the Energy Information Administration (EIA). More coal-fired plants closed in Trump's first two years in office than in the entirety of Obama's first term. Indeed, in 2019 the EIA forecast a 21 percent decline in coal production over the next 20 years.

"We just had another all-time high for our stock market. Just hit. So that will be 149 times in less than three years."

—January 17, 2020 (remarks)

Trump often claims that the stock market has notched record highs more than 100 times during his presidency. (He's silent when the stock market goes down, as it did for much of 2018, but talks about it incessantly when it's going up.) The stock market had performed well, but his scorekeeping is fishy. Just two days earlier, Trump had referenced 141 record highs in his presidency. The correct number was 46. (Little did Trump know that the plunge in the stock market following the coronavirus outbreak in early 2020 would wipe away much of the gain during his presidency.)

"I'M SAVING YOU MONEY"

 "We've eliminated a record number of job-killing regulations, saving the average American household $3,000 a year."

—Jan. 9, 2019 (campaign rally)

This has become one of Trump's favorite statistics, but it's bogus, especially the way he frames it. This statistic comes from a report issued in June 2019 by his Council of Economic Advisers, which calculated such savings five to ten years in the future. Trump speaks as if this pile of money is already lining Americans' pockets.

The report makes several generous assumptions about the impact of deregulation to reach this figure. Experts we consulted found the conclusions dubious. One expert cited in the report called the analysis "just crazy" and "anti-academic." Even if one accepted all of the CEA's numbers, the report does not look at the other side of the ledger—actions taken by the administration that economists say have reduced household income, such as the president's tariff war.

The CEA report has the air of an effort to give the president a shiny new talking point, but according to the administration's own numbers, the supposed $3,000 in additional real income per household might not materialize until after the president finishes his hoped-for second term. Yet he barnstormed around the country telling audiences he was already giving them this money.

> "In the Bush administration, for eight years, $450. In the Obama administration, for eight years, $975. In the Trump administration, for less than three years, almost $10,000, when you include the tax cuts, the energy savings and the regulation cuts. Nobody can believe it."
>
> —Jan. 19, 2020 (speech)

Trump here takes his previous false claim—the $3,000 in regulatory savings—and adds it to a stew of dubious assumptions to cook up a $10,000 figure. Then he tosses out numbers for his predecessors that are not comparable.

This talking point started in October 2019 with an opinion article by Stephen Moore, a former campaign economic adviser whom Trump briefly nominated for a seat on the Federal Reserve Board. Moore argued that the median household income gain under Bush was a little over $400 and under Obama about $1,000, compared with $5,000 under Trump. The Census Bureau shows a gain of only $1,380 from 2016 and 2018, but Moore used data from a private firm, Sentier Research, that spots trends sooner than the annual release of the official census figure.

The numbers for Bush and Obama are low because both men had to deal with recessions on their watch. The Sentier data shows the income trend under Trump was simply a continuation of a trend that started under Obama. When we compared the last 31 months of Obama to the first 31 months of Trump, the trend was clear. In those 31-month periods, median household income rose 5.6 percent under Obama and 7.1 percent under Trump. That gives a slight edge to Trump, but these monthly numbers bounce around a lot, so it's unclear whether the recent pace under Trump can be maintained. (Indeed, it dropped sharply in November and December of 2019.)

On top of those sketchy numbers, Trump ladles $2,500 in "energy savings." That's from another Council of Economic Advisers report that estimated $2,500 in savings for a family of four from the "shale revolution"—which started in 2007, ten years before Trump took office. He also assumes every household got a $2,000 tax cut, but the effect of his tax cut is widely scattered across income groups, with the biggest gains going to the biggest wage earners.

Of course, the president never mentions his actions that have reduced household income. We often wonder whether the crowds hearing this claim are puzzled about why they haven't found this illusionary $10,000 in their bank accounts.

 "We're actually taking in more revenue now than we did when we had the higher taxes because the economy's doing so well."

—Jan. 6, 2020 (interview)

Here, the president makes a basic mistake. He asserts that even though he signed into law a bill cutting taxes in 2017, revenue has continued to rise—a fact he attributes to a robust economy. But revenue was always supposed to increase year after year, despite the tax cuts, according to Congressional Budget Office estimates released when the tax bill was approved by Congress. And revenue is way down from what had been anticipated before Congress approved the tax cuts, which (along with higher spending) is why the federal budget deficit kept soaring despite a good economy.

"OUR TRADING PARTNERS ARE TAKING OUR MONEY"

 "We've been losing, for years, close to $800 billion, not million—$800 million is a lot—but we've been losing $800 billion on trade. Eight hundred billion dollars."

—May 9, 2019 (remarks)

 "China has been taking out $500 billion a year for many years out of our country. Hundreds of billions of dollars, 200, 300, 500, 400, back and forth, but on average, hundreds of billions of, not millions, hard to believe, billions."

—Nov. 26, 2019 (interview)

 "But we lost last year with the European Union $151 billion. This has been going on for many years. Think of it—$151 billion."

—Feb. 25, 2019 (remarks)

 "Mexico has been making, for many, many years, hundreds of mill— of billions of dollars. They've been making an absolute fortune on the United States."

—June 6, 2019 (remarks)

 "With Japan, we had a $68 billion deficit."

—Dec. 18, 2019 (campaign rally)

NOT QUITE SO DIRE: TRUMP'S TRADE DEFICIT CLAIMS

$0B $100B $200B $300B $400B $500B $600B $700B $800B

OVERALL TRADE DEFICIT

Trump claimed $800 billion.

In 2017, the actual deficit was $550 billion.

In 2018, the actual deficit was $628 billion.

CHINA

Trump claimed $500 billion.

In 2017, the actual deficit was $337 billion.

In 2018, the actual deficit was $380 billion.

EUROPEAN UNION

Trump claimed $151 billion.

In 2017, the actual deficit was $101 billion.

In 2018, the actual deficit was $115 billion.

MEXICO

Trump claimed $100 billion.

In 2017, the actual deficit was $67 billion.

In 2018, the actual deficit was $79 billion.

JAPAN

Trump claimed $68 billion.

In 2017, the actual deficit was $57 billion.

In 2018, the actual deficit was $57 billion.

CANADA

Trump claimed $58 billion.

In 2017, the United States had a small surplus of $2.8 billion.

In 2018, the United States had a small surplus of $3.6 billion.

"Canada was taking out $58 billion a year, at least, by the way, at least. Now we're making the deals fair."

—Sept 7, 2018 (interview)

Trump consistently inflates trade deficits, so each of these numbers is wrong. Sometimes he's citing the trade-in-goods deficit—ignoring trade-in-services, where the United States often has a surplus, even though the 2018 Council of Economic Advisers report, which Trump signed, said that "focusing only on the trade in goods alone ignores the United States' comparative advantage in services." Other times, he's simply inventing numbers out of whole cloth. His framing is also wrong: Countries do not make or lose money on trade deficits.

In a March 2018 fundraising speech, Trump admitted that he insisted to Canadian Prime Minister Justin Trudeau that the United States ran a trade deficit with Canada without knowing whether that was true, according to audio of the private event obtained by *The Washington Post*. After *The Post* published an article on the speech, Trump doubled down, insisting in a tweet: "We do have a Trade Deficit with Canada, as we do with almost all countries."

A few months later, he insisted the deficit was $100 billion, citing "a Canada release." That figure was based on a misreading of statistics issued by the Canadian government. These numbers, indicating a $98 billion merchandise trade deficit, include re-exports of goods from third countries (such as a washing machine from China that passed through Vancouver's port on the way to the United States), inflating the number. Think of it this way: Trump frequently complains about the trade deficit with China. That washing machine is recorded in that deficit. But now he was counting the same washing machine as part of a trade deficit with Canada.

"MY TRADE DEALS ARE AMAZING"

 "We will soon be replacing the NAFTA catastrophe, one of the worst trade deals in the history of the world, frankly, with the incredible USMCA."

—Jan. 14, 2020 (campaign rally)

 "We lost thousands of factories and millions of jobs because of NAFTA—thousands. Think of it: Thousands of factories, millions of jobs."

—April 12, 2018 (remarks)

Trump regularly attacks the North American Free Trade Agreement, which took effect in January 1994, as the worst trade deal ever. He frequently describes it in apocalyptic terms, claiming it resulted in the loss of millions of jobs. NAFTA—which created an economically integrated market for the United States, Mexico and Canada—has had strong critics from the start, and it's difficult to separate the impact of trade agreements on jobs from other, broader economic trends such as automation and the explosive growth of low-wage labor abroad. But Trump's attacks on the deal were over the top.

"In reality, NAFTA did not cause the huge job losses feared by the critics or the large economic gains predicted by supporters," concluded the nonpartisan Congressional Research Service in 2015. "The net overall effect of NAFTA on the U.S. economy appears to have been relatively modest, primarily because trade with Canada and Mexico accounts for a small percentage of U.S. GDP. However, there were worker and firm adjustment costs as the three countries adjusted to more open trade and investment."

So NAFTA was not as bad as Trump claimed. But once he

struck a deal for a modest retooling—which was dubbed the United States–Mexico–Canada Agreement (USMCA)—he immediately proclaimed he had struck a deal that was "incredible," "wonderful," "great," and "maybe the best trade deal ever made." About two-thirds of the deal was borrowed from the Trans-Pacific Partnership, the trade deal Trump scrapped at the start of his term, deeming it "one of the worst trade deals ever negotiated." To win support from House Democrats, the USMCA includes more environmental and labor protections and also helped modernize the 26-year-old pact with provisions on intellectual property, pharmaceuticals and the digital economy. The USMCA also makes it harder for companies to close factories in the United States and Canada and move entirely to Mexico. Analysts say the USMCA is 85 percent to 90 percent identical to NAFTA, but that would never be apparent from Trump's description of his deal-making prowess.

"We finished [a new trade deal] with South Korea. What a difference that has made. That was a Hillary Clinton deal. She said, 'This will produce 250,000 jobs.' And she was right, except the jobs were produced for South Korea, not for us, okay?"

—Oct. 23, 2019 (speech)

So many things are wrong here. Clinton, as secretary of state, did not negotiate the United States–Korea Free Trade Agreement (known as KORUS). It was signed under George W. Bush but did not go into effect under his tenure; aspects were renegotiated by Obama, and it went into effect in 2012. Clinton never said it would produce 250,000 jobs. Sometimes Trump claims that a government agency or official predicted a job loss of 250,000, but that's not the case either.

The U.S. International Trade Commission concluded that "aggregate U.S. output and employment changes would likely be negligible." Trump's claim about the number of jobs lost have also ballooned over the years, from 100,000 to 200,000 and then to 250,000.

The Trump administration negotiated mostly cosmetic changes to KORUS, removing some red tape and lifting a cap on car exports to South Korea that automakers were not even reaching. Most of the deal's original 24 chapters were untouched, noted *The Economist*, which headlined its article on the deal: "The trade deal between America and South Korea has barely changed."

 "Just so you understand, China, forever, never paid us 10 cents. Now we have—literally, we will soon have, literally, hundreds of billions of dollars coming in from China. We never got anything from China."

—Nov. 9, 2019 (remarks)

Trump loves tariffs, but he consistently oversells their impact and gets basic facts wrong. Through Jan. 23, 2020, his Chinese tariffs had garnered only about $44 billion, not "hundreds of billions of dollars." And to rescue farmers when China responded to the tariff war by not buying U.S. agricultural products, Trump authorized direct payments to them, totaling $28 billion. So that amounts to only a net gain of only $16 billion. To put that in context, in fiscal 2019, federal revenue exceeded $3.4 trillion, so this is the equivalent of fractions of pennies.

More to the point, China doesn't pay the tariffs. Essentially a tax, the tariffs are generally paid by importers, such as U.S. companies, who in turn pass on most or all of the costs to consumers or producers who use Chinese materials in their products. (Technically, we should note that as a matter of demand and supply elasticities, Chinese producers will pay part of the tax if there are fewer goods sold to the United States.) So, ultimately, Americans foot the bill for Trump's tariffs, not the Chinese. Trump is fooling himself if he thinks otherwise.

As for Trump's claim that the United States never earned tariffs from China before—he often says China "never gave us 10 cents"—tariffs have been collected on Chinese goods since the early days of the Republic. President George Washington signed the Tariff Act of 1789, when trade between China and the United States was already established. Tariffs on China have generated at least $8 billion every year since 2009.

Donald J. Trump
@realDonaldTrump

> **"The unexpectedly good first quarter 3.2% GDP was greatly helped by Tariffs from China. Some people just don't get it!"—May 13, 2019**

Nope. Tariffs reduce economic growth, as even Trump economic adviser Larry Kudlow acknowledged in an interview on "Fox News Sunday" the day before this tweet. He said it would reduce growth by "two-tenths of 1 percent" of the gross domestic product, which translates to $40 billion. Other estimates are bigger—the Trade Partnership has a figure twice as high—which is why the Federal Reserve acted to reduce interest rates as the trade war continued.

> **"So this is phenomenal for the farmers. . . . We just signed one for $40 billion with Japan."**
>
> —Jan. 9, 2020 (interview)

This is grossly misleading. Trump signed a deal with Japan that returns benefits American farmers lost when he pulled out of a broader Asia-Pacific pact, known as the Trans-Pacific Partnership, during his first week in office. Japan went ahead with the agreement with the other nations, putting U.S. farmers at a disadvantage. The deal did not resolve differences over trade in automobiles, but tariffs will be cut on $7 billion worth of agricultural products and markets will be opened on about $40 billion worth of digital trade between the two countries. But Trump often describes it as Americans banking $40 billion, suggesting it's all going to farmers.

 "The WTO, we're winning cases for the first time. We just won a $7.5 billion case. We never won cases."

—Nov. 12, 2019 (speech)

This is false. The United States has prevailed in nearly 90 percent of the cases that it brings against other countries in the World Trade Organization. The United States tends to lose when other countries bring cases to the WTO. Other countries have a similar won-lost percentage.

 "I was doing the final touches on the China deal. And that's going to be one of the great deals ever. And it's going to ultimately lead to the opening of China, which is something that is incredible, because that's a whole, big, untapped market of 1.5 billion people."

Dec. 13, 2019 (remarks)

This is nonsense. Trade relations were normalized with China in 2000. It was first "re-opened" during the Nixon administration. In 2016, the year before Trump became president, the United States sold $170 billion of goods and services to China, making it the country's third-biggest trading partner after Canada and Mexico.

THE STRANGE CASE OF
THE PHANTOM FACTORY OPENINGS

Factories that didn't open (or close) because of Trump

Shell ethylene cracker plant, Monaca, Pennsylvania
Dec. 10, 2019: "Just a few months ago, I visited the new Shell petrochemical plant in Beaver County. At $6 billion, with a B, it is the largest investment in Pennsylvania history. We're ending decades of failed trade policies that devastated communities all across the state."
Trump falsely suggests the Shell plant is the result of his trade policies. Royal Dutch Shell announced the plant in 2012, under the Obama administration, after receiving one of the largest tax incentives in Pennsylvania's history.

Abrams tank manufacturing plant, Lima, Ohio
Jan. 9, 2020: "They have this Army tank plant right, in Lima . . . It was closed, they announced it was closed. It was all set to close. I said you can't close this plant . . . So, that was something I did that I'm very proud of because I really overrode a lot of talented people that wanted to close it."
This story is a fantasy. Trump has steered more funding to this tank plant in Ohio, but it was never in danger of closing.

"Apple" plant, Austin, Texas
Nov. 20, 2019: "Today I opened a major Apple Manufacturing plant in Texas that will bring high paying jobs back to America."
Trump did not open this Texas plant, and it is not even an Apple plant. It is a Flex Ltd. plant that has been making Mac Pro computers since 2012 under a contract with Apple.

Liquefied Natural Gas plant, Hackberry, Louisiana
May 19, 2019: "Yesterday as you probably saw, I was in Louisiana opening up a $10 billion LNG plant that would've never been approved under another type of administration, never."
Sempra Energy announced its plan to create an LNG export terminal in 2012 in a partnership with Japanese companies. The Federal Energy Regulatory Commission authorized the project in June 2014 under Barack Obama.

CHAPTER EIGHT

Trump on Foreign Policy:
"We Fell in Love"

Effective diplomacy requires careful planning, a delicate touch, patience and a certain degree of cynicism. "Man was given speech to disguise his thoughts, and words to disguise his eyes," Charles Tallyrand, the skilled 19th-century French diplomat, said. "Don't trust anything, or anyone."

President Trump's diplomacy leans toward a different approach: bull in china shop. There are lots of scattered shards on the floor; whether anything of lasting value is being created is unclear.

Trump has upended U.S. relations with democracies that have long been allies, berating them as ingrates and demanding payment for the presence of U.S. troops. He has shown an affinity for authoritarian leaders in countries such as Turkey, Saudi Arabia, Brazil and the Philippines, abandoning the traditional U.S. promotion of human rights. He pulled the United States out of the Paris Accord on climate change and the international nuclear agreement with Iran—two signature achievements of Barack Obama. He denounced North Korean dictator Kim Jong Un as "Rocket Man" and then months later agreed to high-stakes summit diplomacy with Kim. "We fell in love," Trump told a rally in 2018, before the relationship faltered after three meetings.

There's always room for innovation in diplomacy. Sometimes shaking things up is necessary to push nations to reconsider their positions. Some effects of Trump's foreign policy won't be clear for years. Certainly, all presidents tend to oversell their diplomatic efforts and play down their setbacks.

But Trump's foreign policy was marked from the start by how consistently his statements on international issues were wrong. One can offer a reasoned critique of the shortcomings of the nuclear accord negotiated between Iran and the United States and five other world powers. But Trump repeatedly utters falsehoods that are easily disproven, undermining his case.

Here are some of the most prominent examples of how Trump has gotten it wrong on international issues, arranged mostly by the key regions or countries that have animated Trump. We also include a section on claims about the U.S. military, since Trump frequently claims he inherited a "depleted" force but has quickly turned it around. These are not just minor flubs; rather, they reflect what many see as a disturbing ignorance about how international relations work. The president's inexperience, inconsistency and unwillingness to change his ways, according to Democratic and Republican foreign policy veterans alike, weaken the trust of allies and make it harder for other countries to negotiate with the United States.

MIDDLE EAST

 "They poured precious American blood and treasure into the Middle East while our great cities fell into disrepair; $8 trillion was spent in the Middle East."

—Nov. 6, 2019 (campaign rally)

This is one of Trump's favorite lines, which he has used more than 60 times as president. It started at $6 trillion, but Trump soon elevated it to $7 trillion, and by late 2019, it had grown to $8 trillion.

First of all, Trump has a bit of a geography problem. He is talking about the wars in Iraq and Afghanistan, but Afghanistan is in Central/South Asia, not the Middle East.

Second, Trump is relying on a study published by Brown University's Costs of War Project, but he misunderstands what it says. The study includes estimates for future obligations through 2056 for veterans' care, estimated at $1 trillion, as well as paying interest on the debt issued to fight the wars, estimated at about $900 billion. It also includes $1 trillion in homeland security spending.

In other words, this is more than just spending on Middle East wars, and a chunk of it is spread out over more than 30 years into the future, but Trump lumps it all together and acts as if it has already been spent. The report indicates less than $2 trillion has been spent directly on the wars in Iraq and Afghanistan (and the conflict against ISIS).

 "But, in Iraq, we're in for probably $5.5 trillion."
—Oct. 16, 2019 (remarks)

This is similar to the previous claim but on steroids. The cost of the Iraq War between 2001 and 2019 was $822 billion, according to the Costs of War Project. The Congressional Research Service provides a similar estimate.

 "[Saudi Arabia has] been a terrific ally. They're creating millions of jobs in this country. They're ordering

equipment, not only military equipment, but $400 billion worth of—and, actually, even more than that over a period time—worth of different things."

—June 29, 2019 (news conference)

 "[The Saudi deal is equal to] 500,000 jobs, American jobs. Everything's made here."

—Oct. 16, 2018 (interview)

 "That's a million and a half jobs [from Saudi deals]."

—Sept. 16, 2019 (remarks)

Trump's first trip overseas was to Saudi Arabia, and he's been enamored of the country and its de facto ruler, Crown Prince Mohammad bin Salman, ever since. Trump defended MBS, as the prince is known, even after the CIA concluded he likely had ordered the 2018 killing and dismemberment of *Washington Post* columnist Jamal Khashoggi.

Trump has justified his support by citing an ever-changing estimate of American jobs that would be created from deals he secured during that 2017 visit. In one media exchange, in the space of minutes the jobs estimate changed from 600,000 to 1 million.

This is all a fantasy.

After the 2017 trip, Trump claimed he had reached $110 billion in military sales agreements and another $270 billion in commercial sales; he later increased the total sales to $450 billion. In 2017, The Fact Checker obtained a confidential White House list of the deals and discovered that most of the items on Trump's $110 billion list had no delivery dates or were scheduled for 2022 or beyond. There appeared to be few, if any, signed contracts. Rather, many of the announcements were MOIs—memorandums of intent. There were six specific items, adding up to $28 billion, but all had been previously reported to Congress by the Obama administration.

One deal that eventually came to fruition in 2019 was Saudi Arabia's $15 billion purchase of THAAD—the Terminal High Altitude Area Defense anti-ballistic missile system. (Trump had to offer a 20 percent price cut in 2018 to get the Saudis to ink the deal.)

As for the commercial deals, the $270 billion number turned out to be the result of double-counting, wishful thinking and fuzzy figures. (For the record, the State Department offered a different accounting, coming to just $80 billion in commercial deals.)

The "millions" of jobs supposedly being created in the United States are also a figment of Trump's imagination. (The White House, in its official news release, only referred to "tens of thousands" of jobs, which was already a stretch.) The jobs being created are primarily in Saudi Arabia. The contract for the Saudis to spend $6 billion on Lockheed Black Hawk helicopters says the helicopters will be manufactured and assembled in Saudi Arabia. Similarly, Raytheon, another U.S. arms manufacturer, agreed to establish an industrial base in the kingdom. Saudi officials said that any contract would require that more than 50 percent of funds for new military equipment be spent in the kingdom, compared to the current 2 percent minimum. But Trump never acknowledges that, if he's even aware of that fact.

 "I was very much opposed to the war in Iraq. I think it was a tremendous mistake, should have never happened."

—Nov. 18, 2018 (interview)

This is one of Trump's signature lies. He made this claim during the campaign, and he has said it more than a dozen times as president.

Trump even falsely claimed that the Bush White House approached him prior to the invasion to ask him to tone down his rhetoric.

We searched high and low—as did other reporters—and there is no evidence Trump was an opponent of the war, let alone a vocal one. In fact, he offered lukewarm support. When radio host Howard Stern asked Trump, a frequent guest, if he supported invading Iraq, Trump replied, "Yeah, I guess so. You know, I wish the first time it was done correctly." In another interview on Fox News, two months before the invasion, he said Bush had to make a decision: "Either you attack or you don't attack."

Shortly after the invasion, he told Fox News: "It looks like a tremendous success from a military standpoint."

Not until August 2004, in an interview with *Esquire*, did Trump publicly express opposition to the war. By then—17 months after the invasion—many Americans had turned against the war, making Trump's position not particularly distinctive.

"This was the anti-Benghazi. This was— Benghazi was a disaster. They showed up a long time after it took place. They saw burning embers from days before."

—Jan. 9, 2020 (speech)

Trump often makes a misleading comparison between the 2012 attack on a diplomatic facility and CIA annex in Benghazi, Libya, and the 2019 attack on the U.S. embassy in Baghdad. The Benghazi facility was not a consulate or even an official site; the U.S. ambassador just happened to be there that night. The U.S. embassy in Baghdad cost $750 million and is heavily secured. While Trump frequently says it took days for additional U.S. forces to arrive in Benghazi, they actually arrived just hours after the attack that killed the ambassador—and right in the middle of a predawn assault on the CIA annex. Glen Doherty, who was killed during the attacks, was part of the force that had been dispatched from Tripoli.

 "When I was elected President two years ago, ISIS was all over Syria and all over Iraq. We've wiped out ISIS in Iraq. We've wiped out ISIS."

—Jan. 6, 2019 (remarks)

 "Everybody gives me credit for decimating ISIS."

—Jan. 2, 2019 (remarks)

 "As you know, we captured 100 percent of the ISIS caliphate. When I took office, we had almost nothing."

—Nov. 25, 2019 (remarks)

From Trump's description, he inherited a mess and quickly mopped up the Islamic State militant group, also known as ISIS. But that's not the real story.

The Islamic State can be traced back to a group called al-Qaeda in Iraq, which was started by a Jordanian terrorist named Abu Musab al-Zarqawi, and arose in response to the U.S. invasion of Iraq in 2003. Eventually, al-Qaeda in Iraq more or less petered out, but the civil war in Syria that started in 2011 created a vacuum of governance in the country, thereby breathing new life into what had become a moribund organization. In 2014, Obama announced the formation of an international coalition to defeat the Islamic State.

As a result, Obama set up virtually all the structure that would do the key fighting against the Islamic State under Trump. Under Obama, all Iraqi cities held by ISIS—such as Fallujah, Ramadi, Tikrit and eastern Mosul (but not the western half of Mosul)—were retaken by the end of his term, as was much of a northeastern strip of Syria along the Turkish border. That amounted to about 50 percent of ISIS's territory. The basic plan of attack that resulted in the liberation of Mosul and Raqqa was also launched under Obama, though Trump sped up the tempo by changing the rules of engagement. The assault on Raqqa began in November 2016—two months before Trump took office, led by the same coalition that ultimately captured the city.

Although the ISIS caliphate has been eliminated, ISIS is still intact as a terrorist network. It has tens of thousands of active members in Iraq and Syria, affiliates around the globe and a proven ability to continue to perpetrate terrorist attacks.

 "Thousands and thousands of ISIS fighters are killed, and thousands and thousands—tens of thousands are in prison right now. And Europe doesn't want them. It's not right. They want to go to France. They want to go to Germany. They want to go to [the] UK. They want to go to these countries where they came from. That's where they—that's their home."

—Jan. 9, 2020 (speech)

Trump often claims that most of the ISIS fighters held in custody are from Europe, but this is false, according to James Jeffrey, Trump's coordinator in the coalition to defeat ISIS. "The liberation of the last areas in Syria has produced both a large collection of foreign—of terrorist fighters—some 10,000 of them are under lock and key in northeast Syria," Jeffrey said at an August 2019 briefing. "Most of them, about 8,000, are Iraqi or Syrian nationals, and we have efforts in place—they're going slowly—to move—but they're going—to move the Iraqis back to Iraq, and the Syrians to be placed on trial."

 "We don't want to be involved in the border. The border between Turkey and Syria—they've been fighting for hundreds of years, they've been fighting for centuries."

—Oct. 25, 2019 (interview)

Trump frequently and misleadingly says there has been a conflict lasting "hundreds of years" or "centuries" between the Turks and the Kurds, apparently to explain why a U.S. role in the region would be fruitless. This is not only simplistic but historically ignorant and false.

The Kurds' struggles began in earnest only after the collapse of the Ottoman Empire in the 1920s, mainly because their lands were carved up among different nation-states. The Ottoman Empire, with Constantinople (now Istanbul) as its capital, controlled much of the Middle East, Turkey and the Balkans from the 1300s through the early 20th century. Within the empire, there were loosely-defined regions where certain ethnicities was more populous. Being "Kurdish" is rooted in culture and language—not in a political ideology. Even under the Ottoman Empire, ethnic Kurds spoke different dialects depending on where they lived. Under the empire, many countries that exist today were only dreams written about by nationalist intellectuals.

That changed in the 1920s, as colonial powers created new borders to serve their own interests. When the country of Iraq was created under British supervision, the map was drawn to include a large Kurdish population in the north. That's because Kurds generally follow the Sunni branch of Islam, and the British wanted more Sunnis in the nascent country to balance out the Shiite population in the south.

In the century since the collapse of the Ottoman Empire, a drive to create a Kurdish state has been stymied by great powers seeking to flex their muscles against one nation or another in the region. The Kurdish people are not natural enemies of the Turks, and the history of the two peoples fluctuates between periods of peace and conflict.

"So I say to David [Friedman, the U.S. Ambassador to Israel], 'David, let me ask you a question. Jerusalem stone. Let's do the whole damn building in Jerusalem stone.' Huh? 'You got so much Jerusalem stone,' I said. 'Is it available, David?' He said, 'We have so much we don't know what the hell to do with it.' So he has a wall opposite the elevators—rich guy. And I got a whole damn building made out of Jerusalem stone. True. So the end of the story is this: I say, 'David, let's go.'"

—Dec. 7, 2019 (speech)

About a dozen times, Trump has regaled audiences with the story of how he had the brilliant idea of covering the new U.S. embassy in Jerusalem in Jerusalem stone and ordered Friedman to make sure it got done. But Trump had no choice in the matter. Ever since the British mandate in then-Palestine, municipal law has required that all buildings be faced with Jerusalem stone, a local form of limestone with an exceptionally warm, golden hue.

IRAN

 "Obama gave them [Iran] $150 billion. . . . Got zero. He got zero out of it. He got zero. I'd love to have that money back. It's a lot of money."

—Jan. 14, 2020 (campaign rally)

This is one of Trump's favorite claims, which he has made almost 70 times. He cites the "$150 billion" figure to portray Obama as Iran's sucker in the negotiations that led to the international nuclear agreement. But it's incredibly misleading

Trump often makes it sound as though the United States cut a check to Iran, suggesting Obama used taxpayer funds. (In December 2018, Trump made the link explicit: "The Democrats and President Obama gave Iran 150 Billion Dollars and got nothing, but they can't give 5 Billion Dollars for National Security and a Wall?")

But this was always Iran's money. It had been frozen in international financial institutions around the world because of sanctions intended to curb Iran's nuclear ambitions. Many of the funds were held in banks in Asia, including China and India, as well as Turkey. Many countries received waivers to buy Iranian oil and gas despite international sanctions against Iran, but they placed the payments in escrow-style accounts that remained off-limits to Iran. The Islamic Republic also transferred assets to Asian banks from Europe in anticipation of financial sanctions.

Moreover, Trump's "$150 billion" is not credible. It was a high-end estimate (the low-end was $70 billion) that did not take into account Iran's outstanding obligations, such as money stuck in illiquid Chinese projects. The U.S. Treasury Department estimated that once Iran fulfilled these obligations, it would receive about $55 billion. The Central Bank of Iran said the number was actually $32 billion. The precise amount is not clear, but no one except Trump says it amounted to $150 billion. And the money was returned only because Iran signed on to the nuclear agreement after years of negotiations.

Obama administration officials, including Secretary of State John Kerry, acknowledged that some of the money released to Iran may have ended up in the pockets of designated terrorist organizations funded by Iran. But they said Treasury would closely monitor the spending and take further action if necessary. Officials anticipated most of it would go to bolster an economy devastated by years of sanctions.

 "President Obama paid $1.8 billion in cash, whoever saw a million dollars piled up as a promotion in hundred-dollar bills?"

—Sept. 9, 2019 (campaign rally)

This is another Trump favorite, which he often mentions in tandem with the alleged $150 billion. Trump gets the number close to right—it was really $1.7 billion—but he always leaves out important context. This again was Iran's money—which was owed by the United States.

Before the 1979 Islamic revolution, Iran under the shah was reputedly the biggest buyer of U.S. military equipment, depositing funds for potential deals into a Defense Department account. When Iran seized U.S. Embassy staffers as hostages, the Carter administration froze the military sales account. This issue—and other outstanding claims—has been litigated ever since through a tribunal established in The Hague. Some of the money in the account was used to pay U.S. companies whose contracts with Iran were canceled, but about $400 million was left in what was known as the Foreign Military Sales Trust Fund account. When Obama became president, that money still had not been paid back to Iran, and interest was building.

The resolution of the long-frozen account certainly looks unusual on its face. On Jan. 17, 2016, the day after four American detainees, including *The Washington Post*'s long-imprisoned Tehran correspondent, Jason Rezaian, were released in a prisoner exchange, a jumbo jet carrying $400 million in euros, Swiss francs and other currencies landed in Tehran. That was the $400 million that had been frozen since 1979. Soon after, $1.3 billion in cash followed. That was the amount the Obama administration negotiated as the interest owed on the debt.

State Department officials insisted the negotiations over the claims and detainees were not connected but came together at the same time, with the cash payment used as "leverage" to ensure the release of detainees.

Obama administration officials claimed that without a deal with Iran, The Hague tribunal might have imposed an even higher interest penalty on the United States. (Experts agreed that was likely.) U.S. officials said the transfer was made in cash, rather than by wire, as previous claims reached through The Hague tribunal were paid, to ease the impact of increasingly tough sanctions imposed on Iran. If time was of the essence, cash was the best way to go.

 "President Obama made a deal that was an outrage. The Iran deal, which, frankly, in five or six years of a short period of time they'd be allowed to make nuclear weapons. They cannot have nuclear weapons."

—June 14, 2019 (interview)

The nuclear accord was reached after years of negotiations over Iran's nuclear ambitions, culminating in 2015 during Obama's administration. It was by many accounts the most complex and detailed international nuclear agreement ever reached—159 pages with five annexes. It was officially known as the Joint Comprehensive Plan of Action (JCPOA).

We doubt Trump ever read the JCPOA closely, but he has denounced it as a "terrible" deal and withdrew the United States from it in 2018. Many of the claims he makes about it are simply wrong, such as saying on numerous occasions that it was going to "expire very soon."

As a signatory to the international Non-Proliferation Treaty, Iran has pledged not to develop nuclear weapons—ever. In agreeing to the JCPOA, Iran recommitted itself to the Non-Proliferation Treaty. Under the nuclear deal, after 2026, Iran would be free to develop, test and use more advanced types of uranium-enriching centrifuges and upgrade a nuclear facility in Natanz. But Iran would continue to be limited to peaceful programs; developing nuclear weapons would remain banned.

Whether one can trust the Iranians not to divert nuclear fuel for weapons-making is another matter. Critics have warned that Iran could develop a "breakout capability" unless great safeguards were added. But rather than work with allies to strengthen JCPOA, Trump dumped it entirely, saying he would seek a new agreement. But no progress has been made on restarting negotiations.

 "They're allowed to test ballistic missiles. You're not allowed to go to various sites to check. And some of those sites are the most obvious sites for the creation or the making of nuclear weapons."

—Aug. 26, 2019 (news conference)

Trump is wrong about inspections. The International Atomic Energy Agency said the Iran deal created the "world's most robust" nuclear inspection effort.

Under the JCPOA, Iran's declared nuclear sites, such as the Natanz uranium enrichment facility, will be under continuous monitoring by the International Atomic Energy Agency—and inspectors would have immediate access. Under the deal, Iran will have limits for 10 years on the enrichment permitted at Natanz; the IAEA can keep close tabs on production. The JCPOA allows international monitoring of Iran's centrifuge production and storage facilities, the procurement chain, and the mining and milling of uranium—verification measures that many experts say exceed previous nuclear deals.

The deal also addressed what to do if regulators learn of suspicious activity at an undeclared site. The IAEA can demand instant access—but Iran could refuse. So the JCPOA sets up a process to resolve the standoff, described in a 29-page document known as Annex 1, that could take up to 24 days to resolve.

This provision was added to remove a loophole in an agreement that requires Iran to give the IAEA access to suspect sites within 24 hours but does not mandate immediate consequences for a nation that refuses access. Some critics have said the 24-day timeframe is too long for resolving conflicts, but that's not the same as having no access, as Trump claimed.

As for missiles, it's worth recalling that the JCPOA was the product of lengthy negotiations. Iran insisted the deal was limited to the nuclear program, not its missile program. Limits on Iran's ballistic missiles thus have been handled under U.N. Security Council resolutions, including the one that implemented the nuclear deal, which helped slow Iran's missile development.

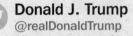

Donald J. Trump
@realDonaldTrump

"Just out that the Obama Administration granted citizenship, during the terrible Iran Deal negotiation, to 2,500 Iranians—including to government officials. How big (and bad) is that?"—July 3, 2018

This claim on Trump's Twitter feed appears to have originated with Mojtaba Zonnour, a hard-line cleric and member of Iran's parliament who has criticized the JCPOA and President Hassan Rouhani for striking the deal. In June 2019, Zonnour gave an interview to the Iranian newspaper *Etemad*, and his comments were then reported by Fars, a semiofficial news agency known for its ties to Iranian hard-liners.

The White House refused to explain why Trump made this claim; neither would the Homeland Security and State departments. We concluded it was bunk.

Two senior Obama administration officials who had authority over immigration matters told The Fact Checker that they had no knowledge of the Obama administration offering citizenship or green cards to 2,500 Iranians as part of the JCPOA negotiations. Both officials said the claim was highly implausible, since such an offer would have required high-level authorization, and they had no indication that authorization was requested or given. Ben Rhodes, a key player in the nuclear negotiations, said he had never heard of the figure and that citizenship visas were not part of the JCPOA talks.

NORTH KOREA

"Look, he [North Korean leader Kim Jong Un] likes me; I like him. We get along. He's representing his country. I'm representing my country. We have to do what we have to do. But he did sign a contract. He did sign an agreement, talking about denuclearization. And that was signed. Number one sentence: denuclearization."

—Dec. 31, 2019 (remarks)

The evolution of Trump's policy on North Korea is astonishing. On Nov. 7, 2017, speaking in South Korea, the president denounced the North Korean regime, saying: "Citizens spy on fellow citizens, their homes are subject to search at any time, and their every action is subject to surveillance. In place of a vibrant society, the people of North Korea are bombarded by state propaganda practically every waking hour of the day. North Korea is a country ruled as a cult."

Seven months later, Trump met face-to-face with Kim in Singapore, the first time a U.S. president sat down with a North Korean leader. "His country does love him. His people, you see the fervor. They have a great fervor," Trump said after the meeting.

Complex diplomatic initiatives usually work the opposite way: Lower-level officials reach a series of agreements over months or years of talks, resulting in a summit meeting to finalize the deal. Trump, eager for a made-for-television event, opted to go straight to the summit without substantial agreements in place.

The problem with that approach is demonstrated by the document Trump and Kim Jong Un signed in June 2018. Trump is wrong to call it "a contract." It was remarkably vague, leaving much to interpretation and debate, especially compared to previous documents signed by North Korea. Pyongyang has a long history of making agreements and then not living up to their obligations, but apparently Trump is not aware that the language in earlier agreements was tougher.

The third sentence—not the first, as Trump claims—of the statement says that North Korea commits to "work towards the complete denuclearization of the Korean Peninsula." The phrase is not defined and "towards" is rather weak. In the past, North Korea viewed "denuclearization" to mean the United States removing the nuclear umbrella it provides to Japan and South Korea. There was no indication in the documents that its definition has changed, and North Korea later confirmed that that remains its interpretation of the phrase.

By contrast, in 2005, North Korea (officially the Democratic People's Republic of Korea, or DPRK) signed a document with the United States and four regional neighbors that said: "The DPRK committed to abandoning all nuclear weapons and existing nuclear programs and returning, at an early date, to the Treaty on the Nonproliferation of Nuclear Weapons and to IAEA [International Atomic Energy Agency] safeguards." (That deal later fell apart.)

> "Our relationship with North Korea has been very good. We've really established a good relationship with Kim Jong Un. I have personally. There's no rocket testing. There's no missile testing."
> —July 22, 2019 (remarks)

Trump and Kim met twice more, in February and June 2019, when Trump stepped over the Demilitarized Zone to become the first U.S. president to set foot on North Korean soil. No further agreements were reached, but Trump continued to depict the relationship as a success even as experts said Pyongyang continued to improve its nuclear and missile programs. Trump even made excuses for Kim, dismissing the missile tests as "short-range," not "ballistic missiles tests" and claiming that Kim was "not happy with the testing." But

North Korea had indeed tested ballistic missiles, and it soon moved on to test submarine-launched ballistic missiles that landed in Japan's territorial waters off its coastline.

The Washington Post reported that U.S. spy agencies are seeing signs that North Korea was constructing new missiles at a factory that produced the country's first intercontinental ballistic missiles capable of reaching the United States. Even the president's national security adviser at the time, John Bolton, said North Korea continues to make the fuel needed for nuclear weapons and testing missiles in violation of sanctions. "North Korea has been building new missiles, new capabilities, new weapons as fast as anybody on the planet with the 115th most powerful economy in the world," Air Force Gen. John Hyten said in January 2020.

 "When I took over—when I became President, North Korea was ready to go to war. We were, I think, headed to a war."

—July 16, 2019 (remarks)

 "I think we've made more progress than anybody has made in—ever, frankly, with regard to North Korea."

—Sept. 24, 2018 (remarks)

In typical Trumpian fashion, the president hypes the problem before he was elected and then oversells his achievements. There is no evidence the United States was ready to go to war under Obama, though Obama had warned Trump that his biggest foreign policy challenge would likely be North Korea.

Trump met with Kim but has little to show for it. Previous presidents made more headway in restraining Pyongyang's nuclear ambitions, though ultimately, they too were unsuccessful. In 1994, Bill Clinton negotiated a nuclear agreement with North Korea that froze its plutonium program, and he was working on a missile deal when he left office. But that agreement fell apart under George W. Bush. Then Bush tried to negotiate a deal working with regional partners, even lifting sanctions on North Korea. But those tentative agreements fell apart as well by the time he left office.

After the failure of the Bush administration's efforts, Obama adopted a policy of "strategic patience," gradually escalating sanctions while refusing to negotiate with Pyongyang until it gave up its nuclear weapons program. The Obama administration reached a short-lived agreement with North Korea in 2012 to suspend its nuclear weapons tests and uranium enrichment and allow international inspectors to monitor its main nuclear complex. By the end of Obama's presidency, he was no closer to resolving the problem, and North Korea had greatly improved its nuclear and missile capability.

Trump never would admit it, but he effectively has adopted the same policy of strategic patience as long as Pyongyang does not make provocative moves, such as nuclear tests.

 "[President Obama] called Kim Jong Un on numerous occasions to meet. President Obama wanted to meet with Kim Jong Un. And Kim Jong Un said no. Numerous occasions he called. . . . During President Obama, they were nuclear testing. They were sending missiles. Right now, everything is nice and quiet."

—July 5, 2019 (remarks)

No public records or news articles show that Obama ever tried to meet with Kim. Former U.S. intelligence officials and experts on North Korea said they knew of no evidence for Trump's claim. Many of Obama's top advisers on North Korea said Trump's claim was false, taking to Twitter to denounce the claim as "horseshit." As we have noted, Obama's strategy after 2012 was to escalate sanctions and avoid entreaties to North Korea. He very clearly told the world he was not interested in a meeting.

> "One of the things that, really, I'm happy, is that the soldiers that died in Korea, their remains are going to be coming back home. And we have thousands of people that have asked for that. Thousands and thousands of people. So many people asked for that, when I was on the campaign. I'd say, 'Wait a minute, I don't have any relationship.' But they said, 'When you can, President, we'd love our son to be brought back home,' you know, the remains."
>
> —June 13, 2018 (interview)

It is all but impossible for Trump to have had such conversations during the campaign—at least as often as he claims. He's frequently suggested that he had conversations with parents of Korean War dead, but a parent of a son who served in the Korean War would likely be well more than 100 years old. Assuming that the average age of mothers of service members born in 1934 was between 20 and 29, such mothers would have been between 102 and 111 years old during the 2016 campaign.

Fifty-five sets of skeletal remains were given to the U.S. military after the first Trump-Kim summit, but the Pentagon later abandoned efforts to work with North Korea on the issue, saying it had been unable to coordinate with the North Korean army regarding any resumption of joint recovery operations.

ALLIES

 "Now, and [NATO] Secretary [Jens] Stoltenberg, I think he's terrific. In my first year, I raised $130 billion from them, not from us, and now he just announced $530 billion all because of me."

—Jan. 10, 2020 (interview)

This is an example of how the president sometimes fails at basic math.

Trump is incorrectly adding together two numbers. As described in Chapter One, since 2006, NATO guidelines have asked each member country to spend at least 2 percent of its gross domestic product on defense. In 2014, NATO decided to increase its spending in response to Russia's seizure of Ukraine's Crimea region.

NATO estimates that its European members and Canada will spend $130 billion on defense over the four years between 2016 and 2020. NATO expected the countries to spend another $270 billion in the following four years, ending in 2024, for an eight-year total of $400 billion. But Trump has repeatedly added the four-year total and the eight-year total together to come up with a fanciful $530 billion—all the while falsely giving himself all of the credit for the spending increase.

 "Well, they [NATO] build an office building for $3 billion. They do lots of things that they shouldn't be doing, before I got here."

—Jan. 10, 2020 (interview)

NATO's new headquarters cost about $1.23 billion, according to the NATO budget and current exchange rates. When Trump first saw the building in 2017, he remarked: "I never asked once what the new NATO headquarters cost. I refuse to do that, but it is beautiful."

 "I picked up $500 million with one phone call to a country. And that's just the beginning. And I've done it with many other countries. Anyway, but just over the last very short period of time—one phone call that lasted for a period of, I would say, five minutes, I picked up $500 million because I said: 'You're not taking care of us. We're taking care of you, but you're not taking care. It's not fair.'"

—May 9, 2019 (remarks)

 "South Korea—we defend them and lose a tremendous amount of money. Billions of dollars a year defending them. . . . And working with Secretary Pompeo and John Bolton, they agreed to pay, yesterday, $500 million more toward their defense. Five hundred million, with a couple of phone calls. I said, 'Why didn't you do this before?' They said, 'Nobody asked.' . . . But South Korea is costing us $5 billion a year. . . . So they've agreed to pay $500 million more."

—Feb. 12, 2019 (remarks)

This is totally false, from the imaginary phone call to the numbers cited by Trump. The United States neither spends $5 billion a year on defending South Korea nor did the Koreans agree to pay $500 million more. The United States and South Korea signed a mutual defense treaty in 1953, after the United States led a U.N. force that helped repel an invasion from North Korea. U.S. troops have been stationed in South Korea for more than a half-century, and the two countries began to share costs under agreements dating to 1991. The United States keeps nearly 28,500 troops in South Korea, not just to defend that country but to further its own interests in the region.

Under a longstanding agreement, South Korea paid nearly $830 million a year to host U.S. forces; by contrast, the United States spent about $1.25 billion annually to maintain its military presence there. Prior to 2009, the two countries paid roughly an equal amount toward the U.S. presence, but the cost of the operation has risen since then, shifting more of the burden to Washington. (Separately, South Korea covered 90 percent of the cost of a new military base that came with a $10.8 billion price tag. It's the largest U.S. military base overseas.)

Trump administration officials asked South Korea to increase their contribution by 50 percent, and after many rounds of negotiations spanning nearly a year—not a single phone call—the two sides agreed to an 8.2 percent increase, the same level as South Korea's defense budget increase in 2019. That's a $70 million jump, not $500 million.

 "As you know, we were having a lot of problems with the Philippines. The relationship with the past administration was horrible, to use a nice word. I would say 'horrible' is putting it mildly. You know what happened. Many of you were there, and you never got to land. The plane came close but it didn't land."

—Nov. 14, 2017 (remarks)

Trump has made this bizarre claim four times, even making a sweeping motion with his hand to indicate a landing plane when he made this last statement. But Barack Obama's two visits to the Philippines, in 2014 and 2015, when Benigno S. Aquino III was president, were unremarkable, and he was greeted warmly.

Trump appears to be confusing a presidential visit with Obama's decision to cancel a 2016 meeting during a conference of leaders in Asia with Philippine President Rodrigo Duterte.

Duterte had said he would call Obama a "son of a bitch" if the U.S. president questioned extrajudicial killings that Duterte had ordered in a sweeping crackdown on drug trafficking. (At the time, more than 2,400 people had been killed since Duterte took office, and Obama made it clear he planned to raise his concerns.) Obama initially shrugged off Duterte's insult, calling him "a colorful guy." Obama wanted to be sure "if I'm having a meeting, it's productive and we're getting something done."

Apparently, he did not get that satisfaction, as the White House announced Obama had replaced the planned meeting with Duterte with one with South Korean President Park Geun-hye. After the cancellation, Duterte scrambled to make amends. His office expressed regret that his comments "came across as a personal attack." Duterte's press service then said he would be seated next to Obama at an Association of Southeast Asian Nations (ASEAN) gala dinner in Laos the next day, but that did not happen. They did shake hands, however.

The number of people killed in the crackdown had risen to more than 7,000 by the time Trump became president. During Trump's 2017 trip to the Philippines, he appears to have barely raised the issue, if at all.

U.S. MILITARY

 "Our military was depleted to a level that we had very little ammunition. I was actually told we had no ammunition. Now we have more ammunition than we've ever had."

—Oct. 21, 2019 (remarks)

 "We had a general come to my office—respected general. And we were having big trouble with one country—first week in office, very early. He said, 'Sir, we have no ammunition.' I said, 'You know what? We're going to have ammunition—a lot of it. And hopefully we'll never going to have to use it, but we have a lot of it.'"

—Oct. 12, 2019 (speech)

This is a good example of how Trump's most-repeated claims tend to become more exaggerated over time. He initially hedged, saying "we were very low . . . I don't want to say 'no ammunition.'" But over time the hedges disappeared.

What's going on? Near the end of Obama's term, military leaders publicly warned that stockpiles of precision-guided munitions (PGM) were running low after targeting Islamic State operatives with tens of thousands of smart bombs and guided missiles.

Trump has taken this claim to the extreme. It's a huge exaggeration to say the U.S. military had run out of ammunition when Trump took office.

Trump never limits his comments to PGMs and instead gives the impression that all ammunition was running out. No military official has claimed that munitions, whether PGMs or for any other kind of weapon, were depleted, and officials in the Obama administration had already started to fix the problem by the time he took office.

 "We are massively increasing our military budget to historic levels."

—Nov. 15, 2017 (prepared speech)

Trump has made a claim along these lines nearly 150 times, but it is misleading. In constant dollars, the military budget peaked in 2010 ($719 billion in 2012 dollars). There was a decline starting in 2011 because Congress passed the Budget Control Act to reduce the federal budget deficit. Under Trump, the effort to reduce the deficit has been abandoned, but in the 2020 budget, the Defense Department is getting $653 billion in 2012 dollars, or almost ten percent less than in 2010.

 "So when you have a system that allows Sergeant Bergdahl to go, and you probably had five to six people killed—nobody even knows the number, because he left—and he gets a slap on the wrist, if that; and then you have a system where these warriors get put in jail for 25 years—I'm going to stick up for our warrior."

—Nov. 25, 2019 (remarks)

Trump referred to the case of Army soldier Bowe Bergdahl to justify his controversial decision to restore the rank and pay grade of a Navy SEAL who was convicted of taking a photo with a deceased teenage ISIS fighter in 2017. Bergdahl deserted in Afghanistan in 2009 and was held by the Taliban until Obama arranged a prisoner swap in 2014.

Trump said "five or six people" were killed after Bergdahl deserted his unit. But *Stars and Stripes* newspaper reported in 2016 that there is no evidence these soldiers died while searching for Bergdahl. "They were all killed in August and September, after the exhausting search effectively had been called off and the mission had changed to secure upcoming Afghanistan elections, according to court testimony," the report said.

 "Iran went in, and they hit us with missiles. Shouldn't have done that, but they hit us. Fortunately for them, nobody was hurt, nobody was killed. Nothing happened. They landed—and very little damage even, to the base."

—Jan. 9, 2020 (speech)

In January 2020, the United States, acting on Trump's order, launched a drone strike and assassinated a top Iranian general, Qasem Soleimani, the commander of the Quds Force and an architect of attacks on American troops. After the assassination, Iran retaliated by lobbing missiles on a facility in western Iraq that housed U.S. service members, the Ain al-Asad air base. Despite Trump's assurances that no U.S. soldiers were hurt in the attack, the Pentagon admitted a week later that eleven U.S. troops had been injured. Eight U.S. service members were evacuated to an American base in Germany, and the other three were sent to Camp Arifjan in Kuwait. The blast from the Iranian attack threw at least two soldiers through the window of a meters-high tower. The Pentagon eventually admitted that 109 U.S. service members had been diagnosed with traumatic brain injuries; the eight soldiers who had been treated in Germany were sent to the U.S. for treatment. Trump later dismissed their injuries as "headaches," prompting a rare complaint and demand for an apology from the Veterans of Foreign Wars.

TRUMP'S CRYSTAL BALL

"I PREDICTED OSAMA BIN LADEN"

In speeches and interviews, Trump has claimed that well before the 9/11 attacks, he warned that al-Qaeda leader Osama bin Laden was a threat—was going to "do damage" to the United States. Trump claims he even predicted the rise of terrorism. "But nobody ever heard of Osama bin Laden until, really, the World Trade Center," Trump told an audience on Oct. 27, 2019. "But about a year—you'll have to check—a year, year and a half before the World Trade Center came down, the book came out. I was talking about Osama bin Laden."

His claim is ridiculous. Trump's book, "The America We Deserve," was published in January 2000, when he was considering a presidential run under the Reform Party banner. There is only a single, offhand reference to bin Laden in the 304-page volume: "One day we're told that a shadowy figure with no fixed address named Osama bin-Laden is public enemy number one, and U.S. jetfighters lay waste to his camp in Afghanistan. He escapes back under some rock, and a few news cycles later it's on to a new enemy and new crisis."

Even if his claim were true, Trump would have been echoing predictions by experts, news organizations and even bin Laden himself, who in media interviews in 1998 indicated that he planned to attack the United States.

For instance, here's a 1999 CNN headline: "Bin Laden feared to be planning terrorist attack." The article started: "U.S. officials fear that suspected terrorist Osama bin Laden 'may be in the final stages' of planning an attack against the United States."

"I PREDICTED BREXIT"

Trump often claims that on the day before Brexit—the June 23, 2016, referendum on whether the United Kingdom should leave the European Union—he predicted that Brexit supporters would win. Polls at the time had indicated a narrow edge for supporters of remaining in the EU.

"You know that I was a fan of Brexit," he told reporters while visiting London on Dec 3, 2019. "I called it the day before. I was opening up Turnberry the day before Brexit."

Trump's timeline is all mixed up, despite his claim to having "one of the great memories of all time."

On March 23, three months before the vote, Trump was optimistic that Brexit would succeed. "I think that Britain will separate from the EU," he said on British TV. "I think that maybe it's time, especially in light of what's happened with the craziness that is going on with immigration, with people pouring in all over the place, I think that Britain will end up separating from the EU."

Trump added, "I'm not endorsing it one way or the other."

But by June 22, the day before the vote, he was no longer so sure. "I don't think anybody should listen to me because I haven't really focused on it very much," he told Fox Business.

As for being at Turnberry, his golf club in Scotland, he was there the day after the vote, not the day before, to cut a ribbon for the ceremonial opening of his golf course.

CHAPTER NINE

Trump on Impeachment:
"A Perfect Phone Call"

On July 24, 2019, the former special counsel, Robert S. Mueller III, testified before Congress about his two-year investigation into possible coordination between the Trump campaign and Russian entities and whether Trump had tried to obstruct the investigation. It was an anticlimactic moment. Mueller's report, released three months earlier, could not establish coordination between the campaign and Russia, though it said Trump welcomed Russia's help. The report also said it could not exonerate Trump of committing crimes in trying to thwart the inquiry—an obtuse formulation that Trump promptly spun into "NO COLLUSION, NO OBSTRUCTION, TOTAL EXONERATION."

During his testimony, Mueller was halting and imprecise. Any effort in the House of Representatives to impeach Trump over the report's numerous examples of possible obstruction quickly lost steam. For Trump, the threat of impeachment had evaporated.

The very next day, sitting in the White House residence, Trump placed a call to Ukrainian President Volodymyr Zelensky. Two years of the Russia investigation had led to a muddled stalemate; now, a single phone call would lead in five short months to only the third impeachment of a president in the nation's history.

On the call, Trump cryptically suggested a link between a Ukrainian investigation of former vice president Joe Biden, Trump's potential 2020 rival, and favors for Zelensky—a promised White House meeting and delivery of U.S. military aid. Some administration officials listening in on the call were so shocked by Trump's blunt and threatening language that within weeks, a whistleblower submitted a report to Congress, resulting in an investigation, a vote to impeach Trump and, eventually, his trial and acquittal in the Senate. The probe uncovered how Trump had urged his personal lawyer, Rudolph W. Giuliani, to press the Ukrainian government to investigate Biden. The president was serious about this: When the U.S. ambassador got in the way, she was fired. The House's investigation revealed how, on a flimsy pretext, the president personally intervened to halt U.S. aid to Ukraine that Congress had authorized.

Mueller's investigation into Russian interference was clearly on Trump's mind as he asked Zelensky to help him out. "I would like you to do us a favor though, because our country has been through a lot and Ukraine knows a lot about it," Trump said on the call, rambling about "the server, they say Ukraine has it. . . . As you saw yesterday, that whole nonsense ended with a very poor performance by a man named Robert Mueller, an incompetent performance, but they say a lot of it started with Ukraine."

Russian intelligence had spread the fiction that Ukraine, not Russia, had intervened in the 2016 election—and Trump's aides had warned him it was a fantasy. Yet he believed it anyway, leading to his request that Ukraine interfere in the 2020 U.S. election process, which in turn led to Trump's impeachment. Testimony from congressional hearings established that Trump was mainly interested in Ukraine announcing an investigation. Trump hoped to get information that could be weaponized for electoral purposes, as questions about Hillary Clinton's email server had been in 2016. Trump didn't care whether the investigations were real, according to Gordon Sondland, Trump's ambassador to the European Union.

Trump responded to the threat of impeachment with a blizzard of misinformation, often echoed by his strongest allies. He barred many top officials from testifying and blocked congressional requests for documents. Then he claimed he did not get a fair hearing from Congress. Whether Trump's actions amounted to impeachable conduct deeply split Democrats and Republicans. About a dozen House and Senate Republicans said they were troubled by Trump's behavior, but only one, Sen. Mitt Romney of Utah, said it warranted removal from office.

Trump refused to admit any error, insisting that his phone call was "perfect," his actions justified and his political opponents guilty of trying to overthrow the government. After his acquittal, Trump made note of the few Republicans who had criticized him, yet he stuck to his claim of perfection: "I had some that said, 'Oh, I wish you didn't make the call.' And that's okay, if they need that. It's incorrect. It's totally incorrect."

THE INITIAL FALSE CLAIMS

 "The Democrats, a lot of it had to do, they say, with Ukraine. It's very interesting. It's very interesting. They have this server, right? From the DNC, Democratic National Committee. The FBI went in and they told them, 'Get out of here. You're not getting it. We're not giving it to you.' They gave the server to CrowdStrike or whatever it's called, which is a company owned by a very wealthy Ukrainian. And I still

want to see that server. You know, the FBI has never gotten that server. That's a big part of this whole thing. Why did they give it to a Ukrainian company?"

—Nov. 22, 2019 (interview)

When Trump made these remarks on "Fox and Friends," his favorite morning TV show, host Steve Doocy was moved to ask: "Are you sure they did that? Are you sure they gave it to Ukraine?" It was a rare moment of doubt on a show that serves as the president's booster-in-chief.

The interview took place the day after Fiona Hill, Trump's former top Russia adviser, told Congress that any notion that Ukraine intervened in the 2016 election was a hoax hatched by the Russian regime to deflect from its well-documented efforts to interfere in the U.S. vote. But Trump wouldn't let go of this theory.

Trump first publicly raised this notion shortly after he became president, in an April 2017 interview with the Associated Press. He brought it up again in his July 2019 phone call with Zelensky: "The server, they say Ukraine has it."

But just about everything Trump says about this is wrong.

- The server (actually, there's more than one) is not in Ukraine; it's in Washington, displayed at the Democratic National Committee's offices beside a filing cabinet the Watergate burglars pried open in 1972. The *New York Times* even ran a photo of this DNC server on its front page in 2016.
- It doesn't matter that the FBI never took physical possession of the DNC servers that were hacked. Agents obtained complete copies of the hard-drive images made by CrowdStrike, the tech security company that first identified that the DNC had been hacked by Russian operatives. Then–FBI Director James

B. Comey testified that his staff told him that this arrangement was an "appropriate substitute" for possession of the servers. Mueller's investigation confirmed CrowdStrike's findings; 12 Russian intelligence officers were indicted in 2018 for their alleged role in the breach.

- CrowdStrike co-founder Dmitri Alperovitch is a cyber and national security expert who was born in Russia and now is a U.S. citizen; he is not Ukrainian.
- CrowdStrike is not a Ukrainian company. Founded in 2011 in Sunnyvale, Calif., it trades on the Nasdaq stock exchange under the symbol CRWD. It went public about a month before Trump's call with Zelensky, earning headlines for a stock price that popped as much as 97 percent in its first day of trading.

 "Biden, he calls them and says, 'Don't you dare prosecute, if you don't fire this prosecutor'—The prosecutor was after his son. Then he said, 'If you fire the prosecutor, you'll be okay. And if you don't fire the prosecutor, we're not giving you $2 billion in loan guarantees,' or whatever he was supposed to give."

—May 19, 2019 (interview)

"We have him [Biden] on tape with corruption. I mean, he's getting the prosecutor for, I guess, John, it was $2 billion—saying, 'We're not giving you the $2 billion'—or whatever the amount was—'unless you get rid of this prosecutor.' And then he goes, 'Lo and behold, the prosecutor was gone.' . . . He's been hit. And he's been caught red-handed."

—Oct. 9, 2019 (remarks)

"You know full well that Vice President Biden used his office and $1 billion of U.S. aid money to coerce Ukraine into firing the prosecutor who was digging into the company paying his son millions of dollars."

—Dec. 17, 2019 (statement)

These false allegations are at the core of Trump's demand for a probe from the Ukrainian government. "There's a lot of talk about Biden's son, that Biden stopped the prosecution," Trump told Zelensky. "It sounds horrible to me." Trump first spelled out his story in a May 2019 interview with Fox News, two months before the Ukraine call, and then repeated the tale in remarks and interviews more than 30 times before his impeachment trial.

Then–Vice President Biden's role in Ukraine, and his son's involvement there, make for a complex story. Trump seized on kernels of truth to build an appearance of scandal that resonated with his supporters and raised questions in some voters' minds. Trump argued that Biden had demanded a quid pro quo from the Ukrainians, the same charge Democrats lobbed at Trump. But at its core, Trump's tale was a fiction: There had been no prosecution or investigation of Biden's son Hunter, and Joe Biden's actions in Ukraine were fully coordinated with the State Department and America's European allies.

Here's what really happened: During Obama's second term, Biden was in charge of the Ukraine portfolio, keeping in close touch with the country's president, Petro Poroshenko. Biden's brief was to sweet-talk and jawbone Poroshenko into making reforms that Ukraine's Western benefactors wanted to see as part of Ukraine's escape from Russia's orbit. But the Americans saw an obstacle to reform in Viktor Shokin, the top Ukrainian prosecutor whom the United States viewed as ineffective and beholden to Poroshenko and Ukraine's corrupt oligarchs.

The U.S. embassy in Kyiv proposed that Biden, during his 2015 visit there, use a pending delivery of $1 billion in loan guarantees as leverage to force reform. Biden addressed the Ukrainian parliament, decrying the "cancer of corruption" in the country and criticizing the prosecutor's office. During that visit, Biden privately told Poroshenko that the loan guarantees would be withheld unless Shokin was replaced. After repeated calls and meetings between the two men over several months, Shokin was removed and the loan guarantees were provided.

Trump had it completely backward. Biden was thwarting corruption, not abetting it.

But Biden had exaggerated what happened. At a January 2018 Council on Foreign Relations event, he bragged about firing the Ukrainian prosecutor, telescoping the timeline from months of diplomacy into hours. "I'm leaving in six hours," Biden claimed he had said. "If the prosecutor is not fired, you're not getting the money. Well, son of a bitch, he got fired."

As the 2020 presidential campaign heated up, Trump's allies circulated a video of Biden's boast, making it appear as if Biden were a shakedown artist.

Meanwhile, in 2014, Hunter Biden had joined the board of Burisma, a Ukrainian natural gas company that was owned by a Ukrainian oligarch, Mykola Zlochevsky. Hunter Biden showed questionable judgment in taking such a position while his father had a high-profile role in U.S.-Ukraine relations, and the possible conflict of interest was well-documented in news reports at the time. Biden had offered U.S. aid to Ukraine to increase its gas production, which could benefit the country's energy industry.

But contrary to Trump's theory, there was no probe of Burisma; rather, Ukrainian prosecutors led by Shokin in 2014 opened an investigation of Zlochevsky for illicit enrichment and money laundering. But then Ukrainian prosecutors let the investigations go dormant, angering the U.S. State Department. The American ambassador said in 2015 that mismanagement of the case was an example of Ukraine's failure to hold corrupt officials to account.

Years after Biden forced the ouster of Shokin, the former prosecutor cried foul, falsely claiming that he was removed because he had had Burisma in his sights—a story he peddled to Trump's allies. The real reason the Americans wanted Shokin out was his own apparent corruption: George Kent, a Ukraine expert who served as deputy assistant secretary of state for European affairs, described Shokin as "a typical Ukraine prosecutor who lived a lifestyle far in excess of his government salary, who never prosecuted anybody known for having committed a crime" and who "covered up crimes that were known to have been committed."

In 2019, the prosecutor general of Ukraine, Yuriy Lutsenko, said "he had no evidence of wrongdoing by U.S. Democratic presidential candidate Joe Biden or his son." He added: "Hunter Biden did not violate any Ukrainian laws."

 "Then [Hunter] Biden flies to China. . . . But he flies with his father, who is then vice president, and in 10 minutes, he picks up $1.5 billion for his fund."

—Nov. 6, 2019 (campaign rally)

 "Hunter Biden walked away with a billion and a half dollars from China."

—Oct. 11, 2019 (remarks)

As part of his campaign against Joe Biden, Trump consistently targeted Hunter Biden. Again, he shamelessly spun a web of allegations based on flimsy evidence.

Any offspring of a prominent politician needs to be wary of even the appearance of a conflict of interest between the child's business interests and the parent's political position. Hunter Biden has led a troubled life, yet he has managed to score big business deals in Ukraine and China that might not have materialized without his father's prominence. Similarly, Ivanka Trump was granted Chinese trademarks in 2018, days before and after President Trump vowed to save jobs at ZTE, a major Chinese telecommunications company. She also was granted Chinese trademarks in 2017, on the same day she sat next to Chinese President Xi Jinping at a dinner.

Trump, naturally, chose to focus on Biden's son, not his own daughter. He claimed that Hunter Biden "made millions of dollars from China" and "took money from China—a lot of money." He also said that Hunter Biden walked out of China with "$1.5 billion in a fund . . . after one quick meeting and he flies in on Air Force Two."

There is no evidence to support those statements, but again Trump exaggerated kernels of truth—just enough to outline a portrait of malfeasance.

In December 2013, Hunter Biden and one of his daughters flew from Japan to China with Joe Biden on Air Force Two as the vice president embarked on a diplomatic mission. Twelve days after arriving in Beijing, Hunter Biden joined an advisory board of a Chinese American fund called BHR Partners, which had announced it would try to raise $1.5 billion for investments outside China. The fundraising apparently fell short of that, but Trump seized on the figure and repeated it at least 30 times.

As far as we could determine, Hunter Biden was not a direct investor in the fund, instead advising those who did invest. George Mesires, a lawyer for Hunter Biden, said the former vice president's son took an equity stake worth $420,000 in BHR Partners in 2017, after Joe Biden was no longer in the White House.

Nevertheless, the *New Yorker* magazine reported that during the China trip, Hunter Biden arranged for his father to shake hands with Jonathan Li, who ran a Chinese private-equity fund and was a co-founder of BHR. Hunter Biden seemed to trade off his father's name, and certainly arranging a handshake between a potential business partner in China and the vice president raised eyebrows. After Trump's frequent attacks, Hunter Biden announced on Oct. 31, 2019, that he had resigned from the BHR board.

THE PHONE CALL

 "I think it's a disgrace that people can make impeachment out of nothing. That was a perfect conversation."

—Dec. 10, 2019 (remarks)

 "This is based on a perfect phone call. Did anybody read the transcript? It's a perfect call."

—Jan. 14, 2020 (campaign rally)

Donald J. Trump
@realDonaldTrump

"I JUST GOT IMPEACHED FOR MAKING A PERFECT PHONE CALL!"—Jan. 16, 2020

When the outlines of the whistleblower's allegations became known, Trump responded with a bold but risky strategy: He authorized the release of a rough transcript of his phone call with Zelensky and then repeatedly—about 100 times—described the call as "perfect." He said the transcript showed that the whistleblower account was false, even though the transcript demonstrated that virtually every detail in the report was correct.

Trump's release of the rough transcript created the illusion of transparency—what did he have to hide if he released the transcript?—even as he ordered top officials not to cooperate with any House inquiry, either through testimony or release of documents. He also signaled to his supporters that he would, as ever, hold a firm line—no regrets, no backsliding, no apology.

The conversation with Zelensky was no typical call. Normally, a president, speaking to a foreign counterpart, works off a set of carefully prepared talking points that cover a range of issues. Trump appeared to have no agenda except to ask the Ukrainian government to work with his private attorney to investigate a potential 2020 presidential rival and look into debunked conspiracy theories about possible interference by Ukraine in the 2016 election. For his part, Zelensky wanted a firm date for a White House meeting, which Trump dangled but did not deliver.

Officials from the White House and the State Department listened in on the call, as usual. Several testified that they were disturbed by it. "I thought it was wrong. I thought it was wrong for the president of the United States to call for an investigation of—call a foreign power to investigate a U.S. citizen," said Lt. Col. Alexander Vindman, the top National Security Council staff member for Ukraine. He reported his concerns to the NSC legal adviser.

Trump's call "struck me as unusual and inappropriate," said Jennifer Williams, an adviser to Vice President Pence. "The references to specific individuals and investigations, such as former Vice President Biden and his son, struck me as political in nature."

Tim Morrison, the NSC's top adviser on Russia, also reported the call to the council's legal adviser "to make sure that the package was reviewed by the appropriate senior level attention." Morrison testified that he was afraid of the impact a leak about the call would have "in Washington's polarized environment."

By focusing on the call, Trump hoped to detract from what happened before and after July 25. He had secretly halted $391 million in aid that the Ukrainians were expecting—and testimony established that Ukrainian officials learned of the hold as early as the day of the call. Before the call, Giuliani and officials such as Sondland, the U.S. ambassador to the European Union, had made clear what was expected of an increasingly uncomfortable Zelensky administration—a commitment to investigations. On July 20, the acting U.S. ambassador to Ukraine, Bill Taylor, spoke with Oleksandr Danyliuk, Ukraine's national security adviser, who told him that Zelensky "did not want to be used as a pawn in a U.S. reelection campaign." Then, the day after the July 25 call, David Holmes, an embassy political officer, overheard Sondland and Trump discuss the conversation as the ambassador spoke on his cell phone with the president.

"So, he's going to do the investigation?" Trump asked, according to Holmes. Sondland told him yes, Zelensky "loves your ass" and would do "anything you ask him to." When Sondland hung up, he remarked to Holmes that Trump "did not give a shit about Ukraine," caring only about a possible Biden investigation.

The hold on the aid was lifted in September, following intense congressional pressure, but only after Holmes learned that Zelensky planned to announce in an appearance on CNN that he was ordering the investigation Trump wanted. Holmes was shocked by the crassness of Trump's demand: "While we had advised our Ukrainian counterparts to voice a commitment to following the rule of law and generally investigating credible corruption allegations, this was a demand that President Zelensky personally commit on a cable news channel to a specific investigation of President Trump's political rival." Zelensky canceled the CNN interview when he learned that the hold on aid had been lifted.

Months later, when Romney, the 2012 GOP presidential nominee, announced he would be the sole Republican to vote to convict Trump, he dismissed the president's favorite phrase. "What he did was not 'perfect,'" Romney said. "No, it was a flagrant assault on our electoral rights, our national security and our fundamental values. Corrupting an election to keep oneself in office is perhaps the most abusive and destructive violation of one's oath of office that I can imagine."

Donald J. Trump
@realDonaldTrump

"I want to meet not only my accuser, who presented SECOND & THIRD HAND INFORMATION, but also the person who illegally gave this information, which was largely incorrect, to the 'Whistleblower.' Was this person SPYING on the U.S. President? Big Consequences!"—Sept. 29, 2019

Donald J. Trump
@realDonaldTrump

"WHO CHANGED THE LONG STANDING WHISTLEBLOWER RULES JUST BEFORE SUBMITTAL OF THE FAKE WHISTLEBLOWER REPORT? DRAIN THE SWAMP!"—Sept. 30, 2019

When the whistleblower report became public, Trump claimed it relied on secondhand information. But Michael Atkinson, the U.S. intelligence community's inspector general, released a statement disclosing that the Ukraine whistleblower relied on both firsthand and secondhand information in drafting the complaint against

Trump: "The Complainant on the form he or she submitted on August 12, 2019 in fact checked two relevant boxes: The first box stated that, 'I have personal and/or direct knowledge of events or records involved'; and the second box stated that, 'Other employees have told me about events or records involved.'"

Atkinson said that even without access to the rough transcript of the July 25 phone call, his preliminary review found that the complaint "appears credible," including that Trump sought to pressure the Ukrainian president to help with his reelection bid.

Trump also seized on an inaccurate report on a conservative website to falsely claim that the rules had suddenly been changed in August to allow the whistleblower to report on his Ukraine phone call. But the key document governing the inspector general's process for handling whistleblower allegations, the ICD 120, has been virtually unchanged since 2014. Contrary to speculation in the right-wing media, the whistleblower filed the complaint on the 2018 version of the form, not on any new online form. In an unusual statement, Atkinson rebutted Trump's claim and the flawed reporting that sparked it. Trump fired Atkinson in April 2020.

"The whistleblower said 'quid pro quo' eight times. It was a little off— no times."

—Oct. 12, 2019 (speech)

This is a good example of how Trump twists information in news reports and then weaponizes it to put false words in the mouths of others.

The whistleblower's report never used the phrase "quid pro quo," let alone said that Trump used the phrase eight times. On Sept. 21, before the rough transcript of the call was released, the *Wall Street*

Journal reported that Trump urged Zelensky "about eight times to work with Rudy Giuliani on a probe that could hamper Mr. Trump's potential 2020 opponent."

When the transcript was released, it turned out that Trump made eight distinct requests for assistance during the call, though Giuliani was not mentioned in each instance. The *Journal's* reporting was essentially correct. But Trump on a half dozen occasions pretended it was false. Here are the eight times Trump made a request during the call:

- "I would like you to do us a favor though, because our country has been through a lot and Ukraine knows a lot about it."
- "I would like you to find out what happened with this whole situation with Ukraine."
- "I would like you to have the Attorney General call you or your people and I would like you to get to the bottom of it."
- "Whatever you can do, it's very important that you do it if that's possible."
- "Mr. Giuliani is a highly respected man. He was the mayor of New York City, a great mayor, and I would like him to call you. I will ask him to call you along with the Attorney General. Rudy very much knows what's happening and he is a very capable guy. If you could speak to him that would be great."
- "There's a lot of talk about Biden's son, that Biden stopped the prosecution and a lot of people want to find out about that so whatever you can do with the Attorney General would be great."
- "Biden went around bragging that he stopped the prosecution so if you can look into it. . . . It sounds horrible to me."
- "I will have Mr. Giuliani give you a call and I am also going to have Attorney General Barr call and we will get to the bottom of it. I'm sure you will figure it out."

TRUMP'S EXCUSES

 "Now, with all of that, of course, you have to look at corruption. Are we going to be sending massive amounts of money to a country, and they're corrupt, and they steal the money, and it goes into everybody's bank accounts? So you have to look at that."

—Nov. 22, 2019 (interview)

 "We have an obligation to investigate corruption. And that's what it was."

—Oct. 21, 2019 (interview)

 "I'm only interested in corruption. I don't care about politics. I don't care about Biden's politics. I never thought Biden was going to win, to be honest."

—Oct. 4, 2019 (remarks)

Trump's main excuse for raising Biden in the phone call and withholding aid was that he was concerned about corruption. It's a bogus explanation. As president, Trump has shown little interest in combating corruption in other countries—and in the case of Ukraine, the U.S. government had already taken action to push the country toward reform.

Congress approved the military aid in September 2018. A top Defense Department official, as required by law, certified to congressional committees on May 23, 2019, that Ukraine had made sufficient progress on anti-corruption efforts to merit the security funds. The Pentagon announced the $250 million aid package June 18.

That's how such aid typically works. But on Trump's orders, the

White House informed the Pentagon on July 18 that Ukraine's aid was being frozen. (The White House also froze a separate $141 million aid package coming from the State Department.) The White House did not release the funds until mid-September, just weeks before the deadline for disbursing the funds.

Trump didn't raise corruption concerns in his July 25 phone call with Zelensky, ignoring his prepared talking points, which suggested he bring up corruption. Instead, as the rough transcript shows, he only asked Zelensky to look into the 2016 election and launch an investigation of the Bidens.

There is no evidence the White House ever conducted a review of corruption in Ukraine during the two months when the aid was on hold. The White House never rebutted the Defense Department's finding that Ukraine had made sufficient progress on corruption to merit the assistance. Moreover, there was never an explanation why the Trump administration, which had approved $510 million in aid in 2017 and $359 million in 2018 when Poroshenko was still in power, was now withholding it, even though Zelensky defeated Poroshenko running on an anti-corruption platform.

Behind the scenes, key players understood what was really happening. Taylor, the acting ambassador to Ukraine, had texted Sondland on Sept. 1: "Are we now saying that security assistance and WH meeting are conditioned on investigations?" Sondland, in a phone call, replied that "everything" was dependent on an announcement of a probe, including security assistance. Trump wanted Zelensky "in a public box," and that required a public statement, Sondland told Taylor.

 "The other thing I look at is, why isn't France and why isn't Germany and maybe, I could say, why isn't Greece—but why aren't all of these countries—why

aren't they paying? Why is it always the United States
that has to pay?"

—Jan. 7, 2020 (remarks)

"It also bothered me very, very much that Germany,
France, and all of these other countries aren't putting up money, but we're always the sucker that does
it. And that bothered me."

—Nov. 2, 2019 (remarks)

Trump also had another excuse for withholding aid to Ukraine: It
was time for the Europeans to step up to the plate. The United States
should stop playing the sucker.

This appears to be a case where Trump assumes something is
true, without bothering to check the facts. During the call with Zelensky, Trump also hit this theme: "I will say that we do a lot for
Ukraine. We spend a lot of effort and a lot of time. Much more than
the European countries are doing and they should be helping you
more than they are."

Trump's premise is wrong. Europe has been a major funder to
Ukraine since Russia annexed the Crimean Peninsula in 2014, often
providing far more aid than the United States. The European Union
has delivered more than $16.5 billion in grants and loans to Ukraine,
according to EU records. By contrast, the United States has provided
nearly $2 billion to Ukraine since late 2013, according to the U.S.
Agency for International Development.

Trump would have been on more solid ground if he had limited
his complaint to *military* aid. The UK, Poland, the Baltic nations and
Canada also contribute military aid, via a NATO assistance package,
but the United States provides most of it; other European nations
are wary of provoking Russia by arming its neighbor. But this is how

the aid burden is usually divided between the United States and the Europeans, with the United States providing the muscle and Europe providing the "soft power" to stabilize troubled nations.

During congressional testimony, State and Defense Department witnesses said concerns about burden-sharing among the allies never came up in interagency meetings as officials struggled to understand why the White House put a hold on the Ukraine aid.

 "In terms of the money, it got there two or three weeks ahead of schedule—long before it was supposed to be there."

—Jan. 7, 2020 (remarks)

Trump also asserted that the aid money for Ukraine eventually was delivered, "ahead of schedule," so no harm was done. But this is incorrect. U.S. officials became increasingly frantic about the aid freeze because the 2019 fiscal year ended on Sept. 30, after which the appropriation would expire. The hold was finally lifted in mid-September, only after intense pressure from members of Congress on both sides of the aisle, but it takes time for the U.S. government to transfer such funds. That's one reason lower-level officials were so concerned.

It turned out that about $35 million of the aid could not be disbursed by the Sept. 30 deadline. For the money to go through, Congress had to pass a law extending the deadline to the fiscal 2020 year.

 "We've done more for Ukraine than President Obama. He sent them pillows and sheets and we sent them very powerful weapons."

—Sept. 22, 2019 (remarks)

Trump, as always, claims he did more than Obama. But to dismiss Obama's aid to Ukraine as "pillows and sheets" is ridiculous.

While the Obama administration did not send lethal aid, in 2015 it provided Ukraine more than $120 million in security assistance and had pledged an additional $75 million worth of equipment, including unmanned aerial vehicles, armored Humvee vehicles, counter-mortar radars, night vision devices and medical supplies, according to the Pentagon's Defense Security Cooperation Agency. The Trump administration provided many of these same items, but in March 2018, the White House also approved the sale of Javelin missiles, a shoulder-fired precision missile system designed to destroy tanks, other armored vehicles and helicopters.

In the July 25 call, Trump asked for "a favor" after Zelensky said Ukraine was ready to buy more Javelins. During the Obama administration, U.S. officials were concerned that the Ukrainian military lacked the capability to handle weapons such as Javelins, but the country had indeed achieved that capability by the time Trump took office.

Ironically, *Foreign Policy* magazine reported, Trump initially did not want to provide Javelins to Ukraine but eventually aides persuaded him that it could be good for U.S. business. Nevertheless, the sale was mostly symbolic. The Trump administration insisted that Javelins could not be deployed in a conflict zone, so they are stored in western Ukraine, far from the front lines of the ongoing conflict against pro-Russia separatists in eastern Ukraine.

 "The president of Ukraine said I did absolutely nothing wrong, he said I had no pressure whatsoever."

—Jan. 10, 2020 (interview)

Trump on Impeachment: "A Perfect Phone Call"

"The Ukrainian president came out and said, very strongly, that 'President Trump did absolutely nothing wrong.' That should be case over. But he just came out a little while ago and he said, 'President Trump did absolutely nothing wrong.' And that should end everything."

—Dec. 2, 2019 (remarks)

Look at it from Zelensky's perspective: There is no upside to admitting he felt pressured during the July 25 call. First, it makes him look weak to his constituents. Second, he does not want to anger Trump, whose support is crucial in Ukraine's ongoing conflict with Russia. So any of his comments on a possible pressure campaign must be viewed skeptically.

Diplomatic text messages revealed during the investigation show that Ukrainian officials had been informed that Trump would make an unusual ask. On the morning of the call, U.S. special envoy to Ukraine Kurt Volker texted a Zelensky aide, "Heard from White House—assuming President Z convinces trump he will investigate / 'get to the bottom of what happened' in 2016, we will nail down date for visit to Washington. Good luck!"

Zelensky's boldest comments came during an interview with *Time* magazine in December, saying, "I don't trust anyone at all." Trump falsely claimed that Zelensky said Trump "did absolutely nothing wrong." Nowhere in the interview did Zelensky say that. In fact, he criticized Trump's comments about corruption in Ukraine and his decision to suspend military aid. "We're at war," Zelensky said. "If you're our strategic partner, then you can't go blocking anything for us. I think that's just about fairness. It's not about a quid pro quo. It just goes without saying."

239

"The transcript was perfectly accurate."

—January 16, 2020 (remarks)

 "They didn't even know, probably, that we had it transcribed, professionally transcribed, word-for-word
transcribed, so beautiful."

—December 10, 2019 (campaign rally)

The White House never released an exact "word-for-word" transcript. Instead, it was cobbled together by officials who took notes
as they listened to the call. The memo released by the White House
includes a "caution" saying that it "is not a verbatim transcript." Current and former U.S. officials, in interviews with *The Washington
Post*, pointed to several elements that indicate the document may
have been handled in an unusual way. Those include the use of
ellipses—punctuation indicating that information has been deleted
for clarity or other reasons—that traditionally have not appeared in
summaries of presidential calls with foreign leaders.

Vindman told House impeachment investigators that the transcript omitted crucial words and phrases, and that his attempts to
include them failed.

 "They kept saying 'me.' It wasn't about me, it was
about us. The word was 'us.' So, they would—kept
saying 'me' instead 'us.' 'Can you do 'us' a favor?'
'Our country,' comma, 'our country.'"

—Dec. 13, 2019 (remarks)

"I said do us a favor, not me, and our country, not a campaign."

—Dec. 17, 2019 (statement)

Weeks after the rough transcript of the July 25 call was released, Trump began claiming that when he said "do us a favor" in the call, the word "us" referred to the United States, not himself or his administration.

This strains credulity. He repeatedly requested that Ukrainian officials meet with his personal lawyer, Giuliani. In a May 2019 letter to Zelensky requesting a meeting, Giuliani said he represented Trump "as a private citizen, not as the president of the United States," and said he was carrying out this mission with Trump's "knowledge and consent."

 "Ambassador Sondland testified that I told him: 'No quid pro quo. I want nothing. I want nothing. I want President Zelensky to do the right thing, do what he ran on.'"

—Dec. 17, 2019 (statement)

Trump misleadingly seized on a small part of the mainly damaging testimony by Sondland, who was named U.S. ambassador after donating $1 million to Trump's inauguration.

Sondland told the House impeachment panel that the White House held back an invitation to Zelensky to meet with Trump in Washington to pressure the Ukrainian president into announcing the investigations Trump sought. "I know that members of this committee frequently frame these complicated issues in the form of a simple question: Was there a quid pro quo?" Sondland said. "With regard to the requested White House call and the White House meeting, the answer is yes."

Sondland said he later came to believe that $391 million in aid to Ukraine had also been made contingent on Zelensky announcing that the investigations were underway.

Trump chose to ignore that testimony and instead highlighted a quote from a phone conversation that Sondland said he had with Trump on Sept. 9—after Congress announced its investigation into the hold-up of aid to Ukraine. "President Trump was adamant that President Zelensky himself had to clear things up and do it in public," Sondland said. "President Trump said it was not a quid pro quo."

Sondland said he told Zelensky that, "Although this was not a quid pro quo, if President Zelensky did not 'clear things up' in public, we would be at a 'stalemate.'" That conversation persuaded Zelensky to schedule the CNN interview to announce the investigations.

Sondland testified that he did not know if Trump was telling the truth, at least about the funding portion of the quid pro quo.

Although Trump repeatedly cited the "I want nothing" snippet of Sondland's testimony, the president fired Sondland two days after his acquittal.

THE CONGRESSIONAL INVESTIGATION

 "You talk about Pinocchios—that should get 10 Pinocchios. . . . He made up a story. It was a phony story. Adam Schiff."

—Oct. 4, 2019 (remarks)

"Adam Schiff is a corrupt politician. He's corrupt. He got up—he made a speech, said something I never said."

—Dec. 31, 2019 (remarks)

Trump often makes up quotes and falsely attributes them to people. But he never lets go if he thinks someone has done the same thing to him.

Rep. Adam Schiff (D-Calif.), chairman of the Intelligence Committee, led the impeachment inquiry and thus became a constant target of Trump's attacks. At one hearing, Schiff made a misstep that gave Trump an opening: He summarized the content of Trump's July 25 call with Zelensky, paraphrasing the call for dramatic effect. Schiff's disclaimer—"this is the essence of what the president communicates"—was meant to signal to listeners that he was not quoting verbatim from the rough transcription. But the theatrics backfired.

Much of what Schiff said tracks the thrust of Trump's call. But Schiff added some eyebrow-raising embellishments. He suggested that Trump, after asking for "a favor," said something like "I'm going to say this only seven times, so you better listen good. I want you to make up dirt on my political opponent." Biden's name actually came up twice in the call, not seven times, and Trump asked Zelensky to launch an investigation, not "make up dirt."

In Trump's telling, which he repeated nearly 70 times, Schiff was guilty of a "crime" for paraphrasing his call and should be tried for "treason." Schiff is guilty of taking dramatic license, but he engaged in protected political speech. "Treason," defined by the Constitution, is giving "aid and comfort" to "enemies" or "levying war" against the United States.

"[Schiff] made up a conversation. He made a conversation that didn't exist. He never thought in a million years that I was going to release the real conversation. And when it did, the whistleblower turned out to be totally inaccurate."

—Oct. 12, 2019 (interview)

"Nancy Pelosi said, 'Well, that's what he said. Isn't it?' But she was angry as hell when she got to read the transcript. Because she said, 'Wait a minute, that's not what I was told.' But she was stuck, she was stuck."

—Oct. 11, 2019 (campaign rally)

This is totally mixed up. The rough transcript was released on Sept. 25, and Schiff held the hearing on Sept. 26. Republicans at the hearing were able to call out Schiff's embellishments precisely because they had the president's words in front of them.

But Trump repeatedly reversed the order of events in his version of this hearing, telling audiences that he released the transcript because Schiff had given a phony account of the call.

As Trump knocked Schiff for putting words into his mouth, he repeatedly attributed a fake quote to Pelosi. In Trump's own dramatic retelling, Pelosi authorized the impeachment inquiry on Sept. 24—only to be shocked when the rough transcript was released a day later.

There is no evidence that Pelosi said what Trump claims. Her staff denies it. Pelosi issued a scathing statement after the rough transcript was made public: "The release of the notes of the call by the White House confirms that the President engaged in behavior that undermines the integrity of our elections, the dignity of the office he

244

holds and our national security. The President has tried to make law-lessness a virtue in America and now is exporting it abroad."

 "Then, you have Vindman—you have all these characters. You know these are people I've never met. I never even met. I never even heard of these people and they're either Never Trumpers, some were appointed by Obama, but they could be Never Trumpers."

—Nov. 15, 2019 (interview)

 "This ambassador that everybody says is so wonderful, she wouldn't hang my picture in the embassy. Okay? She's in charge of the embassy. She wouldn't hang it. It took like a year and a half or two years for her to get the picture up."

—Nov. 22, 2019 (interview)

There's no evidence that any of the impeachment hearing witnesses—including former U.S. ambassador to Ukraine Marie Yovanovitch; acting ambassador to Ukraine Bill Taylor; State Department officials George Kent, David Holmes and David Hale; national security aides Vindman and Hill; vice presidential aide Williams or former U.S. special envoy Volker—are or were "Never Trumpers." Many people who testified were recruited to serve in his administration or had served multiple presidents from both parties.

Trump forced out Yovanovitch on May 20 after Giuliani and other players badmouthed her to the president. In his July 25 call with Zelensky, Trump complained about her: "The former ambassador from the United States, the woman, was bad news and the people she was dealing with in the Ukraine were bad news, so I just want to let you know that."

Yovanovitch, a highly regarded foreign service officer, worked in high-level posts for presidents George W. Bush and Barack Obama. The claim that she refused to hang Trump's portrait is not true. Trump's official portrait for display in federal facilities was not released until October 2017, after *The Washington Post* reported on a strange bureaucratic snafu that had delayed delivery of the pictures. "Nearly eight months after Donald Trump's inauguration, pictures of the president and Vice President Pence are missing from thousands of federal courthouses, laboratories, military installations, ports of entry, office suites and hallways, and from U.S. embassies abroad," *The Post* reported in September 2017.

Lewis Lukens, the former deputy chief of mission for the U.S. embassy in London, tweeted, "I was in charge of the US embassy in London for much of Trump's first year. We didn't hang his picture either. Why? It took the WH almost 15 months to get official photos sent to embassies to hang. And we were instructed not to print other photos."

> "What the Democrats did in the House was a disgrace. What they did—how unfair it was. We didn't get lawyers. We didn't have witnesses. We didn't do anything."
>
> —Dec. 31, 2019 (remarks)

Trump often claimed that House Democrats violated his due-process rights in the impeachment inquiry because he wasn't allowed to have counsel present during closed-door depositions and couldn't call or cross-examine witnesses. This is a great example of how politicians use legalese to mislead the public.

The Constitution gives wide discretion to the House and Senate to establish rules for impeachment proceedings, and it doesn't require that officeholders get due-process rights. Near the end of the impeachment inquiry in the House, the Judiciary Committee invited Trump's legal counsel to appear, but the White House declined the invitation.

Under the Constitution, the House assumes the role of prosecutor in any impeachment, making the decision to file charges. The Fifth and Fourteenth Amendments guarantee due process for defendants in court who could be "deprived of life, liberty, or property." But impeachment is a political process, with a maximum penalty of removal from office. The Constitution gives the Senate responsibility for holding impeachment trials, and an impeached president may defend himself at that stage, as Trump did after he was impeached.

 "They come up with two articles that aren't even a crime."

—Jan. 6, 2020 (interview)

Trump was wrong to claim that a statutory crime is required for the House to impeach a president. The standard for conviction in an impeachment trial is not the same as the standard in the criminal justice system. The outcome of an impeachment trial relies largely on senators' personal judgments.

"The historic meaning of the words 'high crimes and misdemeanors,' the writings of the founders and my own reasoned judgment convince me that a president can indeed commit acts against the public trust that are so egregious that while they're not statutory crimes, they would demand removal from office," Sen. Mitt Romney said in his speech announcing he would vote to convict Trump. "To maintain that the lack of a codified and comprehensive list of all the outrageous acts that a president might conceivably commit renders Congress powerless to remove such a president defies reason."

CHAPTER TEN

Trump and Coronavirus: "Their New Hoax"

In early 2020, the global outbreak of coronavirus sickened hundreds of thousands of people, shook financial markets and threatened to usher in a worldwide recession. Trump responded to the crisis with a dizzying mix of bluster, ignorance and suspect claims.

When the Ebola outbreak took place in 2014, private citizen Trump used his Twitter account to blast Obama for his handling of the situation. "President Obama has a personal responsibility to visit & embrace all people in the US who contract Ebola!" Trump, a lifelong germaphobe, tweeted. But as a far more pervasive public-health crisis unfolded on his watch, Trump turned on his critics, accusing them of purposely hyping the seriousness of the epidemic. At one campaign rally, Trump even said that media coverage of the virus's spread was the Democrats' "new hoax."

In the first three years of his presidency, Trump had shown little interest in health issues beyond the country's borders. He proposed big reductions in spending on global health programs created after the Ebola outbreak and he took a White House pandemic office that Obama had created and folded it into a nonproliferation bureau. Whether having a separate office on pandemics in the White House would have made the administration react more swiftly to the emerging coronavirus threat is questionable. "There isn't any organizational chart in the U.S. government that makes any difference in the Trump administration," a former administration official told The Fact Checker. "Trump is more likely to say to Jared [Kushner], 'What do you think we should do?' That's the big problem."

For Trump, talking about the virus was often a numbers game. For many weeks, he emphasized how few cases had developed in the United States. Only after the scope of the pandemic could no longer be dismissed did the president acknowledge that the death toll could be staggering. The virus, he said after it had killed several thousand people, was a "great national trial unlike any we have ever faced before."

 "We have it totally under control. It's one person coming in from China, and we have it under control. It's going to be just fine."
—Jan. 21, 2020 (interview)

Trump was asked whether he had any concerns about a pandemic after the Centers for Disease Control and Prevention (CDC) identified the first case of coronavirus in Washington state. That was the initial sign that the virus might eventually spread via community transmission, but Trump dismissed any concern. Within weeks, Washington state would become the first epicenter of the outbreak in the United States.

"A lot of people think that goes away in April with the heat—as the heat comes in. Typically, that will go away in April."

—Feb. 10, 2020 (remarks)

Trump predicted the virus's quick demise around the time the World Health Organization said the virus had infected more than 46,000 people, killed at least 1,116 and was on a path to spread vastly more widely. His administration's own public health officials disputed Trump's prediction, which appeared to be rooted in the idea that flu season in the United States generally ends in the spring. The virus was already spreading in Singapore, where February temperatures are akin to summer in the United States.

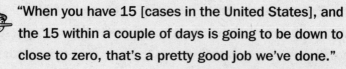 "When you have 15 [cases in the United States], and the 15 within a couple of days is going to be down to close to zero, that's a pretty good job we've done."

—Feb. 26, 2020 (news conference)

Trump apparently was not listening to his own news conference. He made this remark moments after Health and Human Services Secretary Alex Azar said that "the degree of risk has the potential to change quickly. And we can expect to see more cases in the United States." Within three days, 12 more cases were identified in the United States and one person had died. Within five days, there were more than 100 confirmed U.S. cases and six people had died. Two weeks later, there were 800 cases and 27 deaths. And the numbers kept rising.

"The flu in our country kills from 25,000 people to 69,000 people a year. That was shocking to me. And so far, if you look at what we have with the 15 people and their recovery, one is—one is pretty sick but hopefully will recover, but the others are in great shape."

—Feb. 26, 2020 (news conference)

Trump appeared nonplussed at learning basic public health information—the number of deaths annually from the seasonal flu. Estimates of U.S. deaths from influenza in the past decade range from a low of 12,000 in the 2011–2012 season to a high of 61,000 in 2017–2018. But Trump misleadingly compared those numbers with the known cases of covid-19 in the United States. Tens of millions of people each year come down with the flu. The fatality rate in the United States from seasonal flu is 0.1 percent. The new coronavirus appears to have a much higher fatality rate, possibly 10 times higher, but the outbreak was too new for a firm death rate to be determined.

 "But the same vaccine could not work? You take a solid flu vaccine—you don't think that would have an impact or much of an impact on corona?"

—March 2, 2020 (remarks)

"No," replied Leonard Schleifer, chief executive of Regeneron, which develops and makes vaccines. The health company executives meeting with Trump explained that the coronavirus was new and therefore could not be protected against by vaccines developed to immunize people against other viruses. Drug company executives repeatedly explained to Trump that it would take more than a year to develop, test and bring to market a coronavirus vaccine. But moments later, the president told reporters that the scientists' timetable could be much shorter: "I don't think they know what the time will be. I've heard very quick numbers — matter of months."

 "The H1N1, that was swine flu . . . I had heard it was 13,000 [deaths], but a lot of deaths. And they didn't do anything about it."

—March 4, 2020 (interview)

Under fire for a sluggish response, Trump started to target the Obama administration, especially its handling of the 2009 swine flu outbreak. But it's false to say Obama "didn't do anything about it." In fact, Obama's handling was widely praised at the time as the right mix of taking action and avoiding panic.

On April 26, 2009, when only 20 cases of H1N1—and no deaths—around the country had been confirmed, the Obama administration declared the virus a public health emergency. The administration quickly sought funding from Congress, receiving almost $8 billion. Six weeks later, the World Health Organization declared a pandemic.

On Oct. 24, after more than 1,000 Americans had died of H1N1, Obama declared a national emergency. The estimated death toll in the United States during the H1N1 epidemic was 12,469 from April 2009 to April 2010, but that was much less than a government forecast of 30,000 to 90,000 deaths that had been made in August of 2009.

"The Obama administration made a decision on testing that turned out to be very detrimental to what
we're doing. And we undid that decision a few days
ago so that the testing can take place in a much
more accurate and rapid fashion."

—March 4, 2020 (remarks)

Trump was looking for scapegoats to excuse his administration's lack-
adaisical efforts to expand testing. But there was no Obama rule on
testing; rather, there were simply "guidance" documents from 2014
about how to deploy laboratory-developed tests. The guidance never
took effect and was withdrawn before Trump took office. Trump's
administration suggested, without evidence, that labs gearing up to
produce coronavirus tests were confused because of previous regulatory actions by the Obama administration. But Trump had been president for three years and his administration already had been working
with Congress on legislation concerning lab tests. If lab directors were
confused, the administration could have taken action creating emergency authorization to develop coronavirus tests sooner than it did.

 "When people have the flu, you have an average of
36,000 people dying. I've never heard those numbers. I would've been shocked. I would've said, 'Does
anybody die from the flu?' I didn't know people died
from the flu—36,000 people died."

—March 6, 2020 (remarks)

Trump said he did not know that people died of the flu. But his
paternal grandfather was a victim of the first wave of the Spanish flu
pandemic in 1918.

"Anybody that wants a test can get a test."

—March 6, 2020 (remarks)

The day after these remarks, Health and Human Services Secretary Alex Azar said, "You may not get a test unless a doctor or public health official prescribes a test." Reports from across the country documented the scarcity of tests. Moreover, the United States lagged far behind other major countries in providing tests for possible cases. The CDC initially distributed flawed tests to state and local health departments. The lack of tests in the United States, compared with countries such as South Korea that had tested tens of thousands of people by March of 2020, made it impossible to measure accurately the extent of the virus's spread in the United States.

"I met with the leaders of [the] health insurance industry, who have agreed to waive all co-payments for coronavirus treatments."

—March 11, 2020 (speech)

This is wrong. Insurance companies agreed to waive co-payments for testing, but not for treatment if it turned out a person was diagnosed with covid-19.

"This is the most aggressive and comprehensive effort to confront a foreign virus in modern history."

—March 11, 2020 (speech)

Beyond the unverifiable claim about his administration's efforts, there is no such thing as a "foreign virus." Viruses can emerge anywhere on Earth. The Spanish flu that emerged in 1918, killing 20 million to 50 million people, is believed to have started in the United States—the first case was reported here—though no one knows for sure, except that it almost certainly did not start in Spain.

 "We have a problem that a month ago nobody ever thought about."

—March 16 (news conference)

This was a ridiculous claim. There were plenty of warnings if Trump had been paying attention. China's government sealed off the city of Wuhan on Jan. 23 to halt the spread of the virus. And on Jan. 28, two former Trump administration officials published an opinion article in the *Wall Street Journal* titled "Act Now to Prevent an American Epidemic." The article identified steps that needed to be taken immediately, such as partnering with the private sector before the CDC was overwhelmed with testing requests — but it took the administration another month to issue guidance that would encourage private-sector tests.

 "So you're talking about 2.2 million deaths. 2.2 million people from this. If we can hold that down as we're saying, to 100,000, it's a horrible number. Maybe even less, but to 100,000, so we have between 100 and 200,000, we all together have done a very good job."

—March 29 (news conference)

Only four weeks earlier, Trump had touted as "a pretty good job" the fact that there were only 15 cases in the United States and predicted they soon would be down to zero. But the long delay in testing masked the scope of the problem. With the number of cases in the United States nearing 150,000 and more than 2,500 people already dead from the virus, the president conceded that the U.S. economy had to be locked down for weeks and likely months. But he changed the definition of "a very good job." Now he would claim victory with less than 200,000 deaths on his watch.

CONCLUSION

Toward a Resurgence of Truth

"Falsehood flies, and truth comes limping after it, so that when men come to be undeceived, it is too late; the jest is over, and the tale hath had its effect."
—Jonathan Swift, "The Art of Political Lying," 1710

When Bill Clinton was impeached by the House of Representatives, he told reporters, "I have accepted responsibility for what I did wrong in my personal life." He said he hoped to be censured by the Senate for his failure to tell the truth about his sexual relationship with Monica Lewinsky.

When the House Judiciary Committee voted for articles of impeachment against Richard Nixon over Watergate, he resigned from office, informing the nation, "I regret deeply any injuries that may have been done in the course of the events that led to this decision."

And although Ronald Reagan was never seriously threatened with impeachment over the Iran-Contra affair, he nevertheless took responsibility, fired key staff members and hired a new chief of staff to fix problems exposed by the scandal.

Donald Trump expressed no such regrets and acknowledged no

mistakes as he faced months of investigation and then an impeachment trial. Following the advice of his longtime lawyer and mentor, Roy Cohn, to always counterattack, Trump constructed an alternative and false narrative—his phone call with the Ukrainian president was "perfect," not a possible abuse of power—and rallied his supporters behind a series of fictions that carried him to his acquittal in the Senate.

The president's technique—shaped by Cohn and refined over half a century by Trump—is relentless and unforgiving: Never admit any error, constantly repeat falsehoods, and have no shame about your tactics. In this book, we have documented how lies and misleading and exaggerated claims form the vital core of Trump's political persona. He misleads about things both big and small; he seizes on flimsy, conspiratorial claims if they fit with his current position; and he is unconcerned about contradicting himself from day to day. He gets many of his facts wrong, no matter how important or sensitive the venue. And he attacks his opponents with outrageously false claims and hyperbolic rhetoric.

Trump's management style arguably has hampered his success as president. Trump runs the country much as he did his small family business—with a flat organization and a cast of advisers and hangers-on who rarely challenge his authority. But where the family business was mostly stable—key top executives stayed with Trump for decades—the White House presented a very different challenge. White House advisers are part of a larger Washington ecosystem that includes Congress, the courts, the political parties and the news media. The boss found that he was not absolutely in charge.

As he began his fourth year in office, Trump was on his fourth national security adviser and his fourth chief of staff. Countless Cabinet members had been fired and replaced. Many departed with bitter memories and unflattering tales about how Trump was poorly informed, on policy issues and about how the U.S. government works. They described a president who was impervious to information that conflicted with what he already believed.

It's a fool's errand to try to predict the impact of a presidency while the incumbent is still in office. Each president brings a unique set of skills and personal experiences to the office. Trump's impact would deepen in a second term; defeat, by contrast, likely would be viewed as a repudiation of his character and approach to the office.

Still, as fact-checkers who try to shine a light on the truth behind political rhetoric, we wonder: Does Trump offer a template for a future president—for a more skilled liar with a firmer grasp on how to harness the reins of government? Has he changed the nature of the presidency?

There are certainly troubling signs that Trumpism is beginning to infect and distort politics in the United States.

Trump's aides frequently suggest there is no such thing as absolute, verifiable truth. Kellyanne Conway, the counselor to the president who advises Trump on policy and communications strategy, coined the phrase "alternative facts" to defend the White House's false claims about the attendance numbers at Trump's inauguration. Trump's personal lawyer, Rudolph W. Giuliani, argued that the president should avoid testifying before special counsel Robert Mueller because he could be trapped into a lie that would lead to perjury charges. "Truth isn't truth," Giuliani argued, explaining that everyone has their own version of the truth.

A hallmark of authoritarian regimes is to call truth into question—except as the regime defines it. Russian president Vladimir Putin offers up a fog of disinformation to maintain power, including denying obvious facts (such as Russian involvement in the downing of Malaysia Airlines Flight 17), spouting falsehoods and deflecting attention with nonsensical comparisons (dubbed "whataboutism").

"A cumulative effect of all these tactics is nihilistic debasement of the very concept of truth," said Michael McFaul, a former U.S. ambassador to Russia. "Putin is not trying to win the argument; instead, his propaganda machine aims to convince that there is no truth, no right and wrong, or no data or evidence, only relativism, point of view and biased opinion."

Trump used all three tactics to combat the investigation that led to his impeachment. He denied verified facts; his phone call to the Ukrainian leader was not, as he insisted, "perfect" but was so troubling that numerous administration officials listening in immediately reported their concerns. He told easily disproven falsehoods, such as claiming that the whistleblower wrote "a fake report" when it was correct on virtually all details. And he regularly engaged in whataboutism, seeking to direct attention to the actions of former vice president Joe Biden's son Hunter, even though Hunter's business dealings, if suspect, were irrelevant to whether the president abused power.

The president is aided in his disinformation effort by cheerleaders in the right-leaning media, especially evening talk-show hosts such as Sean Hannity and Lou Dobbs on Fox News and Fox Business, respectively, as well as Republican lawmakers who generally refuse to criticize his actions publicly. The few GOP lawmakers who dared to challenge the president's version of the truth quickly found themselves under attack, either from the president's Twitter account or by his fervent supporters. Rep. Justin Amash of Michigan read the Mueller report and declared it was clear the president should be impeached. Amash was immediately drummed out of the Republican Party and became an independent. He ended up voting for Trump's impeachment.

Trump has targeted traditional news-media organizations as unreliable, corrupt, "fake news" and most alarmingly "the enemy of the people." His aim is to undermine straight reporting that uncovers malfeasance, corruption or unflattering information. Trump appears to view any critical story as "fake news," even if it's true. Without evidence, he accuses news organizations of making up sources—even though that would be a firing offense at any reputable media outlet. "The LameStream Media, which is The Enemy of the People, is working overtime with made up stories in order to drive dissension and distrust," he tweeted in November 2019. His strategy is to undermine the very concept of neutral, unbiased reporting, hoping to replace neutral accounts with the hagiography he creates or embraces.

Trump's attacks on the media have been effective enough that some of his allies have adopted his tactics. When a CNN reporter tried to ask Sen. Martha McSally (R-Ariz.) a straightforward question about calling witnesses in the impeachment trial, she responded, "You're a liberal hack. I'm not talking to you. You're a liberal hack." McSally, who was facing a tight election race, immediately posted the exchange on YouTube and used it to raise money. Her reward? A tweet from a Trump 2020 Twitter account: "THIS is how you handle FAKE NEWS." Similarly, Secretary of State Mike Pompeo publicly attacked as a "liar" the co-host of National Public Radio's "All Things Considered," Mary Louise Kelly, when she brought up Ukraine in an interview that he claimed was supposed to be devoted only to questions on Iran. She proved Pompeo was the liar when she revealed emails showing she had told his staff she would ask about Ukraine.

Trump offers supporters a binary choice—you are with me, or you are not. That simplistic approach takes advantage of how Americans increasingly view party identification as a basic, essential sign of character. In 1960, a survey found that only 4 percent of Democrats and 4 percent of Republicans said they would be disappointed if their child married someone from the opposite political party. In a 2019 survey, 45 percent of Democrats and 35 percent of Republicans said they would be somewhat or very unhappy if their son or daughter married someone from the other party. Strikingly, a child's decision to marry someone from a different race, ethnicity or religion raised far less concern, especially among Democrats.

Trump's presidency is both a product of this tribalism and an exacerbating force. Going far beyond the traditional rhetorical flourishes politicians use to rally supporters, Trump routinely depicts Blue America as evil. "Democrats are now the party of high taxes, high crime, open borders, late-term abortion, socialism, and blatant corruption," Trump declared at a January 2020 rally. "The Republican Party is the party of the American worker, the American family, and the American dream!"

By exploiting this sense of grievance against the Other—whether that means the other party, people of other races or ethnicities, or people with different values—Trump makes it easier for his supporters to ignore or even embrace his falsehoods.

A 2018 study in the *American Sociological Review* found that Trump's lying endeared him to supporters, rather than turning them off. The researchers surveyed 400 people, split evenly by sex and political inclination, and then manipulated them into thinking they were part of an in- or out-group as they assessed a student government election and a debate over an alcohol ban on campus. When the study described a "crisis of legitimacy" on campus, members of the anti-establishment out-group consistently were attracted to a lying candidate, seeing his dishonest behavior as evidence that he was fighting for them. "If that constituency feels its interests are not being served by a political establishment that purports to represent it fairly, a lying demagogue can appear as a distinctively *authentic champion* of its interests," the report concluded.

This attitude might help explain why Trump retains such a hold over his core group of supporters, despite constant chaos in the administration, relatively few domestic or foreign-policy accomplishments—and a persistent inability to tell the truth.

But there are also signs that Trump may be an aberration—and that once he leaves the White House, either in defeat in 2020 or at the end of a second term, no other president would consider lying on such a grand scale.

Every action in politics results in a reaction, so the immediate consequence of Trump may be a successor who distinguishes himself from Trump by refusing to engage in hyperbole and falsehoods. Nixon, after all, was replaced by Jimmy Carter, who assured voters during his 1976 campaign that "I'll never tell a lie. . . . I'll never knowingly make a misstatement of fact. I'll never betray your trust. If I do any of these things, I don't want you to support me." Those lines appeared not only in his stump speech but also in his television commercials. (Carter's willingness to answer any question forthrightly nearly backfired on him when he told *Playboy* magazine in a campaign interview: "I've looked on a lot of women with lust. I've committed adultery in my heart many times." The interview reduced his lead over President Gerald Ford, Carter believed, but he narrowly won in the end.)

Similarly, Democrats running for their party's nomination to face Trump emphasized truth-telling. For instance, Sen. Kamala Harris (D-Calif.), who dropped out before any primary votes were cast, titled her 2019 campaign memoir "The Truth We Hold" and included the line "Let's speak truth" in her stump speech.

At The Fact Checker, we noticed during the early months of the 2020 presidential campaign that many of Trump's potential Democratic rivals sought to avoid getting Pinocchios. They were quick to provide detailed explanations for any questioned statements. Some dropped a talking point simply in response to a query from The Fact

Checker team. Several issued apologies for misspeaking to avoid a Pinocchio rating. (We generally do not award Pinocchios when a politician admits error, but few politicians took advantage of this standing offer until the 2020 campaign cycle.)

More broadly, there is evidence that Trump's falsehoods may have hurt him more than they have helped him. That may limit the appeal for other politicians to follow his path.

Trump may have survived impeachment with a blizzard of falsehoods, but through the first three years of his term, he failed to ever win majority support of Americans in public opinion polls. A 2019 Gallup poll found that by a narrow margin, 51–49, Americans considered Trump a strong and decisive leader. But only 34 percent believed he is honest and trustworthy, what Gallup described as "among his weakest personal characteristics."

Trump has earned 33 or 34 percent on the trustworthiness question throughout his presidency. By contrast, Americans were more likely to consider Bush (65 percent), Obama (61 percent) and Clinton (46 percent) honest and trustworthy.

Paradoxically, Trump's attacks on the media appear to have helped revive trust in the media, which had been falling for decades and reached a low in 2016. During the Trump presidency, trust in the media jumped substantially, especially among Democrats, though it dipped from 2018 to 2019, according to Gallup.

As we catalogued Trump's thousands of claims, we wondered whether his constant repetition of proven falsehoods made an impact. Numerous studies have documented what is known as the "illusory truth effect"—that if a falsehood is repeated often enough, people will start to believe it.

The Fact Checker worked with *The Washington Post*'s polling team to assess whether Americans believed many of Trump's most repeated falsehoods. The survey presented 18 pairs of opposing statements—one true, one false—without identifying who made the statement. Eleven questions gauging belief in Trump's false claims were mixed among four false claims from Democrats, one true claim by Trump and two other factual statements. The poll found that fewer than 3 in 10 Americans—including fewer than 4 in 10 Republicans—believed Trump's claims.

Indeed, one result from the survey suggests that doubts about Trump's honesty may lead some to be skeptical of him even when he says things that are true. Fewer than half of adults, 47 percent, believed Trump's oft-repeated (and true) statement that the U.S. unemployment rate was at its lowest level in roughly 50 years.

The *Post* poll also found that clear majorities across party lines said it is never acceptable for political leaders to make false statements. But there was an important distinction between the two parties: Forty-one percent of Republicans said false claims are sometimes acceptable "in order to do what's right for the country," while only 25 percent of Democrats and 26 percent of independents agreed.

Such low marks on trustworthiness undermine a president's authority and make it harder to rally public support for his domestic proposals and foreign-policy initiatives. Trump's proclivity for exaggeration and falsehoods has made it harder for him to build popular consensus even for his most successful actions.

Trump ordered the assassination of Iranian general Qasem Soleimani even though Bush and Obama had been wary of such a step. Despite Soleimani's clear involvement in attacks on American troops, the other presidents had held back because of the possible military and diplomatic consequences of an assassination. Trump charged ahead, consequences be damned.

But the president bungled his explanation for ordering the strike. He initially claimed it was necessary because Soleimani was plotting "imminent" attacks on Americans—a key word because otherwise the assassination might have been illegal under international law. The administration resisted explaining what "imminent" meant, but then Trump said during a media event six days after the killing that the Iranians had been looking to blow up the U.S. embassy in Baghdad. Later that day, he told a campaign rally that an undisclosed number of embassies were going to be attacked. Finally, a week after Soleimani's death, he blurted out during an interview on Fox News, "I can reveal I believe it probably would've been four embassies."

That was too much for Defense Secretary Mark T. Esper, who said he had not seen any evidence that four embassies were targeted. The State Department had not even sent a warning, as would be typically done about any potential threat against the Baghdad embassy. Some reporting suggested that Trump had misunderstood a line in one of his briefings that speculated about how Iran might respond to the killing of Soleimani.

After Iran retaliated, Trump quickly proclaimed that no U.S. soldiers had been hurt. That announcement allowed him to back away from a potential military conflict, but the Pentagon later admitted that 109 U.S. service members had been diagnosed with traumatic brain injuries.

The president had managed to turn an apparent triumph—eliminating the head of a terror organization—into a controversy over his honesty about the reasons for the strike and his understanding of the serious injuries suffered by military personnel. A more traditional presidency likely would not have fallen into such a briar patch of controversy—the talking points on the reasons for the attacks would have been vetted carefully, and the president would have been circumspect both about the intelligence leading up to the attack and about the injuries suffered by U.S. troops.

But Trump was elected expressly to disrupt the traditional norms of Washington, and he has consummate confidence in his direct link to his supporters—his use of social media to promote his personal brand. Just as Franklin D. Roosevelt harnessed the power of radio with regular "fireside chats" and John F. Kennedy was the first made-for-television president, Trump has shown politicians around the world how to make an impact with a well-timed tweet. Future presidents may be a bit more circumspect in their rhetoric on Twitter—and whether they use it to spread falsehoods and attack rivals—but they certainly will not ignore the power of social media to make their case. Besides Twitter, Trump has mastered Facebook, micro-targeting supporters to keep them engaged and supportive—and to go after political rivals.

It is no coincidence that the rise of social media has been accompanied by an astonishing growth of fact-checking organizations. When The Fact Checker was launched in 2007—one year after the creation of Twitter and when Facebook had only 50 million users—it was one of the first fact-checking initiatives. Five years later, in 2012, there were about two dozen active fact-checking websites around the world, according to the Duke Reporters' Lab, which conducts an annual census. The number metastasized to 44 in 2014, 149 in 2018 and more than 230 in 2020.

The growth has been especially strong in places—such as India (12 fact-checking organizations) and South America—where democratic norms are weakening and would-be authoritarian leaders have gained power. These fact-checkers debunk viral rumors, claims and videos that spread quickly across social-media platforms, including WhatsApp, a Facebook app that is popular outside the United States. (As of 2020, there are 2.5 billion monthly Facebook users, 1.5 billion WhatsApp active users and 330 million Twitter monthly users.)

The growth of fact-checking is largely possible because of the Internet. We could not write The Fact Checker column on a daily basis without the vast digital resources that allow our team instant access to government databases, think-tank reports and other materials. In 1996, as chief political correspondent for *Newsday*, I wrote what may have been the first extended fact-check in a U.S. newspaper—a guide, published before the first presidential debate, on the accuracy of claims and counterclaims that Bill Clinton and his Republican opponent, Bob Dole, were making on the campaign trail. I spent weeks tracking down the data and information needed to vet the candidates' statements, even dispatching messengers to pick up hard copies of reports written at various think tanks. Now, such information is often just a few clicks away.

Similarly, back in 1996, when the Internet was in its infancy, readers did not have easy access to presidential transcripts, White House pool reports, congressional hearings or those think-tank reports. (In 1996, Americans with Internet access spent fewer than 30 minutes a month surfing the web, compared to nearly 200 hours a month in 2019.) The raw materials used to assemble news reports are now readily available to anyone with Internet access.

But technological change that has empowered people has come at a cost. Newspapers and the evening news shows once provided Americans with a common point of reference—a basic foundation of fact. Now, citizens are increasingly sorted into ideological cul-de-sacs, deciding if they want their news slanted left or right. On top of that, Facebook and Twitter have built algorithms that guide users toward material with ever more extreme perspectives, based on what you already have read.

The question facing news consumers and government leaders alike is whether additional access to news and faster dissemination of information leaves us better informed—or renders us increasingly intolerant of other points of view. The Internet opened a world of information and facts for non-journalists, but that freedom is wasted if people see or select only the facts and opinions that match their own inclinations. We seem to have gotten richer in information—but poorer in knowledge and understanding.

More than anyone else, President Trump exemplifies the social-media creature who exists in a partisan, secluded world of his own, refusing to let conflicting facts and information get in his way. But that does not mean Americans should accept such limits and silos in their own lives. By diversifying your social-media and news diet, you learn from people who challenge your assumptions and preconceived notions. Be open to new ideas, and don't jump to conclusions. Read the article, not just the headline.

For many people, even these simple steps may be hard. A 2017 study found that two-thirds of liberals and conservatives surveyed were simply uninterested in hearing the views of the other side on contentious issues such as guns and climate change—even when they were offered extra money to do so. Another study, from 2018, found that people exposed to tweets from political opponents for a month actually made them less tolerant; liberals became somewhat more liberal and conservatives became substantially more conservative.

At the very least, remember this: Just because a politician you support makes a claim, don't take it at face value. They're trying to sell you something. Buyer beware. Check the facts.

"*THEY'RE* PINOCCHIO"

The Fact Checker's Pinocchios are a constant source of fascination (and annoyance) for President Trump.

> "You wouldn't believe that's possible, but I know it's true because I've said it 50 times and the fakers back there, they've never corrected me. No, it's true. If I were slightly off, if it were, if I was off by two factories, there'd be a head-line, 'Donald Trump told a fib. Donald Trump gets to be a Pinocchio again.'"
>
> —Jan. 9, 2020 (campaign rally)

> "I have to tell you, I have to be always very truthful because if I'm a little bit off, they call me a liar. They'll say, he gets a Pinocchio, the stupid *Washington Post. They're* Pinocchio."
>
> —Dec. 18, 2019 (campaign rally)

> "They catch it within, you know, 'Two dollars, he was $2 off. He gets a Pinocchio.' Though [Rep. Adam] Schiff got four Pinocchios for making up what I said on a phone call."*
>
> —Oct. 11, 2019 (campaign rally)

---

* No, Schiff didn't. He got them for another reason.

"You know I never say this. I don't think I've ever said it in a speech but maybe they'll find out if I did. Then they'll give me Pinocchios, 'He said it before,' but I don't know if I ever said it."

—Oct. 10, 2019 (campaign rally)

"I heard Adam Schiff got four Pinocchios. That's good. He should have gotten them two and a half years ago."

—Oct. 4, 2019 (remarks)

"If you notice, they don't mention the call that I had with the president of Ukraine. They don't mention that because it was so good. The only time they mentioned it was when Adam Schiff made it up. You talk about Pinocchios—that should get 10 Pinocchios."

—Oct. 4, 2019 (remarks)

"Shifty Schiff. How about Shifty Schiff? He got four Pinocchios today in *The Washington Post*. He lies like a son of a gun."

—Oct. 4, 2019 (speech)

"I don't want to be specific, because if I give you the wrong number, we'll have breaking news. It will be on every newspaper that I said 112 and it was actually 111. And it will be breaking news. They'll give me Pinocchio."

—Sept. 20, 2019 (remarks)

"When I say it, they don't correct me. They don't say, 'Oh, he gets a Pinocchio.' They can't because it's true."

—July 23, 2019 (speech)

"That was a lie. What you should do is give them Pinocchios."

—Jan. 10, 2019 (remarks)

"If I would have said that during the campaign, oh they would have given me a hard time. They would have said 'Pinocchio,' you know, they do the whole thing."

—Nov. 2, 2018 (campaign rally)

"They never questioned me on that. You know they want to. Because, you know, they'd say—I'd like to give him a Pinoc-chio, four Pinocchios."

—Oct. 20, 2018 (campaign rally)

"Nobody's ever challenged it. Maybe they have. Who knows? I have to always say that, because then they'll say they did actually challenge it, and they'll put like—then they'll say he gets a Pinocchio. So maybe they did challenge it, but not very much."

—Oct. 18, 2018 (campaign rally)

"The one thing with them, they fact-check, but even their fact-checking is wrong. If I'm right, or if I'm 97.3 percent right, they will say he's got a Pinocchio or he's lying. They are bad people."

—Aug. 13, 2018 (speech)

"Even a certain newspaper that I don't like very much came out today and they gave [Sen. Chuck] Schumer four Pinocchios, and they said because he was not telling the truth."

—Nov. 2, 2017 (interview)

"I better say 'think.' Otherwise they'll give me a Pinocchio—and I don't like those—I don't like Pinocchios."

—July 17, 2017 (speech)

"The, you know, fake media. They never correct me because it's true. Oh, believe me, if it's off by 100th of a percent, it's like I end up getting Pinocchios, right?"

—March 21, 2017 (speech)

Schumer: "*The Washington Post* today gave you a whole lot of Pinocchios because they say you constantly misstate how much of the wall is built and how much is there."
Trump (laughs): "Well, The Washington Post!"

—Dec. 11, 2018 (Oval Office meeting)

Anatomy of a Trump Rally:
"Is There a Better Place?"

It was the "Moby-Dick" of fact-checking assignments, a two-hour tornado of false and bewildering claims. On Dec. 18, 2019, in Battle Creek, Mich., President Trump held his longest campaign rally to date just as the House was voting to impeach him.

Trump's rallies are a roving mecca for his supporters. They come by the thousands, many traveling for hours from other towns and states to experience the reality-TV-star-turned-president. The sea of red caps, Trump's well-worn attack lines, the crowd's "lock her up" chants, the booing of the media, the disparagement of trade deals as the root of America's woes, the stories of grisly crimes committed by undocumented immigrants, the dark theories about a "deep state" and the sunny claims about economic growth—each rally is a raucous spectacle of grievance and triumph unlike any other in modern politics.

In 2016, Trump's rallies were ratings gold for cable networks and a key ingredient in Trump's narrow victory. And the rallies continued throughout Trump's presidency—until the coronavirus pandemic forced the show to close down for at least a few months—their script so familiar that even Fox News stopped regularly carrying them live.

This book presents Trump's claims by subject and shows the purpose his deceptions and lies serve, but to get the full impact of his rhetoric, you have to see how he puts it all together in a single performance. To conduct an anatomical investigation of one rally—to find out whether the president speaks more fiction or fact in front of his crowds—we had to comb line-by-line through his remarks, checking each assertion, a task we assigned ourselves for that marathon rally in Battle Creek. We focused only on material statements, avoiding trivialities and opinions. We didn't double-count statements when the president repeated himself.

Our analysis showed that the truth took a beating. From a grand total of 179 factual statements, we identified 120 that were false, mostly false or unsupported by evidence. That's 67 percent, or two-thirds of what Trump said.

In a similar analysis in September 2018, we found that 70 percent of Trump's statements were false, misleading or lacking evidence; the tally was 76 percent for a rally in July 2018. Trump's rallies have grown longer and the number of claims worth fact-checking has nearly doubled over the years, yet Trump's rate of false and misleading claims has remained largely consistent.

"Did you notice that everybody is saying Merry Christmas again? Did you notice?"

FALSE. This claim is a Trump favorite and also popular on Fox News and in right-wing media, but evidence of a "War on Christmas" is flimsy. The phrase "Merry Christmas" continues to be ubiquitous in retail advertisements, popular culture and public spaces even as some people and businesses use more secular holiday greetings. There's no evidence anything has changed under Trump.

"We have tremendous support in the Republican Party like we've never had before—nobody's ever had this kind of support."

FALSE. George W. Bush, George H.W. Bush, Ronald Reagan, Richard Nixon and Dwight Eisenhower had more support among Republicans than Trump, according to the Gallup poll.

"What's happening now—and by the way, your state, because of us, not because of local government, but because of us, because of the job that we've done. . . . Michigan's had the best year it's ever had. Best year it's ever had. And that's because we have auto companies expanding and thriving and they're coming in from Japan and they're coming in from a lot of other places."

FALSE. Trump is taking credit for an employment picture in Michigan that actually had been just as strong under previous presidents. Unemployment in the state fell to 4 percent in November 2019, but it had dropped below 4 percent in several of the previous years.

"I understand she's not fixing those potholes [referring to Michigan Gov. Gretchen Whitmer, a Democrat]. That's what the word is. It was all about roads, and they want to raise those gasoline taxes, and you—we don't want to do that. But she's not fixing the potholes."

MOSTLY FALSE. Michigan's transportation department spends about $9 million a year repairing potholes. Some experts say much more funding is needed to keep up with the state's pothole epidemic. Whitmer took office in 2019 and proposed raising the state gas tax to generate new funding for roads, but the state's Republican-led legislature so far has blocked her plan.

"I don't know if you know this, but probably 10 years ago, I was honored. I was the Man of the Year by, I think, somebody, whoever. I was the Man of the Year in Michigan. Can you believe it?"

FALSE. Trump claims he won Michigan's "Man of the Year" award, but there's no evidence any such award exists. Trump apparently was referring to a 2013 dinner hosted by a county Republican Party organization, which presented him with token gifts, including a statuette of Abraham Lincoln. A former Republican congressman who organized the dinner said Trump was not given an award and that the group has never named a "man of the year." Nevertheless, Trump has made this false claim at least seven times over three years.

"We just made the USMCA—we're getting rid of NAFTA."

MOSTLY ACCURATE. The Trump administration negotiated a new free-trade deal with Canada and Mexico that revises portions of NAFTA, which was adopted in 1994.

"[USMCA] makes it very, very prohibitive [to outsource auto industry jobs]. They can do it, but they've got to pay a hell of a big price to do it. And history has proven that stops 'em."

MOSTLY ACCURATE. The USMCA includes wage requirements stipulating that 40 to 45 percent of a car's parts be made by workers earning at least $16 per hour, as opposed to NAFTA, which had no wage requirement.

"Now, from the standpoint of the farmers, you know, what's going on, we had tremendous trade barriers in Canada. We had a tax on dairy

products, 297 percent tariff. Nobody talked about it with Canada, and we had some really bad things with Mexico."

MOSTLY FALSE. Trump suggests he reduced Canadian tariffs on U.S. dairy products. But it's not so simple. The Canadian dairy sector operates under a system that limits production, sets prices and restricts imports. Canadian tariffs, which range between 200 and 300 percent, come into effect when a fixed quota of U.S. exports is reached, though Canada already ranks as the second-biggest market for U.S. dairy products. In the reworked trade agreement, Trump won some narrow concessions on dairy, including higher quotas. But tariffs as high as 300 percent can be imposed on the purchase of dairy products that exceed those quotas.

"You know I had a lot of union labor vote for me, tremendous amount of labor."

MOSTLY ACCURATE. According to Politico, Hillary Clinton "carried union households by 9 points over Trump—a narrow margin when compared to the 20- and 18-point leads Barack Obama held in 2008 and 2012" over his Republican opponents.

"So we left a little stuff for the union because we figured to get it signed, we'll give a little bit and we did it and we have one great deal, and now you have the Democrats tried to take credit for this deal [USMCA] and that's okay. Whatever it takes."

ACCURATE. House Democrats and labor unions said the Trump administration made concessions to them to secure passage of the USMCA.

"We did a [trade] deal with South Korea."

ACCURATE. In 2018, Trump signed a revised United States–Korea Free Trade Agreement that paves a path for increased American exports such as cars.

"We did a [trade] deal with Japan, $40 billion deal with Japan, and we're not—that was just a little piece of a deal."

MOSTLY FALSE. Trump signed a trade deal with Japan in 2019. The $40 billion figure Trump used refers to the size of the market for digital products covered in the deal, but it says nothing about the reduction of tariffs.

"Get her out of here. . . . There's a slob, there's a real slob, wait, wait a minute. She'll get hell when she gets back home with Mom. . . . Okay, so there's one disgusting person who made—wait, wait—who made it—I wouldn't say this, but made a horrible gesture with the wrong finger, right? Now, they won't say that, the fake news. They won't say. If one of us did that, it would be like the biggest story ever. . . . I don't know who the security company is, but the police came up, but they want to be so politically correct, so they don't grab a likely risk and get her out. They say, 'Oh, would you please come?' 'If you'd please come with me.' 'Sir, ma'am, would you—' And then she gives the guy the finger and you—oh, oh. You got to get a little bit stronger than that, folks. Now, I hate to say it. I hate to say it, but, of course, the guy's afraid that, you know, he'll grab a wrist lightly and he'll be sued for the rest of his life, that you've destroyed her life."

UNSUBSTANTIATED. Trump went on an extended tangent in response to a protester at the rally. He falsely claimed that news reports whitewash the fact that some anti-Trump protesters use vulgarities. Then he claimed that police and security at his rallies avoid removing protesters for fear of getting sued. Then he theorized that this reticence to quickly eject protesters casts a bigger spotlight on criticism of Trump.

"The USMCA, which is going to be great for the automobile business, should even be good for the cereal business."

UNSUBSTANTIATED. Some industry experts say the USMCA gives a minor lift to U.S. dairy exporters, but neither the USMCA nor NAFTA included tariffs on cereal, and there's been no evidence of a major boost in cereal exports.

"We made a great deal with China. And you know, China's paying us billions and billions of dollars a year, they never gave us 10 cents."

FALSE. Tariffs have been collected on Chinese goods since the earliest days of the republic.

"We're leaving the 25 percent tariffs on $250 billion [of Chinese goods]. . . . We're leaving, you know, we're making another group of tariff, seven and a half percent."

ACCURATE. The Trump administration agreed to halve a 15 percent tariff on about $120 billion in Chinese products while negotiations began on "Phase Two" of a trade deal with China. A separate, 25 percent tariff on $250 billion worth of Chinese products remained.

"But we'd take it in, billions of dollars and to help the farmers who were targeted—$16 billion and $12 billion the previous year—helps

the farmers. . . . Out of that big check that we get out of, money flows into the Treasury, right? Out of the big check, we gave the farmers $16 billion and $12 billion."

MOSTLY ACCURATE. This is accurate in the sense that the Trump administration provided subsidies of $28 billion over two years to U.S. farmers who were targeted by China in retaliation for Trump's tariffs. Trump, however, fundamentally misrepresents how international trade works. Multiple economic studies show the cost of Trump's tariffs is mostly passed on to consumers.

"I was with a group of 36 farmers at the White House. You know what they said to me? I said, 'Don't worry about it, we're going to take care of you guys.' And I used a bad word. You know what word I used? We're going to get you a subsidy, and they said this two years ago. I said, 'How much were you targeted for?' This was the first year. 'Twelve billion, sir.' The second year was 16 [billion]. They were a target; that's what they didn't get from China. So I said, 'It's all right. We're going to give you a subsidy of the same, and we're going to take it out of the tariffs, and we're gonna have billions and billions of dollars left over.' And they said, 'Sir, we don't want money. We just want a level playing field.'"

INACCURATE. The Trump tariffs garnered about $39 billion on products from China through December 2019, according to Customs and Border Protection, and the administration announced $28 billion in farm subsidies over two years to offset domestic producers' losses from the trade war. That means the tariff revenue from China has been largely eaten up by payments the government has made to farmers who lost business.

"We made the largest-ever investment in our military, $738 billion."

MOSTLY FALSE. In inflation-adjusted dollars, this is not a record. Trump had requested $750 billion. The 2010 defense budget amounted to about $810 billion in current dollars.

"Our military, by the way, in all due respect to the previous two administrations, our military was—was depleted, it was depleted, it was in bad shape."

FALSE. The military budget had declined as a result of decreases in funding for Overseas Contingency Operations as both the wars in Iraq and Afghanistan came to a close, not because the military's resources were depleted. The bipartisan Budget Control Act also helped keep down defense spending.

"We had fighter jets that were 35 years old. We had planes that were 60, as you heard, where the father flew him, the grandfather flew him, and now the young son comes in."

MOSTLY FALSE. The Air Force uses an updated version of the U-2 spy plane, not the same model that was flying six decades ago. Two Cold War–era B-52 planes have been refurbished—one in 2019 and another 2015. They did not fly continuously for 60 years. The last B-52 was built in 1962.

"We've got the best [military] equipment in the world, now spent $2.5 trillion, made in the USA, two and a half trillion."

FALSE. Trump appears to be combining three fiscal years of military funding, but the money is not all spent, only a portion of it is destined for new equipment, and the equipment is not all built.

"We're building a lot of ships now."

ACCURATE. The Navy is building dozens of new ships over five years.

"We're building submarines, the power of which nobody's ever seen before."

ACCURATE. The United States is building a new generation of Virginia-class submarines with more firepower and "the ability to launch strikes with 40 Tomahawk cruise missiles, compared to just 12 on the current ships," according to CNN.

"These countries that come in, prime ministers, presidents, sometimes dictators—those we can't deal with too much—'Sir, we'd like to buy a nuclear submarine.' I say, 'No, thanks.' I turn them all down. You have no idea how many people."

UNSUBSTANTIATED.

"Very early on, I thought we were going to have a problem someplace and one of the generals came up to me and said, 'Sir, don't go, don't do it.' 'Why?' 'We don't have the ammunition.' And I said two things . . . We never want to have a president hear that again, nor do we want a president to have to go through the crap that we're going through right now."

MOSTLY FALSE. Trump often repeats this claim that the military had run out of ammunition when he took office. Toward the end of the Obama administration, after targeting Islamic State operatives with tens of thousands of smart bombs and guided missiles, U.S.

military officials began to say publicly that stockpiles were growing thin. But Trump never limits his comments to precision-guided missiles (PGMs) and instead gives the impression that all ammunition was running low. U.S. officials already were working on rebuilding PGM stockpiles before Trump took office.

"U.S. Armed Forces, the last branch was the Air Force, right? That was many, many decades ago."

ACCURATE. The Air Force was established as an independent military branch in 1947.

"We are now building, and we have now gotten funding for, the sixth branch of the United States Armed Forces: the Space Force, the Space Force."

ACCURATE. Congress allocated $40 million for the Space Force in 2019, less than the $72.4 million requested by the Defense Department.

"We just provided record funding for our nation's historically black colleges and universities."

MOSTLY ACCURATE. The Trump administration has increased funding for historically black colleges and universities, though some experts say cuts to other programs indirectly hamper these institutions.

"Another 266,000 jobs last month. . . . But they said they were guessing, could be 70,000, could be 80,000, maybe 90, maybe 110, somebody said. Then the number comes out: 266,000 with an adjustment."

MOSTLY ACCURATE. Trump got the November jobs report right; it showed a solid gain of 266,000. But he exaggerated the degree to which it beat forecasts. Economists surveyed by Dow Jones, for example, had predicted a gain of 187,000 jobs.

"As of yesterday, we've had 133 record days in the stock market now, and that's in less than three years."

MOSTLY FALSE. The stock market was doing well, but Trump's scorekeeping is fishy. For example, on Oct. 10, 2019, he said "The stock market today just hit another all-time high." Trump didn't say which index he was talking about, but his statement was not true of any of the major indexes, and the Dow Jones industrial average had been higher nine days earlier.

"I'm not allowed to have stock. I can't have stock. They considered the conflict of interest, and that I can't understand, I mean, I can't."

UNSUBSTANTIATED. These claims from Trump—who has declined to release his tax returns or divest from his business—should be taken with a grain of salt.

Trump's transition team claimed in December 2016 that he had sold all his stocks. "President-Elect Trump has already disposed of his investments in publicly traded or easily liquidated investments," said a January 2017 white paper from Trump's attorneys.

A year and a half later, on his 2018 financial disclosure form, Trump reported at least $250,000 in income from stocks, specifically listing Apple, Caterpillar, Halliburton, Microsoft, PepsiCo, Phillips 66 and a publicly traded New Jersey textile company now named Global Fiber Technologies. Then, on his 2019 financial disclosure form, Trump no longer listed income from stocks in these or any other companies.

Trump perhaps was advised he couldn't hold stocks while in office, but the law itself is unclear. The president and vice president are not considered federal employees and technically are not subject to federal ethics rules or criminal penalties covering conflicts of interest. Former presidents such as George W. Bush and Bill Clinton placed their investments, including stocks, in a blind trust.

"The 401(k)s, where people are up 90 percent, they're up 97 percent, they're up 82 percent."

FALSE. Trump often boasts that the value of 401(k) retirement accounts has skyrocketed during his presidency, even though there's no evidence of such huge gains and even though the Census Bureau reports that only 32 percent of Americans are saving for retirement with such plans. An analysis by Fidelity Investments showed the average 401(k) balance increased less than 1 percent from the first quarter of 2018 to the same period in 2019.

"Ford Motor Company just announced that it is investing $1.5 billion in two auto factories in the Detroit area, creating another 3,000 Michigan jobs."

ACCURATE.

"Many other investments we've gotten from Japanese companies, car companies and other companies, but they're all coming in, and a lot of them are coming to Michigan."

MOSTLY FALSE. Some automobile industry investments have been announced in Michigan, but not by Japanese companies.

"We're doing so well in Michigan with the auto companies. Now you're back, you're back. . . . Very proud of it. But while we're creating jobs, fighting for Michigan workers and achieving numbers that you've never seen before, incredible victories for the American people are happening."

FALSE. Car-manufacturing jobs are essentially flat in Michigan since Trump took office, at 42,000. Michigan's total for parts manufacturing jobs fell slightly from July 2016 to November 2019.

"I have the greatest economy in the history of this country."

FALSE. By just about any important measure, the economy is humming along, but it is not doing as well as under Eisenhower, Lyndon B. Johnson, Clinton or Grant.

"Let me just tell you a little secret, if Crooked Hillary would have won, your economy would have crashed."

UNSUBSTANTIATED. Trump often makes this claim, but there's no evidence to back him up. Until the coronavirus epidemic hit, the U.S. economy under Trump continued to grow, as it did for most of the Obama administration.

"You were going down. The regulations were taking it down, the taxes were taking it down. Instead of being up 92 percent or whatever— you're up a lot—you would have been down. . . . . It was crashing. For all those people that would say, 'Oh, it's the Obama,' let me tell you something, you were dying. . . . It was heading south as sure as you're standing."

FALSE. The economy was not "going down," "crashing," "dying" or "heading south" when Trump took office; GDP was growing and unemployment was declining.

"I'm sorry we couldn't get your seats; we didn't have any room. And by the way, 20,000 people outside had to leave."

FALSE. Trump often inflates the crowd size at his rallies. Local officials at this event in Battle Creek said 5,400 people were admitted to the venue while 2,000—not 20,000—were left outside.

"This is about a 5,500-seat arena, and I said to my people, 'Why so small?'"

MOSTLY FALSE. Kellogg Arena seats up to 6,200, according to its website. Local officials said Trump filled the venue with approximately 5,400 attendees.

"I watch these guys come in like Biden, he has a—he has a big rally, and they get 93 people show up. No, it's true."

FALSE. Biden has never held a campaign rally with that few people attending, and the Biden campaign said no such rally had taken place.

"And did you see the new polls from USA Today? *Came out, I'm killing everybody, and . . .* USA Today *hates me. But there's a poll, we're beating everybody."*

MOSTLY FALSE. A poll from *USA Today* and Suffolk University released the day before this rally indeed showed Trump beating every major Democrat by between three and 10 points, but the poll tested Trump against both a Democrat and a third-party candidate, not in a head-to-head matchup with a Democrat. In the poll, a generic third-party candidate garnered support in the double digits. Other reputable polls from that period that did not include a third-party option showed that several leading Democrats would defeat Trump.

"Biden has this rally like, you know, they got 200 seats, but only a small number of people. So you know what they do? They set up a roundtable. So think of these people. They come in, they think they get to listen to the speech, they end up sitting at a roundtable discussing. They must have been happy, right?"

FALSE. There's no record of this happening, and the Biden campaign denies it.

"You finally got a choice [referring to the Veterans Choice program]. They've been trying to get it for almost 50 years."

FALSE. Trump often takes credit for laws enacted years before he took office. In response to a 2014 scandal over wait times and patient care at Veterans Affairs facilities in Phoenix and other locations, a bipartisan group of lawmakers and Obama created the VA Choice program, which allows vets to get private care when VA wait times exceed a certain limit. Trump signed the MISSION Act, an expansion and update of the Choice program.

"I've had crowds over the last couple of weeks—we went to different Pennsylvania and Florida—but I mean, thousands and thousands of people can't get into these NBA arenas, right? Big arenas and we set records."

MOSTLY FALSE. Trump sometimes draws an overflow crowd of thousands to his rallies, and he sometimes fails to fill the seats. The NBA does not play in the Hershey, Pa., and Sunrise, Fla., venues where Trump recently had held rallies, and the president did not break attendance records at those arenas.

"We set records at every arena—they never even mention the crowds. They never mentioned the crowds, it's sort of amazing. You know what? I don't think we've ever had an empty seat from the time I came down the escalator—that's a long time ago. I don't think we've ever had an empty seat. Now, what the crooked media does, though, if you got like over here—look how packed it is and it's thousands outside. . . . But here's the thing, if this man and that beautiful woman happened to get up because they want to go to the bathroom, those cameras will turn to those two seats and they'll say, 'Trump wasn't able to fill up the arena.' . . . Nobody ever leaves our speeches because is there a better place to be in the world than a Trump rally? Never. Nobody."

FALSE. This claim is as silly as it is old. People leave Trump rallies. The evidence abounds. These events are long. They start late. Trump often complains that news reports don't mention his crowd sizes, but they do. Often, it's necessary to do so because Trump's claimed attendance is way off the mark and requires a fact check.

"After three years of sinners and witch hunts, hoaxes, scams, tonight the House Democrats are trying to nullify the ballots of tens of millions of patriotic Americans."

DISTORTED. The Constitution allows the House to impeach the president for "high crimes and misdemeanors," but that's not the same as nullifying an election. The Senate holds a trial in impeachment cases, and a two-thirds majority is needed to convict and remove an officeholder. If Trump had been removed, Vice President Pence would have assumed the presidency.

"Grand Rapids. We have 32,000 people that night, it was one o'clock in the morning. That means it was Election Day [2016] when I started speaking. Hillary, Barack Obama, Michelle Obama, and Bill Clinton, they did an emergency trip, they did an emergency trip to Michigan at six o'clock. They got here at prime time, they started to speak. She had 500 people."

FALSE. The Michigan venue where Trump rallied in the early-morning hours of Election Day 2016 has a capacity of 4,200, a fraction of the 32,000 claimed by Trump. Hillary Clinton held a rally the same day at nearby Grand Valley State University; it was described as a "capacity crowd" in a venue that holds 4,100 people. Neither Barack nor Michelle Obama attended this Clinton rally, so this claim by Trump is false in every way.

"The problem is the newspaper polls are more fake than the news they write. They write fake polls. It's true. They write fake polls. You call them suppression polls, you read them and you get depressed because it looks like you're doing badly. They do that."

FALSE. News and polling organizations do not publish "suppression polls," which in Trump's parlance are polls that relay false information to demoralize and dissuade people from voting.

"They told him [Bill Clinton], 'What do you know?' Remember they shut him out at the end, they didn't want him talking? He was right. . . . He talked about Wisconsin, he talked about Michigan."

MOSTLY FALSE. Former president Clinton made appearances for his wife's campaign through the end of the 2016 election; he wasn't shut out. Clinton reportedly raised concerns that the campaign was failing to reach undecided voters such as working-class whites, but we couldn't find reports that Clinton specifically raised alarms about Michigan and Wisconsin, as Trump claimed.

"[Bill Clinton] said, 'Crooked, I'm telling you, Crooked, I don't like what I see in Michigan. I was in Michigan and I'm telling you that those damn signs, I saw some houses where that four of them on one lawn and two of them on the car.' And he said, 'You horrible human being. You better start listening to me because you're going to get your ass whipped.'"

FALSE. Trump appears to have made up this crude conversation between Bill and Hillary Clinton.

"[Hillary Clinton] didn't come to Michigan enough and she didn't come to Wisconsin, I think, at all, right? Because her polling data look good."

MOSTLY ACCURATE. Clinton did visit Michigan shortly before the 2016 election, though some of her supporters say it was too little, too late. She did not travel to Wisconsin after losing the state's Democratic primary to Sen. Bernie Sanders (I-Vt.).

"We won Michigan."

ACCURATE.

"The word is that we're much higher right now in the polls than we were ever in 2016 in Michigan."

FALSE. Most polls in 2019 showed Trump losing Michigan in head-to-head matchups with leading Democratic contenders.

"Congressional Democrats are directly attacking 2.3 million Michigan voters who rose up in 2016, won the state, and now, the Democrats are very upset. They want to get Michigan back. They just don't know how to do it because they didn't do a thing for Michigan. . . . All they did was take away your companies and let them go to Mexico and other places."

MOSTLY FALSE. Experts say automation, international labor-wage disparities and trade policies caused the United States to lose millions of manufacturing jobs in recent decades. Democrats are not solely responsible for those shifts or policies.

"Mexico has 32 percent of your car business. You know that, right? . . . Thirty-two percent of our car business moved to Mexico."

UNSUBSTANTIATED. It's unclear where Trump gets this estimate. Millions of manufacturing jobs and thousands of U.S. factories have disappeared since NAFTA took effect in 1994, but it's difficult to isolate how many were relocated to Mexico or how many left because of NAFTA.

Studies we reviewed indicate NAFTA had a modest effect on the U.S. economy. Auto industry representatives and independent analysts seem to agree that NAFTA's impact helped rather than hindered automakers with U.S. operations.

Mexico was a relatively small player in North American vehicle production before NAFTA, producing only 3 percent of the continent's vehicles in 1987; it now makes about 20 percent of light vehicles. The U.S. share of North American vehicle production was 70 percent in 2007 and is projected to be about 60 percent in 2020, according to a 2016 report by the Center for Automotive Research.

"Today's illegal, unconstitutional and partisan impeachment . . . Democrat lawmakers do not believe you have the right to select your own president."

FALSE. Impeachment is neither illegal nor unconstitutional. It's literally spelled out in the Constitution. Democrats alleged that Trump committed "high crimes and misdemeanors" by attempting to extort Ukraine for help in the 2020 U.S. election.

"This lawless, partisan impeachment is a political suicide march for the Democrat Party. Have you seen my polls in the last four weeks? It's crazy."

FALSE. Support for impeaching Trump was about 47 percent and hardly moved in the four weeks before these remarks (or even before that), according to an analysis by FiveThirtyEight. Trump's approval ratings, mostly in the low 40s, were largely stable at that point, but they rose just after the impeachment trial to Trump's highest level to that date, at 49 percent in a Gallup poll.

"They've been trying to impeach me from Day One. They've been trying to impeach me from before I ran, okay?"

MOSTLY FALSE. Some Trump critics have been calling for his impeachment for years. But House Speaker Nancy Pelosi (D-Calif.) rebuffed calls to impeach the president until she announced an inquiry into the Ukraine scandal in September 2019.

"If you remember, when I ran, I went immediately to number one, never came off number—we had center stage from Day One, in the debates."

MOSTLY ACCURATE. Trump dominated Republican primary polls once he declared his candidacy in mid-2015, though Ben Carson briefly topped him in November 2015.

"I said, wait a minute. This is no good. I want odd numbers [of participants in a debate] because if you're center stage, if you have 10, that means two people are in the middle. So, I said make it 11 or make it nine, okay? Or I'm not showing up. And generally, they did it because we were way ahead from the beginning."

UNSUBSTANTIATED.

"You know what? These guys are a part of the Democrat Party. They are a part of it. You might as well call them Democrats. No, the media, look, look, I don't—you know, it's hard for somebody to know if you're not the subject because how do you know the New York Times *is totally dishonest or* The Washington Post *or* ABC *is so bad? CBS, so bad."*

FALSE. When Trump doesn't like what's being reported, he calls it fake news or complains about media bias. But in almost every case, the reports are proven to be accurate. Reputable news organizations follow ethical codes and correct mistakes promptly, something Trump knows since he often celebrates these corrections on Twitter.

"NBC, I made a lot of money for NBC with 'The Apprentice,' right? A lot of money, a lot. Plus, we had the number one show a lot, and they

had nothing in the top 10, except for a thing called 'The Apprentice,' and they treat me so bad."

PARTLY FALSE. Trump's reality-television show was highly profitable for NBC and was the seventh-most-watched TV show in 2004, when it premiered, with about 21 million viewers a week. That was the show's only year in the top 10, and ratings tanked in following seasons.

"CNN and MSNBC, their ratings are down the tubes."

EXAGGERATED. Although both CNN and MSNBC suffered ratings declines in 2019, their audiences shrank by 9 percent and 3 percent, respectively, so Trump's characterization is a big exaggeration.

"You have the greatest economy in the history of the world. Other countries come to see me, all of their leaders, and they say, 'Sir,' first thing. 'Sir, congratulations on your economy.' . . . And these guys [the news media] don't like talking about it. And if they do, they say Obama did it."

FALSE. Trump first made this grandiose claim when the U.S. economy expanded at an annual rate of 3.5 percent in the third quarter of 2018. Many other countries had faster growth rates at the time, including China and India, but the president persisted with his assessment. News reports about the U.S. economic expansion are published on a daily basis. Trump succeeded Obama during a sustained period of economic growth, which he fails to acknowledge.

"Remember, Obama said, 'You will never be president.' 'He will never be president.'"

ACCURATE. Obama predicted in 2016 that Trump would not win the presidency.

"[Obama] said, 'I will consider it a personal affront if you allow him [Trump] to be president.'"

FALSE. Obama said he would be insulted if his supporters sat out the 2016 election. "After we have achieved historic turnout in 2008 and 2012, especially in the African American community, I will consider it a personal insult, an insult to my legacy, if this community lets down its guard and fails to activate itself in this election," he said in September 2016.

"I go upstairs, downstairs, all around. They take me up three flights, go down one, I said, 'Are we almost there?' 'Yes, sir, another four flights.' And I say, 'You think Hillary could do this?' I don't think so. They'd bring her back home, she wants to go to sleep."

UNSUBSTANTIATED. Hillary Clinton was secretary of state, a demanding job involving extensive travel.

"They shouldn't even be allowed to have an impeachment because it was based on dishonesty. It was based on illegality. She [Hillary Clinton] went out, and they paid for a fake dossier."

MOSTLY FALSE. The House impeached Trump based on evidence that he attempted to extort Ukraine in exchange for help in the 2020 election. The Steele dossier had nothing to do with it. The dossier was commissioned by the opposition research firm Fusion GPS for a law firm affiliated with the Democratic National Committee and the Clinton campaign. Fusion has said the former British spy who wrote the report received $168,000 for it.

"The FBI then took that fake dossier and they used it in the FISA [Foreign Intelligence Surveillance Act] court to get approval to spy on my campaign. . . . So, they use this fake dossier and they brought it before this big deal court. It's a big deal, the FISA court, and they said this stuff—and they lied about it."

MOSTLY FALSE. The Justice Department inspector general issued a report in late 2019 affirming that the investigation into Trump's campaign and Russia stemmed not from the Steele dossier but rather from a tip from a friendly foreign government—Australia.

"This information provided the FBI with an articulable factual basis that, if true, reasonably indicated activity constituting either a federal crime or a threat to national security, or both," the report said.

A judge approved a warrant authorizing secret surveillance of Trump foreign policy adviser Carter Page after he had departed the campaign. The warrant was renewed three times. The inspector general later found numerous errors in the warrant application and concluded that the Steele dossier was a key source on one topic: Page's alleged coordination with the Russian government on 2016 U.S. campaign activities. However, the inspector general found that the FBI did not act with political bias when it applied for the warrant.

"Because Comey, who's another beauty. Did I do a great job when I fired his ass? What a great job. Oh, no, they had bad plans. No, I did a great thing. That was like throwing a rock at a hornet's nest. Did that place explode? And then, we learned about Lisa Page and her wonder-

ful lover, Peter Strzok. I love you, Lisa. I love you more than anybody in the world. I love you more than anybody in the world. Causes problems with the wife, but we won't talk about that. . . . I've never loved anyone like you. He's going to lose one hundred million to one, Peter, right? That's right. He's going to lose one hundred million to one, but there's no bias. How about the insurance policy?"

MOSTLY FALSE. The Justice Department inspector general found that bias did not taint FBI leaders' decisions in the investigation of Trump's campaign and Russia.

Trump mentioned an "insurance policy" that he believed meant the FBI would target him if he won. But former FBI agent Peter Strzok has insisted the reference in his text to former FBI lawyer Lisa Page had nothing to do with targeting Trump. The issue was whether an important source could be burned.

"The [Justice Department] inspector general . . . don't forget, he was appointed by Obama."

ACCURATE.

"They said, there's nobody in the world that could have handled that stuff that happened and still created one of the greatest economies and done more than any other president ever before in the first three years."

MOSTLY FALSE. Trump has signed few major pieces of legislation compared with other presidents after three years in office. Scholars of the presidency say the whirlwind of accomplishments under presidents such as Franklin D. Roosevelt, Johnson, Reagan and Obama exceeded Trump's efforts.

"They have nothing [referring to the impeachment evidence gathered by Democrats]."

FALSE. Senior Trump administration officials, including John Bolton, the president's former national security adviser, raised concerns about the administration's dealings with Ukraine.

The House Intelligence Committee gathered evidence that Trump withheld $391 million in security assistance funds for Ukraine while he pressed that country to announce investigations into a potential Democratic opponent, Joe Biden, and into a debunked conspiracy theory that Ukrainians, not Russians, interfered in the 2016 presidential election.

The testimony of senior officials was corroborated by text messages, emails, documents, Trump's own public remarks and a rough transcript of his July 25 call with Ukrainian President Volodymyr Zelensky.

The Senate acquitted Trump, though more than half of senators said they disapproved of his conduct.

"You got this guy Schiff. He makes up a statement and he goes in front of Congress where he has immunity, and he makes up a statement from me that's totally fictitious, totally out of thin air, the worst statement I've ever heard, many people saw it."

PARTLY FALSE. Schiff inserted some dramatized, paraphrased comments in Trump's voice as he described Trump's July 25 phone call with Zelensky.

Much of what Schiff said tracked the basic thrust of the call, but he stretched the truth in claiming that Trump asked Zelensky to "make up" or "manufacture" dirt.

"I then sent him the transcript. . . . I call it perfect. He called it perfect. Everyone calls it if you read it."

FALSE. Many outside experts say Trump's July 25 call with the Ukrainian president was highly unusual. Trump appeared to have no agenda except to ask for the Ukrainian government to work with his private attorney to investigate a potential rival and a debunked conspiracy theory about possible interference by Ukraine in the 2016 U.S. election. National security officials were so alarmed that they lodged objections with a White House lawyer before and right after the call.

"I never even think about looks anymore. I don't talk about looks of a male or female."

FALSE. This is objectively untrue. Trump routinely praises or mocks the physical appearance of others. For example, at this rally, he said that Schiff was unattractive and that some F-35 pilots he met were "better looking than Tom Cruise."

"Where's the proof? It's coming, it's coming. Then, we get the Mueller report—nothing."

FALSE. Special counsel Robert S. Mueller III revealed significant criminal activity by some of Trump's campaign advisers and by Russian individuals and entities.

Mueller concluded that Russian government actors had successfully hacked into computers and obtained emails from people associated with the Clinton campaign and Democratic Party organizations, and then publicly disseminated those materials through various intermediaries, including WikiLeaks, to sow discord in the United States, hurt Clinton and help Trump.

The special counsel's report says, "Although the investigation established that the Russian government perceived it would benefit from a Trump presidency and worked to secure that outcome, and that the Campaign expected it would benefit electorally from information stolen and released through Russian efforts, the investigation did not establish that members of the Trump Campaign conspired or coordinated with the Russian government in its election interference activities."

Mueller declined to reach a decision on whether to bring charges against Trump for obstructing justice. The special counsel also did not make an explicit recommendation to Congress on impeachment. But Mueller spent nearly half of the report laying out a sustained effort by Trump to derail the investigation, including an effort by the president to have Mueller removed.

"If we had confidence after a thorough investigation of the facts that the President clearly did not commit obstruction of justice, we would so state," the report says. "Based on the facts and the applicable legal standards, however, we are unable to reach that judgment. The evidence we obtained about the President's actions and intent presents difficult issues that prevent us from conclusively determining that no criminal conduct occurred. Accordingly, while this report does not conclude that the President committed a crime, it also does not exonerate him."

"Did Mueller do a good job? Did he do? How was his performance in front of Congress? Not the best, but think of this, $45 million they spent, and you know, I heard somebody say, 'Well, we got back some of that money.' Let me tell you, you cost this country billions and bil-

lions and billions of dollars in all of the things that didn't get done, in all of the embarrassment to our country. You cost billions and billions of dollars and it was a hoax."

FALSE. The special counsel's office reported $32 million in direct and indirect expenses. According to CNN, Mueller recouped approximately $17 million for the U.S. government from assets seized from Paul Manafort, Trump's onetime campaign manager, who was sentenced to prison for fraud as part of the Russia probe.

"I said, I haven't spoken to Russia in years. What the hell do I have to do with Russia?"

MOSTLY FALSE. Trump signed a letter of intent to build a Trump Tower Moscow in October 2015, and his former attorney, Michael Cohen, has testified that he was pursuing the project on Trump's behalf in 2015 and 2016. The Mueller report says Trump declined to answer questions from the special counsel about the Moscow project.

"Oh, I think we have a vote [on impeachment] coming in. So, we got every single Republican voted for us. Whoa, wow, wow, almost 200. . . . We didn't lose one Republican vote and, and three Democrats voted for us."

MOSTLY ACCURATE. Two Democrats voted against Trump's impeachment. A third Democrat, Rep. Tulsi Gabbard of Hawaii, voted "present." No House Republicans voted to impeach Trump. However, Rep. Justin Amash (I-Mich.), a Republican until five months before the impeachment, voted to charge the president.

"The Democrats . . . they've got horrible policies: open borders, crime is fine, drugs pouring through."

FALSE. Many Democrats support tougher border controls, but they have not reached an agreement with Republicans on comprehensive immigration reform. Almost all research shows that immigrants commit crime at lower rates than the native-born population. Government data shows that most drugs are smuggled through legal checkpoints.

"The individual mandate, just a little while ago, came over the wires, it was just upheld. The individual mandate is now gone."

MOSTLY ACCURATE. On the same day as this Trump rally, a federal appeals court ruled that the Affordable Care Act's requirement that all adults either have health insurance or pay a financial penalty was unconstitutional. (Republicans had already neutralized the individual mandate after Trump took office by reducing the penalty to zero.)

"When you watch some of these people get up and speak today, they don't even—'Look, you have violated the Constitution.' Well, what has he done wrong? 'Well, we don't know that.' They don't even have any crime. This is the first impeachment where there is no crime."

FALSE. A statutory crime is not required to impeach. But the House Judiciary Committee's report on Trump and Ukraine said the first article of impeachment against Trump "encompassed impeachable 'bribery' and violations of federal criminal law."

The House Intelligence Committee's report says Trump "personally and acting through agents within and outside of the U.S. government, solicited the interference of a foreign government, Ukraine, to benefit his reelection." Requesting foreign assistance in U.S. elections is illegal.

"I see a woman, Carolyn Maloney. . . . I was with her. Her first race, I helped her. She was always so nice. 'Oh, thank you. Thank you.' I made lots of contributions over the years. You know in New York, it's like, purely Democrat, especially Manhattan. So, what happens? I make lots of contributions for years and years and years. . . . 'I raise my hand to impeach.' Well, give me back the damn money that I've been paying you for so many years."

MOSTLY ACCURATE. Trump contributed $4,000 to Maloney's congressional campaigns from 1993 to 2009. According to Federal Election Commission records, the donations started when she was already a freshman member of Congress, not when she was running her first race.

"Debbie Dingell, that's a real beauty. So, she calls me up like eight months ago. Her husband was there a long time, but I didn't give him the B treatment. I didn't give him the C or the D. I could have. Nobody would ask. You know, I gave the A-plus treatment. Take down the flags. Why are you taking them down for ex-Congressman Dingell? Oh, okay. Do this, do that, do that, rotunda, everything. I gave them everything. That's okay. I don't want anything for it. I don't need anything for anything. She calls me up: 'It's the nicest thing that's ever happened. Thank you so much. John would be so thrilled. He's looking down, he'd be so—thank you so much, sir.' I said: 'That's okay. Don't worry about it.' Maybe he's looking up. I don't know. . . . No, but I look at her and she's so sincere and what happens? 'I vote to impeach Trump.'"

FALSE. Leaving aside Trump's suggestion that Rep. John Dingell is in hell, Rep. Debbie Dingell (D-Mich.), who succeeded her late husband in Congress, said she didn't call Trump. "He called me to tell me he was lowering the flags," she said. "And that meant a lot. But John Dingell earned his burial at Arlington Cemetery because he's a World War II veteran."

Trump also implied that he arranged for Dingell to lie in state in the Capitol Rotunda, but Dingell did not lie in state there (and such decisions are made by congressional leaders, not by the president).

"I say basically, very simple, 'Do us a favor'—our country, do us, do us, not me, our country. And then, what do I say? I say the United States attorney general. Attorney general of the United States could speak to you would be great, okay? Because it's known for major corruption. . . . I used the word 'us,' us as the United States, our country."

FALSE. Trump seems to have been attempting to whitewash his requests of Zelensky. Weeks after the rough transcript of the July 25 call with the Ukrainian president was released, Trump began claiming that when he said "do us a favor" in the call, "us" referred to the United States, not to himself or his administration.

This is a real stretch. Trump repeatedly requested that Ukrainian officials meet with his personal lawyer, Rudolph W. Giuliani, whom he didn't mention at the Michigan rally. Senior U.S. officials with responsibility over Ukraine matters have said that the allegations Trump wanted investigated were baseless.

"In fact, the new leader of Ukraine got in on a . . . platform where he looks for all of the problems of dishonesty and everything that was going on in Ukraine, right? He looked for it. That's how he got into office."

ACCURATE. Zelensky campaigned on an anti-corruption platform, and many experts said Trump complicated the Ukrainian's agenda by placing unexplained holds on U.S. security assistance funds and dragging Ukraine into the 2020 presidential campaign.

"The president of Ukraine, who is a quality person, said there was no pressure exerted whatsoever. That was a killer for the Democrats, right? Then, his foreign minister said the same thing. He said there was no pressure exerted whatsoever."

MOSTLY FALSE. U.S. officials have testified that Zelensky's government knew the Trump administration was delaying security assistance funds and that the Ukrainian leader was preparing to give CNN an interview in which he would announce the investigations Trump wanted. The interview was canceled. But the Ukrainian leader later criticized Trump for holding up the security funds. "If you're our strategic partner, then you can't go blocking anything for us," Zelensky told *Time* magazine. "I think that's just about fairness."

"Did you see what the Democrats did a couple of days ago? They tried to say that [Zelensky was] not a strong person, that he was weak. They used the word 'weak,' that he was weak and under the power of Trump, he said. Well, do you know how insulting that is?"

MOSTLY FALSE. Democrats and independent experts have pointed out the large power disparity between Trump and Zelensky. Ukraine has been at war with Russia since 2014 and relies on U.S. military and diplomatic support to defend itself. It's not an insult to point out that under such precarious circumstances, the Ukrainian president would be hard-pressed to refuse any request from his American counterpart.

"You know in 2018, in 2018, I didn't run. . . . Well, actually we picked up two seats in the Senate that these guys never talk about."

MOSTLY FALSE. Republicans already held the Senate majority, and they picked up one seat, not two, in 2018. The result was expected and widely reported at the time.

"We just approved 171 Supreme Court justices—federal court justices, 171 federal justices, including Courts of Appeal, 171, will be up, probably by the end of the year, to 182."

ACCURATE. Trump had appointed more than 170 federal judges at this point.

"I thank President Obama. He gave me 142 openings."

MOSTLY FALSE. When Trump took office, approximately 100 judicial seats were vacant. He should thank Senate Majority Leader Mitch McConnell (R-Ky.) as well as Obama. Before Trump took office, Senate Republicans stonewalled many of Obama's judicial nominees instead of giving them hearings.

"I have to tell you, I have to be always very truthful because if I'm a little bit off, they call me a liar. They'll say, he gets a Pinocchio, the stupid Washington Post. *They're Pinocchio."*

FALSE. Trump has earned all of his Pinocchios fair and square. We tend not to bother writing about claims that are "a little bit off" when there are so many fantastically false claims emanating from the president.

313

"Our drug price is down for the first time in 51 years, drug prices came down."

MOSTLY FALSE. Prices for generic drugs seem to be declining, but branded drugs are becoming costlier.

The consumer price index for prescription drugs in 2018 fell for the first time in 46, not 51, years. But a range of independent studies we found shows drug prices have not declined, especially when it comes to branded drugs.

"We're approving very soon for the governor of Florida, Ron DeSantis. . . . We're giving him the right to go and buy from a foreign country where the prices for the identical drug, identical drug, are 50 percent less, and he's going to do that for the people of Florida and we're going to do that for your governors if they want to do that."

MOSTLY ACCURATE. The Trump administration has announced plans to allow states to buy cheaper drugs from Canada. "But officials could not say when the plan might go into effect, and many questions about its possible scope remain unanswered," *The Washington Post* reported.

"[The New York Times*] came out with a story that was—where it was a great headline for me—and the people that read it, the super-radical left, they called and complained so much that they changed the headline and took it from positive to negative on a good story. Can you believe it?"*

MOSTLY ACCURATE. Trump has made a slew of divisive and, at times, racist statements directed at minorities. After mass shootings in Ohio and Texas left more than 30 people dead during one week-end in August 2019, the *Times* was criticized for its headline on a front-page story: "Trump Urges Unity vs. Racism." The headline was later changed to "Assailing Hate but Not Guns." Times editors said the first headline was "bad" because it didn't accurately reflect the article's focus on both Trump's condemnation of racism and on "his brand of divisive politics."

"They made more money 24 years ago than they were making when I got elected president, and they worked one job versus two or three jobs."

MOSTLY FALSE. Data from the Bureau of Labor Statistics shows that the percentage of people working two jobs has declined since the Great Recession—and has held relatively steady, at about 5 percent, since 2010. Going back 20 years, it was about 6 percent.

Adjusted for inflation, the purchasing power of paychecks has barely budged over the last 40 years, though the Congressional Budget Office found that wages grew for all income groups during this period. The rate of increase, however, was most dramatic for the top 1 percent, while everyone else saw relatively modest increases.

"The salaries—and you know, the number one group of people that are going up is the blue-collar worker."

MOSTLY ACCURATE. Some research and data show that pay grew fastest for low-wage workers, increasing 16 percent since Trump's election in 2016.

"African American unemployment is the lowest it's ever been in the history of our country."

MOSTLY ACCURATE. The black unemployment rate has reached record lows since Trump took office, though it ticked up slightly in November 2019 before soaring during the paralysis of the economy during the epidemic. The Labor Department began to report this rate in 1972, so it's a stretch to call it the lowest "in the history of our country."

"[Black] poverty levels are the best they've ever been in the history of our country."

ACCURATE. Poverty has been declining for decades, and black poverty rates have reached new lows since Trump took office, though nearly 25 percent of the African American population still live under the poverty line, which is about double the rate for all Americans.

"With Hispanic Americans, the best unemployment numbers and employment numbers."

ACCURATE. Hispanic unemployment reached record lows under Trump, hitting 4.2 percent in November.

"With Asians, the best unemployment."

ACCURATE. The jobless rate for Asian Americans reached a record-low 2 percent in May 2018, but data for this category goes back only to 2000, so there's not a lot of room for historical comparison.

"The best unemployment, and women, I'm sorry, 71 years, best in 71 years."

MOSTLY ACCURATE. Under Trump, the unemployment rate for women has attained its lowest levels since 1953. That's about 67 years.

"They're accusing me really of doing what Joe Biden admitted. . . . He's on tape saying that he's holding back $1 billion from Ukraine unless you change the prosecutor."

FALSE. Trump accuses Biden of something he did not do. The Ukrainian prosecutor general's office had opened an investigation into a Ukrainian oligarch who owned Burisma Holdings, a natural gas company. Hunter Biden, the vice president's son, joined Burisma's board in April 2014 and left in 2019. Ukraine's prosecutor general, Viktor Shokin, let the investigation go dormant, as he had for other investigations. The United States and its allies decided Shokin was not effective in his job and had let corruption flourish.

Biden traveled to Ukraine in December 2015 and said the United States would withhold $1 billion in loan guarantees unless Shokin was removed; it was not a demand to stop the Burisma prosecution. And there's no evidence that Shokin was after Hunter Biden or that he was ever under investigation. The vice president's trip was part of a larger anti-corruption push by the United States and its allies.

"I've been doing this for a long time and I have much bigger crowds than anybody's ever had in history."

FALSE.

"I want to be here because this area supported me so overwhelmingly. . . . I didn't get 100 percent, but we got a damn good percentage, right?"

317

EXAGGERATED. Trump won Calhoun County, Mich., by 12 percentage points in 2016.

"Your congressmen, all of your congresspeople—been wonderful people—they're in a place called Congress right now. They're doing an unbelievable job of supporting your president and supporting you. So they had a choice. 'Sir, should we leave and be there?' I said don't leave, stay right where you are."

ACCURATE. Republican House members from Michigan were in Washington voting against impeachment on the night of this Trump rally.

"We've eliminated more job-killing regulations than any administration in the history of our country, whether it's four years or eight years or, in one case, much more than eight years. In a period of two and a half years, we have eliminated more regulations than any other president by far."

UNSUBSTANTIATED. Trump may have grounds to brag, but there is no reliable metric on which to judge his claim—or to compare him with previous presidents. Many experts credit Jimmy Carter with historic deregulation of the airline and trucking industries; he also lifted the ban on brewing beer at home, resulting in an explosion of new breweries.

"You're saving almost $3,000 a year because of regulation cuts."

MOSTLY FALSE. This statistic comes from a report issued in 2019 by the White House Council of Economic Advisers, which calculated such savings five to 10 years into the future, though Trump frequently suggests the savings are already being realized.

"Total income gains for median households will reach $10,000 a family. I'll give you a couple of quick numbers. So under President Bush, for eight years, you saved $450, meaning you took in $450. Okay, fine. Under President Obama, you took in $975. Under President Trump, including the energy savings and the regulation savings and the tax cuts savings, it's more than $10,000 in less than three years."

FALSE. Trump is mixing up all kinds of apples and oranges for maximum spin. The claim that households are saving $3,000 a year from regulatory cuts earned Three Pinocchios. The president never mentions actions taken by the administration that reduced household income. For instance, the Federal Reserve Bank of New York said Trump's tariffs cost the typical U.S. household $831 a year.

"We've ended the war on American energy, and the United States is now the number one producer of oil and natural gas on planet Earth."

MOSTLY FALSE. Trump is taking credit for something that happened under Obama. The United States has been the world's biggest energy producer since at least 2014.

"They [Democrats] want to close up your steel mills. They don't want your steel mills."

FALSE. No Democrat has pledged to close steel mills or supports policies specifically targeting the industry.

"Look at what I've done for steel. I mean the steel is back. We taxed all of the dumped steel coming in from China and other places, and U.S. steel mills are doing great. They're expanding all over the country and

they were all going to be out of business within two years. The way they were going, they were gone."

FALSE. Steel mills were not going to be out of business in two years when Trump took office, and they are not expanding all over the country. In fact, primary metal manufacturing jobs are below the levels seen during the Obama administration.

"United States Steel is spending now billions of dollars on expansions."

MOSTLY ACCURATE. The steelmaker announced a big expansion in Pennsylvania, but it also announced in 2019 that it was idling two blast furnaces due to slumping demand and laying off hundreds of workers, including 1,500 in the Detroit area.

"Every major Democrat running for president has pledged to eliminate gas-powered automobiles and destroy the U.S. auto industry forever."

FALSE. Some leading Democrats, but not all, pledged to transition away from fossil fuels over a 10-year period.

"We're even bringing back the old lightbulb. You heard about that, right? The old lightbulb, which is better. . . . The new light, they're terrible. You look terrible. They cost you many, many times more, like four or five times more. And you know, they're considered hazardous waste."

MOSTLY FALSE. The Trump administration is blocking a rule meant to phase out older lightbulbs, saying consumers should have the choice to keep using them. Some newer lightbulbs, compact fluorescent, or CFL, bulbs, contain mercury and tend to have harsher color quality. Light-emitting diode, or LED, bulbs are the dominant environmentally-friendly technology and currently account for more than 70 percent of sales.

"When a lightbulb is out, you've got to bring it to a dump. So let's say over here at Battle Creek, where's your nearest dump? Okay, that's what, a couple of hundred miles away. So every time you lose, drive a couple of hundred miles. I said how many people do that? Nobody."

FALSE. Residents of Battle Creek don't have to travel far to dispose of their CFL lightbulbs. Local officials organize collection events, and the local Home Depot and Lowe's stores also take them.

"You turn on the shower, you're not allowed to have any water anymore."

FALSE.

"Dishwashers, we did the dishwasher, right? You press it—remember the dishwasher, you press it, boom, there'd be like an explosion. Five minutes later, you open it up, the steam pours out the dishes. Now, you press it 12 times. Women tell me, again, you know, they give you four drops of water."

FALSE. Where to begin?

"We just came out with a reg [regulation] on dishwashers."

ACCURATE. The Trump administration is proposing to allow faster dishwashers and to exempt them from energy-efficiency standards.

"I mentioned all three. I said sinks, showers and toilets. The headline was Trump with the toilets, toilets. That's all they were."

ACCURATE. Trump without evidence said on Dec. 7, 2019, that "people are flushing toilets 10 times, 15 times, as opposed to once," and that exaggerated claim did dominate news coverage of his speech. He did also complain about low water pressure in sinks and showers.

"In the last two decades before my election, we lost one in five auto-manufacturing jobs in this country."

MOSTLY ACCURATE. Manufacturing jobs in the auto industry declined nearly 23 percent from 1996 to 2016, according to federal data.

"Among the very first acts that I did was to stop the deal that would have dealt a death blow to the U.S. auto industry. I withdrew from the horrible Trans-Pacific Partnership that would have ended your auto industry."

MOSTLY FALSE. Trump withdrew from the TPP, but the rest of his claim falls flat. The United States would have had up to 30 years to phase out tariffs on cars and light trucks imported from Japan under the terms of the TPP as negotiated by the Obama administration. Overall, the impact on the auto industry was believed to be limited.

The pact essentially preserved the status quo on trucks in the United States, the most profitable part of the market. Tariffs on trucks brought into the United States have forced foreign car makers to build truck and SUV plants here. Meanwhile, the TPP would have bolstered auto exports as other countries would have been forced to eliminate tariffs, such as Malaysia's 30 percent foreign tax on autos, and Vietnam's foreign tax of 70 percent on autos.

"Like the one [trade deal] in Korea, that was a Hillary Clinton special. She said this will produce 250,000 new jobs, and I said, well, what

happened? He said, well, she was right except it was for South Korea, not for us. So it produced 250,000 jobs for South Korea."

FALSE. Trump is referring to a free-trade agreement with South Korea that was negotiated by George W. Bush's administration and then tweaked by Obama's. Clinton did not negotiate it. One of Trump's top trade aides claimed 100,000 U.S. jobs—not 250,000—would be lost in the deal, but even that's a dubious number disputed by mainstream economists.

"The new USMCA has powerful protections to keep auto-manufacturing jobs right here in Michigan."

MOSTLY ACCURATE. Among other measures, the USMCA requires that 75 percent of vehicles be made of North American content, up from 62.5 percent under NAFTA.

"Since the election, we've created 41,000 brand-new motor vehicle and parts jobs, manufacturing jobs."

MOSTLY ACCURATE.

"Remember the statement by President Obama, 'You'd have to wave a magic wand'? Remember the magic wand, because of manufacturing? And I said, you know, that sounds strange. What do you do if you don't have manufacturing? How do you make things?"

MOSTLY FALSE. Trump often riffs on Obama's 2016 comment blasting candidate Trump for promising to restore manufacturing jobs. At a town hall in 2016, Obama said that more manufacturing jobs had been created during his term than at any time since the 1990s, adding that although some manufacturing jobs were recoverable, many were gone for good because of automation and other economic shifts.

"We've got 600,000 manufacturing jobs."

MOSTLY FALSE. Manufacturers had at that point added about 480,000 jobs since Trump took office.

"They're opening these massive—Foxconn in Wisconsin—they're opening these massive plants."

MOSTLY ACCURATE. Foxconn has announced a big investment in Wisconsin, but there have been bumps in the road. "Whatever Foxconn is building in Wisconsin, it's not the $10 billion, 22-million-square-foot Generation 10.5 LCD factory that President Trump once promised would be the 'eighth wonder of the world,'" the Verge reported. "At various points over the last two years, the Taiwanese tech manufacturer has said it would build a smaller LCD factory; that it wouldn't build a factory at all; that it would build an LCD factory; that the company could make any number of things, from screens for cars to server racks to robot coffee kiosks; and so on."

"Fiat Chrysler recently announced a $4.5 billion investment in Michigan, including the first new auto plant in Detroit in more than a generation."

ACCURATE.

"General Motors recently announced a $300 million investment at its Orion assembly plant right here in Michigan."

ACCURATE.

"Every Democrat running for president wants to open the flood-gates to unlimited refugees from all around the world, overwhelming your communities and putting our national security at grave risk."

FALSE. Refugees do not overwhelm communities because U.S. officials usually place them in different parts of the country. There's no evidence that refugees, many of them women and children, endanger national security. Trump often makes false claims associating immigrants with crime. No leading Democrat running for president voiced support for unlimited refugee admissions, though Joe Biden and Sen. Elizabeth Warren (D-Mass.) favored raising the annual cap from 18,000, where Trump set it after a clampdown in 2019, to more than 100,000.

"Democrat immigration policies are resulting in brutal assaults and wicked murders against innocent Americans."

FALSE. Trump is referring in part to catch and release, the policy of releasing some undocumented immigrants into the country while they await court hearings. This policy is bipartisan, cobbled together through Democratic and Republican administrations.

"We've moved out thousands and thousands of MS-13 thugs out of our country."

MOSTLY ACCURATE. The Trump administration had deported more than 2,000 MS-13 gang members as of the end of 2018.

"We have agreements now with Guatemala, Honduras, El Salvador, you know they didn't use to take them back. If we had a murderer and we said get them the hell out, you know, we don't really want them in our prisons."

FALSE. The United States had deported hundreds of thousands of immigrants from all three of those countries in the years before Trump took office. From 2013 to 2018, there were 550,186 such deportations.

"In June, two illegal aliens in Sandusky, Michigan, were convicted of sadistically beating and stabbing a woman to death with a kitchen knife. Then they hid her body in a water drain."

ACCURATE.

"A criminal alien with two previous deportations was just arrested in Michigan and convicted of brutally beating and strangling to death a single mother of five young children."

DECEPTIVE. This individual had not been "just arrested." The arrest happened in 2016.

"Far-left politicians support deadly sanctuary cities, which deliberately release dangerous violent criminal aliens out of the jails and directly onto your streets."

MOSTLY FALSE. Sanctuary cities generally comply with ICE requests to detain undocumented immigrants when they have allegedly committed serious crimes. Sanctuary generally refers to rules restricting state and local governments from alerting federal authorities about people who may be in the country illegally. A handful of studies of the connection between sanctuary cities and crime found no statistically-significant impact of the policies on crime, nor any reduction in crime because of immigrant-friendly policing strategies.

"Earlier this year, authorities in the sanctuary jurisdiction of Kent County, Michigan—anybody know Kent County?—released an illegal alien charged with assault with intent to murder after he repeatedly and viciously stabbed a man in the head with a broken bottle. They let him go to roam free in Michigan communities."

ACCURATE.

"We had a great election in North Carolina recently. Two great congressmen got elected. . . . When they win, you don't ever hear about it. . . . And they got elected because . . . you have sanctuary cities and they had some horrible crimes happening from those sanctuary cities. As soon as I mentioned that, boom, they went up like rocket ships and they won their elections."

FALSE. Both congressional seats in North Carolina were already held by Republicans, only one race was considered close, and the GOP candidate was ahead in every poll. The races did not turn on Trump's sanctuary-city comments.

"We're getting these prosecutors and, you know, you murder somebody, they give you two months. They fight, then you don't even have to go to jail."

FALSE. This is a gross exaggeration. Some prosecutors have decided to use their discretion to be more lenient with low-level drug offenses or nonviolent cases. There is no evidence of prosecutors going easy on murderers by seeking the kinds of sentences Trump mentions.

"Illegal crossings are down 75 percent since May."

ACCURATE. Southwest border apprehensions declined 75 percent from May to November 2019, when 33,510 people were caught trying to cross into the United States without authorization.

"We've ended catch and release. We've ended it."

FALSE. The Trump administration has come up with policies to whittle away at catch and release, but some of them have been tied up in litigation or rejected by federal judges, and authorities continue to release people into the country despite the president's claim.

"You catch him and then you release him into a country. That's what you had to do by law and if you don't do that, they arrest the Border Patrol people. Do you believe this? The Border Patrol people were in more danger than the criminal aliens coming in."

FALSE. There's no record of Border Patrol agents being arrested for failing to release immigrants into the country. Federal courts have required that undocumented immigrant children be released from custody after a certain number of days, but many adults who cross the border without authorization are quickly returned to their home countries without an immigration hearing. Those with criminal records are not eligible for catch and release.

"Remember the caravans coming up, we call them caravans, and they're interviewing the people? I'll never forget it. One nice citizen

reporter, female reporter: 'And what did you do?' 'Well, I want to come to America.' 'Okay, good. What did you do?' 'Murder.'"

ACCURATE. The interview was broadcast on Fox News.

"I used to be a big contributor [to Democratic Sen. Charles E. Schumer]."

MOSTLY ACCURATE. Trump contributed $8,000 to Schumer's campaigns from 1996 to 2009, according to FEC records.

"Democrats are pushing a socialist takeover of health care that will take away your coverage and take away your doctor. . . . They want to take away 180 million people—great, private, highly-negotiated health care where you have your own doctor."

MOSTLY FALSE. Several leading Democrats proposed to expand Medicare to cover all Americans. This would render the private insurance industry obsolete. But the people on private plans wouldn't be left uncovered, as Trump suggests, because they would be absorbed into the expanded Medicare system. Under a socialized system, all doctors are theoretically open to all patients, but all doctors would be required to accept the government's pay structure.

"Remember Obama? Twenty-eight times, 28 times: 'You can have your doctor, you can have your plan.' Didn't work out that way, did it?"

MOSTLY ACCURATE. This was one of Obama's famous whoppers—claiming patients could keep their doctors despite changes brought on by the Affordable Care Act. Trump says Obama repeated this false claim 28 times. PolitiFact found 37 instances in which Obama or administration officials repeated it.

"How about giving Iran $1.8 billion in cash, how about that?"

MOSTLY FALSE. This is related to the settlement of a decades-old claim between the two countries. An initial payment of $400 million was handed over on Jan. 17, 2016, the day after Iran released four American detainees. That cash payment was money Iran had deposited in the United States before the 1979 revolution to buy U.S. military equipment. The rest of the payment was a negotiated agreement on interest accrued from that deposit.

"I ended the Iran nuclear deal."

MOSTLY FALSE. Trump in 2018 withdrew the United States from the Iran deal, the Joint Comprehensive Plan of Action (JCPOA), but the other signatory nations remained in the deal. Experts say the JCPOA may now be on its last legs. Iran announced it would no longer abide by key restrictions after a top military commander, Maj. Gen. Qasem Soleimani, was killed in a U.S. drone strike in 2019.

"Republicans will strongly protect patients with preexisting conditions."

FALSE. In an ongoing court case, the Trump administration is supporting a total repeal of the Affordable Care Act—including its guarantee that patients can't be denied coverage for preexisting conditions. Republicans in Congress tried for years to repeal the whole law. Trump has not presented an alternative plan in case the court challenge is successful.

"Virtually every top Democrat also now supports late-term abortion, ripping babies straight from the mother's womb, right up until the moment of birth."

FALSE. Most leading 2020 Democrats have not explicitly weighed in on late-term abortion. Trump often mischaracterizes remarks by Virginia Gov. Ralph Northam (D), who said late-term abortion procedures are "done in cases where there may be severe deformities" or "a fetus that's not viable."

"I've asked Congress to prohibit extreme late-term abortion."

ACCURATE.

"To protect the health and safety of our citizens, we awarded $100 million to improve water infrastructure in Flint."

MOSTLY ACCURATE. Trump's Environmental Protection Agency awarded this grant in March 2017, but the funding had been approved by Congress and Obama in 2016.

"We're lowering taxes."

ACCURATE. Trump signed the Tax Cuts and Jobs Act in late 2017, which reduced rates mostly for wealthy earners and corporations.

"I recognized Israel's true capital and opened the American embassy in Jerusalem, and we also recognized Israeli sovereignty over the Golan Heights, a big deal."

ACCURATE.

"We've done so much, even Right to Try. You know Right to Try? People were traveling—they're terminally ill—they're traveling all over the world. We have the best medical in the world, the best doctors, the best labs, the best hospitals—they're traveling all over the world, right, to try and get—because it takes years to get something approved [in the United States]. And I said, 'Wait a minute, folks. Why aren't we doing this?' And they've been trying to do it for 49 years. They couldn't get it done."

MOSTLY FALSE. Trump signed the Right to Try Act, which allows the use of unapproved treatments for some patients. The concept emerged in 2013, though advocates had been calling on the Food and Drug Administration to loosen its restrictions on unapproved drugs for years before that. The FDA already approved 99 percent of requests for access to such medications, but supporters said the agency's policies were still too restrictive.

"What we've done in the last three years with the FDA and even the speed of what we're doing, it would take 12, 13, 14 years to get things approved. It's down to a much smaller number."

UNSUBSTANTIATED. Trump's FDA is approving generic drugs at a record clip, but we couldn't find support for his claim that the process once took up to 14 years and is now much shorter.

"You know some of these [MS-13] guys, they knife people, they don't even need a gun because it's more painful."

ACCURATE.

"These are animals [MS-13 gang members], and then, Nancy Pelosi said they shouldn't use the term 'animal.'"

MOSTLY FALSE. On May 16, 2018, Trump appeared to suggest that undocumented immigrants were "animals," but he clarified on Twitter two days later that he was referring only to MS-13 members. The day after Trump's "animals" comment, Pelosi defended undocumented immigrants, saying that "calling people animals is not a good thing."

"San Francisco . . . the police officers are getting sick just from walking the beat. They're getting sick."

FALSE. The San Francisco Police Department has denied Trump's claim. A police union said three Los Angeles police officers contracted a staph infection after attending to a homeless individual at a police station, but a medical expert said the infection could have come from any number of sources.

"Diseases are coming back that this world hasn't seen for 30, 40, 50 years."

MOSTLY ACCURATE. Some medical experts say that measles, for example, had been nearly eradicated but is reemerging in communities that shun vaccines.

"This is the state where Henry Ford invented the assembly line."

MOSTLY FALSE. Henry Ford did not invent so much as sponsor the invention of the moving assembly line, according to contemporaneous Ford accounts. A Ford worker in Michigan came up with the rough concept after visiting Chicago and seeing a slaughter-house where carcasses were taken apart step by step on a conveyor belt. Between 1908 and 1913, Ford workers finessed that idea onto an auto assembly line. Another Michigan auto pioneer, Ransom Olds, had invented the stationary assembly line years earlier.

"I went to NATO, where we were being ripped off because the other countries, you have 29 countries, and the other countries weren't pay-ing their bills. They were delinquent."

FALSE. NATO members were never "delinquent" in their pay-ments. That's not how NATO works. Before Trump announced his candidacy, NATO member nations agreed to ramp up their defense spending to 2 percent of GDP by 2024.

"I raised, not from us, nothing from us, $130 billion, but that's nothing. And over a short period of time, they will be paying $530 billion more, all of those [NATO] countries."

FALSE. We gave Four Pinocchios to Trump for this claim. He takes credit for increased defense spending by NATO members even though those increases began years before he became president, after Russia invaded Crimea. The $530 billion figure is just wrong. NATO members (not including the United States) are expected to spend an additional $400 billion by 2024, not $530 billion as Trump claims.

"We were spending 100 percent of NATO."

FALSE.

"We're protecting Europe. They rip us off on trade, right? They rip us off like crazy. We lose hundreds of billions of dollars on trade. . . . It's

been going on a long time. They don't take your product. They don't take your cars. They don't take your farm product. They don't take your medical machines."

FALSE. The E.U. is the largest export market for the United States, and those exports supported an estimated 2.6 million U.S. jobs in 2015, according to the Office of the U.S. Trade Representative. The United States runs a trade deficit with the E.U. when looking only at goods, and runs a trade surplus of about $60 billion on services. Combined, the U.S. goods and services trade deficit with the E.U. was $109 billion in 2018. In international trade, some countries dominate some markets and don't compete as much in others. The French have trade restrictions on U.S. wine, just as the United States has trade restrictions on French clothing.

"In France, President Obama's more popular than President Trump."

ACCURATE.

"I just taxed [French] wine and champagne coming into our country because they're ripping us off on the Internet, okay?"

MOSTLY ACCURATE. The Trump administration is preparing these tariffs but has not yet implemented them. Who needs a drink, by the way?

"My father came from Germany."

FALSE. Fred Trump was born in the Bronx to German immigrants.

A NOTE ON SOURCES

Every fact check in this book is derived from those published by The *Washington Post* Fact Checker, which can be found at www. washingtonpost.com/factchecker or from The Fact Checker's database of Trump claims, at washingtonpost.com/graphics/politics/ trump-claims-database. These resources include links to the data and reports we used to assess Trump's statements. We always sought information and comment from White House and administration officials, though they often ducked our calls or emails. They have not disputed our findings, though few politicians are ever happy with the Pinocchio ratings.

During Trump's presidency, fact checks were written by Glenn Kessler, Salvador Rizzo, Meg Kelly, Michelle Ye Hee Lee and Nicole Lewis.

Each of us was responsible for organizing and summarizing fact checks in individual chapters. Sal wrote Chapters Three, Four, Six and the appendix. Meg wrote Chapters One, Two and Five. Glenn wrote Chapters Seven, Eight, Nine and Ten.

The Trump database, designed by *Washington Post* graphics reporter Leslie Shapiro, is updated about every two months. As of Jan. 20, 2020, it contained 16,241 false or misleading claims. The search engine is fast, so it is easy to locate claims with a word or phrase, and it will direct you to our longer fact checks. We welcome academic research into the database. Please let us know the purpose of your research, via an email to factchecker@washpost.com, and we will send you the necessary data files.

The introduction referred to the following studies: Dan M. Kahan, Ellen Peters, Erica Dawson and Paul Slovic, "Motivated Numeracy and Enlightened Self-Government," *Behavioural Public Policy* (2013, last revised 2017); Brendan Nyhan, Ethan Porter, Jason Reifler and Thomas Wood, "Taking Fact-checks Literally But Not Seriously?: The Effects of Journalistic Fact-Checking on Factual Beliefs and Candidate Favorability," *Political Behavior* (January 2019); Bella DePaulo, "How President Trump's Lies Are Different From Other People's," *Psychology Today* (December 2017); and Bill Frischling, "Not 'Stable Genius' Again, Or Please Stop Making Us Run This Analysis," blog.factba.se (Oct. 3, 2019). Neuroscientist Ryan McGarry conducted the experiments that monitored brain activity during the 2016 presidential debates.

The conclusion referred to the following studies: Oliver Hahl, Minjae Kim and Ezra W. Zuckerman Sivan, "The Authentic Appeal of the Lying Demagogue: Proclaiming the Deeper Truth about Political Illegitimacy," *American Sociological Review* (2018); Jeremy A. Frimer, Linda J. Skitka and Matt Motyl, "Liberals and Conservatives Are Similarly Motivated to Avoid Exposure to One Another's Opinions," *Journal of Experimental Social Psychology* (2017); Christopher A. Bail, Lisa Argyle, Taylor Brown, John Bumpus, Haohan Chen, M. B. F. Hunzaker, Jaemin Lee, et al., "Exposure to Opposing Views Can Increase Political Polarization: Evidence from a Large-scale Field Experiment on Social Media," *SocArXiv Papers* (March 2018). The 1960 study on marriage across political parties is Gabriel Almond and Sidney Verba, "Civic Culture Study, 1959–1960," *Inter-university Consortium for Political and Social Research* (1960); the more recent study on marriage is Maxine Najle and Robert P. Jones, "American Democracy in Crisis: The Fate of Pluralism in a Divided Nation," *Public Religion Research Institute* (February 19, 2019).

ACKNOWLEDGMENTS

The Fact Checker would not be possible without tremendous institutional support across *The Washington Post*. Executive editor Marty Baron; managing editors Cameron Barr, Emilio Garcia-Ruiz and Tracy Grant; national editor Steven Ginsberg and politics editor Peter Wallsten have given us the freedom to chart our own course, from the statements we select for fact-checking to experimenting with new platforms to reach readers. Under the ownership of Jeff Bezos and the leadership of publisher Fred Ryan, the staff has expanded from just one person to four people, including two video editors.

People are often surprised to learn that more people watch Fact Checker videos than read the fact checks. But it's true. The Fact Checker's collaboration with the *Post*'s video department—especially editorial video director Micah Gelman, deputy director Phoebe Connelly, producers Nadine Ajaka and Peter Stevenson, video editor Elyse Samuels and video graphics editor Atthar Mirza—has helped us break new ground in visually presenting fact checks. We're excited about the vision Sarah Cahlan is bringing to the team.

We also want to thank The Fact Checker's founder. In 2007, Michael Dobbs, a former *Washington Post* diplomatic correspondent, was between books and approached the editors of *The Post* with

ACKNOWLEDGMENTS

a proposal for a fact-checking feature that would run daily during the 2007–2008 presidential campaign cycle. Working with then–national editor Susan Glasser, Dobbs designed the Pinocchio rating scale and laid the foundation for a column that both enthralled and infuriated readers. (The iconic Pinocchio image was created by illustrator Steve McCracken.) When the campaign ended in November 2008, Dobbs closed up shop and went back to writing books.

But readers kept reading. Ginsberg, then a *Post* politics editor, noticed that online traffic remained high for Dobbs's old fact checks as people searched for information on the web. So, he and then–national editor Kevin Merida persuaded Glenn Kessler to give up his longtime job covering diplomacy and national security to relaunch The Fact Checker in 2011 as a permanent feature—focusing not just on the campaign but on all politicians and interest groups.

We often say we have the best readers. Many of our fact checks come from reader suggestions or queries—and readers are quick to tell us when they believe they have additional information that would improve the fact check (and even change the rating). We also have the best competitors. FactCheck.org and PolitiFact keep us on our toes and help make us better. The growth of the fact-checking community across the globe in the past nine years has been remarkable. We often learn from the innovations of our overseas brethren who are verified members of the International Fact-Checking Network.

Michelle Ye Hee Lee, who was Glenn's partner on The Fact Checker during the 2016 campaign and at the start of the Trump presidency, originally suggested creating a database of Trump's false or misleading claims. Leslie Shapiro, a *Post* graphics reporter, brought that idea to fruition and keeps improving it with every update.

Colin Harrison, editor-in-chief of Scribner and editor of this book, first approached Baron with the idea of turning the Trump claims database into a book. His enthusiasm convinced us to take the plunge. Thanks also to associate editor Sarah Goldberg and the extraordinarily eagle-eyed copy editor, Andrea Monagle. Ginsberg and Barr helped us shape the book proposal. Senior graphics editor Tim Meko oversaw the wonderful graphics by Adrienne Tong, and senior photo editor Bronwen Latimer tracked down the photographs. We especially want to thank *Washington Post* senior editor Marc Fisher, co-author of his own Trump book, "Trump Revealed," who coordinated with the publisher and edited the first drafts of our chapters. He ensured we didn't get too deep in the weeds—an occupational hazard for fact checkers.

Glenn: This book is dedicated to my children: Andre, Hugo and Mara Kessler. They were youngsters when I wrote my first book, but now they are adults—passionate about their career choices, engaged in politics and human rights and eager to make a difference. I could not be a prouder father. It will be up to their generation to fix the messes left behind by mine. My late parents, Adriaan Kessler and Else Bolotin, were immigrants to the United States from the Netherlands; their vivid memories of living under Nazi occupation taught me to cherish the freedoms enshrined in the U.S. Constitution. Finally, none of this would have been possible without my wife, Cindy Rich. Moving from diplomacy to fact-checking was supposed to mean I would be home more often. But I have spent far too many late nights and weekends in our study, either in tense conversation with an angry flack or working on the dreaded database. For nearly four decades, Cindy has been my best friend and partner, and I will always be sustained by her love and support.

Salvador: I would like to thank my parents, Salvador Rizzo and Anna Maria Saenz, for the example they set and for their selfless devotion to their family and community. I am blessed to be their

ACKNOWLEDGMENTS

son. I would like to thank Glenn Kessler, Steven Ginsberg and Marty Baron for their leadership and courage on behalf of our democracy. Most of what I know about journalism and politics I learned covering New Jersey. My thanks to Charlie Stile, Matt Friedman, Jarrett Renshaw, David Tucker, John McAlpin, Marty Gottlieb and Deirdre Sykes for their friendship and mentoring. And I would be remiss if I left out my sidekick, Moonshine, the friendliest cat in the world.

Meg: I want to dedicate this book to my late grandfather, my hero, Otto Hirschfeld, who risked his life to write critically in Germany about Hitler. His bravery inspires me every day. Two generations later, I doubt he would believe his granddaughter has the privilege to cover politics in his adopted home. That of course would never have been possible without my tough-as-nails mother, Barbara Kelly, whose hard work and dedication to fairness is unmatched; my late father, Richard Kelly, whose intellect and endless curiosity are inspirational; and Isabel Lopez, my late father's ever graceful and generous (but forever title-less) partner of three decades. I also want to thank Glenn Kessler, Kainaz Amaria, the late Bob Hirschfeld, Marcia Lawther, Karen Fairbanks, and Beth Donovan for opening doors that I didn't know were there. Glenn, goodness knows why you let a video editor write stories, but I'm glad you did. Last but certainly not least, I want to thank my brilliant, talented fiancé, Brandon Hill, who is a fountain of patience and encouragement. Nothing would work without you, B.

Glenn Kessler has been editor and chief writer of The Fact Checker since 2011 and has worked at *The Washington Post* since 1998. In an award-winning journalism career spanning nearly four decades, Kessler has covered foreign policy, economic policy, the White House, Congress, politics, airline safety and Wall Street. Kessler and his team earned honorable mention in the Toner Prize for Excellence in Political Reporting. He is the author of *The Confidante: Condoleezza Rice and the Creation of the Bush Legacy*. He is a graduate of Brown University and Columbia University's School of International and Public Affairs and lives in McLean, Virginia. Visit www.glennkessler.com.

Salvador Rizzo is a national politics reporter for *The Washington Post*. He writes for the newspaper's Fact Checker unit and has fact-checked hundreds of claims from politicians and advocacy groups. He previously covered Governor Chris Christie and New Jersey politics, with stints at the *Star-Ledger*, the *Bergen Record* and the *New York Observer*, where he was editor of New Jersey's top politics blog, PolitickerNJ.com. He is a graduate of Emory University, where he was editor-in-chief of the student newspaper. Born in San Benito, Texas, he lived in Monterrey, Mexico, for a decade.

Meg Kelly is a video editor and reporter for The Fact Checker at *The Washington Post*. She has covered national politics since 2015—first as a visual producer at National Public Radio and, since 2017, with the *Post*'s Fact Checker team. She grew up in Denver, graduated from Barnard College in New York and was a Fulbright-Nehru Scholar in Mumbai. She lives in Washington, D.C. Visit www.mmountfields.com.

31901065830673